TOWARDS A NEW EUROPE

Stops and Starts
in Regional Integration

Edited by Gerald Schneider,
Patricia A. Weitsman,
and Thomas Bernauer

Westport, Connecticut
London

Library of Congress Cataloging-in-Publication Data

Towards a new Europe : stops and starts in regional integration /
   edited by Gerald Schneider, Patricia A. Weitsman, and Thomas Bernauer.
       p. cm.
   Includes bibliographical references and index.
   ISBN 0–275–94865–X (alk. paper)
    1. Europe—Economic integration. 2. European federation.
   3. European cooperation. I. Schneider, Gerald. II. Weitsman, Patricia A.
   III. Bernauer, Thomas.
   HC241.T68   1995
   337.1′4 —dc20   95–7553

British Library Cataloguing in Publication Data is available.

Library of Congress Catalog Card Number: 95–7553
ISBN: 0–275–94865–X

First published in 1995

Praeger Publishers, 88 Post Road West, Westport, CT 06881
An imprint of Greenwood Publishing Group, Inc.

Printed in the United States of America

The paper used in this book complies with the
Permanent Paper Standard issued by the National
Information Standards Organization (Z39.48–1984).

10 9 8 7 6 5 4 3 2 1

CONTENTS

FIGURES AND TABLES

FIGURES

TABLES

PREFACE

The 1990s have thus far proved to be a decade of dramatic progress for the European integration process. The genesis of the European Union was, perhaps, the most striking advance. Observers of the developments in Europe may be aware, however, that most periods of integration success are followed by periods of stagnation; periods of integration failures are often followed by breakthroughs. What governs this stop and go logic of integration? This volume was initiated in quest of an answer to that question, since prevailing theories in the field of international politics explain the process only partially or inadequately. To address this gap, we solicited articles that further our understanding of integration from the vantage point of formal modeling in general, and rational choice in particular. All contributors address, in some manner, the ups and downs that characterize cooperation in the European Union.

The volume is divided into three conceptual segments. The first part contains articles that explain the evolution of the integration process. The contributions to the second section of the book assess the major institutions of the Union, as well as the process of deepening and expanding cooperation among European states. The final segment of the volume addresses some of the major policy questions facing the European Union today.

The editors would like to thank Peter Moser (University of Zürich) and Claudia Seybold (University of Bern) for their help during the editorial process, as well as Evelyne Homberg and Denise Ducroz at the Graduate Institute of International Studies, Geneva, Switzerland, for administrative support.

I

THE EVOLUTION OF INTEGRATION

1

Explaining the Stops and Starts in Regional Integration

Gerald Schneider and Patricia A. Weitsman

In 1952, six European states ratified an agreement that granted power to a supranational authority to govern a pool of the participating states' coal and steel. Forty years later, the twelve member states of the European Community (EC) signed the treaty on European Union (EU). The history of regional integration in Europe has been marked by these watershed instances of success, yet it is filled too with long periods of stalemate and integration failures. To date, however, there are no theories that adequately explain this ever-evolving and ever-stagnating process of integration. Despite the development of theories with significant explanatory power in other subfields of international relations, we have few tools to explain the stops and starts in European cooperation. Because shifts from progress to stalemate are the predominant pattern of this process, a theory of integration has ultimately to be a theory of disintegration.

THE STATE OF THE ART

The prevailing theoretical approaches to understanding regional integration provide either an explanation for integration success or integration failure; thus far, extant regional integration theory cannot account for both. For neorealists cooperation is puzzling given their assumption that the anarchy prevailing in the international system makes conflictual relations among states unavoidable. They see the integration process as a largely unsuccessful endeavor (Waltz 1979). Cooperation seems possible only if advanced countries are able to effectively address the relative-gains concerns of disadvantaged partners (Grieco 1990:105) or if specific features of the system of interaction among states require it (Waltz 1993:70). In the long run, however, stalemate or open conflict should be the dominant features of European interaction; the self-help system, a consequence of anarchy, endangers any kind of long-term agreement.

The prediction of structural realism that integration is impossible is in stark contrast to the optimism of liberalism. For scholars who believe the state system is composed of a network of social links, integration is almost taken for granted, although coordination problems continue to frustrate attempts to cooperate (Milner 1992). Despite the predominance of neorealism in other subfields of international relations, liberal thinking has been more influential in explaining the process of political integration. Functionalism and its successor neofunctionalism were developed to explain the need for a strengthening of international organization. Functionalist thought was based on the conviction that changing social and economic needs induce the flexible creation and adaptation of institutions to social and economic needs. As a "functional" need arises, changes, or diminishes, organizations developed to solve the problems will be created, changed or diminished as well. Integration proceeds through "spillovers" into other functionally related spheres (Mitrany 1966).

The proponents of neofunctionalism challenged the notion that integration is merely a consequence of technical demands. Scholars like Haas (1958, 1964) argued that social and political goals of participants must be taken into account before cooperation can be realized. Once in place, domestic loyalties would gradually shift to the supranational organizations created to perform the necessary functions. From the vantage point of transactionalism (Deutsch et al. 1957, Deutsch et al. 1967), the "sense of community" was a major condition for successful integration.

It became clear in the mid-1960s that linear development towards a unified Europe was not to be when French President Charles De Gaulle continually blocked progress towards integration through the establishment of a *de facto* veto power in the Council of Ministers. De Gaulle's capacity to frustrate integration invited sharp criticism of liberal optimism by realists (Hoffmann 1966) and sparked modifications to the explanations supplied by functionalism and neofunctionalism. The revisions (Lindberg and Scheingold 1970, Nye 1971) stressed the possibilities of stalemate and crisis, focusing partly on the role of political leadership. However, as the promised "supranational" organism never took life during the 1970s, neofunctionalism gradually receded along with its promises. Students of the Community developments began to argue that "interdependence" rather than "integration" was a better label for the collaborative web the EC represented (Keohane and Nye 1977). During the "Eurosclerosis" of the 1980s, intergovernmentalism came to be seen as the dominant decision making mode of the European Community (Taylor 1983, Scharpf 1988, Schneider 1995). This approach adopts, to a certain extent, neorealist assumptions; power is ultimately vested in the governments of the member states. The intergovernmentalist perspective, however, has only generated several *ad hoc* amendments to functionalist reasoning (Scharpf 1988).

The study of European integration has been characterized by shifts from liberalism to neorealism and back to liberalism. The ups and downs of scholars' disenchantment and enchantment with certain paradigms go hand in hand with the stops and starts of the process of regional cooperation. Yet the interest in international organizations has survived (see Kratochwil and Ruggie 1986). Since the revival of the EC in the mid-1980s, traditional liberal explanations have been enjoying a renaissance. However, the propensity of nations to forgo national sovereignty in exchange for free-trade agreements or other manifestations of increased political integration has not yet led to any major progress in our understanding of regional collaboration.

AN ALTERNATIVE APPROACH

This volume was motivated out of a belief that more focused research questions should be devised in order to generate a better theoretical understanding of the European Union, and regional integration more generally. As long as we do not explain the microfoundations of political integration, no approach to the study of regional integration will reach the standards of a social science theory. This book proposes an alternative set of tools for framing studies on regional integration. The research program we advance draws on questions from the older literature, yet embeds them in a rational choice framework. We maintain that limiting the scope of the research questions we ask will provide a framework that will facilitate the development of theory from the ground up.

Rational choice theory, broadly conceived, allows us to uncover some of the problems of inductive reasoning. A re-orientation of the studies of regional integration, however, does not imply that the research topics have to change as well. The major contribution of traditional studies is still their ability to frame some important questions of research. To answer these questions, different rational choice traditions might be valuable. Three approaches appear to be the most promising; these are game-theoretic, collective action, and transaction cost models. These perspectives are not mutually exclusive. All of these approaches share the general rational choice assumptions: That actors are goal-oriented and develop transitive preferences orders over different sets of outcomes. Game theory additionally focuses on strategic interactions. This enables the researcher to explicitly study the use of threats and other manipulations. Collective action approaches, by contrast, examine whether a society is able to provide public goods, which are characterized by various degrees of non-exclusion and non-rivalry (Olson 1965, Sandler 1992). Models that refer to the transaction costs approach developed by Coase (1960) allow for an examination of institutional change (North 1990).

ASSESSING THE PROGRAM

To assess the potential of the proposed research program, we contrast three rational choice perspectives with political culture approaches and "reflective" institutionalism (Keohane 1988). We argue that only the rationalist paradigm is able to meet some of the crucial challenges required for a rigorous and realistic theory of integration. First, such a theory must explain the *institutional evolution* of organizations like the EU. The integration literature that dates back to the 1960s and even earlier discusses "spillovers" as mechanisms of change. Second, integration theories have to *lay the micro-foundations of political cooperation*. This implies the need to specify how individual preferences are aggregated. The older literature introduced the metaphor of a "shift of loyalties" to address this issue. The third and related requirement is that the theory has to specify the *formation of preferences*; what are the roots of a "sense of community"?

We will discuss whether or not rational choice approaches or other theories of international politics are better able to meet these challenges. Whereas transaction cost approaches are able to explain the long-term evolution of a regional organization, game-theoretic approaches do not incorporate an explicit mechanism for aggregating individual preferences. Public goods theory, or social choice theory in general (Arrow 1951, Sen 1970), is devoted to the analysis of the latter issue. The biggest drawback of current rational choice approaches is the absence of an explanation of the formation of preferences. According to the neoclassical orthodoxy, there is no endogenous change of tastes (Stigler and Becker 1977). However, it seems reasonable to imagine that preferences regarding regional integration are in fact altered by socialization and other processes. It has been argued that rational choice could be reconciled with these questions (Achen 1992). Although some interesting work in evolutionary game theory might provide microfoundations of learning in the future (Binmore and Samuelson 1994), no convincing model linking the formation of preferences to actual decision making exists. Neither the way preferences are formed nor the way they are ordered is inherently clear from the assumptions of rational choice theory.

Political Culture

One school of thought that developed to explain the process of integration is that of political culture. This approach focuses on public and elite opinion and advances within Community states in support of integration. One of the most influential expositions of this approach was put forth by Ronald Inglehart (1970a, 1970b, 1977, 1990). According to Inglehart, the unprecedented wealth attained in the postwar period in Western Europe set off a process that induced attitudinal change among the populous concerning the desirability of integration. "Postmaterialists" identify with the European ideal; they are relatively unconcerned with material goals and instead are intellectually drawn to the concept of a single Europe.

Can political culture approaches meet the three challenges specified above? A recent evaluation (Janssen 1991) persuasively argues that the theory Inglehart puts forth is not wholly empirically accurate. The results of his study suggest that the process of attitude change towards integration in France, Italy, West Germany, and Great Britain does not follow the course one of Inglehart's central hypotheses would suggest. Instead, it appeared that public opinion towards integration is unstable (Janssen 1991:468). In other words, current political culture approaches cannot explain the evolution of the European Union.

Janssen's evaluation also indicates that postmaterialist cultures are not necessarily more integrationist than "materialist" cultures. Further, even if we were able to detect the link between postmaterialist culture and pro-integration attitudes, how are individual preferences aggregated into collective ones? The *Silent Revolution* implies enhanced support for integration at the domestic level increasing over time. If this support translated directly into increased integration, once more we would have a theory that could explain integration success but not failure.

Non-Rational Choice Institutionalism

An alternative institutional approach is one that views formal organizations as embedded in the web of international life. (For an overview of this perspective see Shambaugh and Weitsman 1992:7-17, March and Olsen 1989, Keohane 1988:386-393, and Kratochwil 1989.) This perspective emphasizes the impact of norms, rules, and decision making procedures on behavior and preferences, as well as the reverse. These informal institutions both guide behavior and drive preferences; behavior results from an interplay between the knowledge base, norms, rules, interests, and expectations. Further, institutions do not emerge as a consequence of purposive behavior; rather, they develop as by-products of habit driven individuals. The extent to which this framework of analysis can explain integration is limited. It may lead to interesting insights about how norms and routines affect the development of an organization. However, since there are no axiomatic foundations to guide the choice of specific rules, our understanding of organizational change remains ad hoc. We would need to know whether learning means trial and error or is based on more sophisticated algorithms to achieve a non-rationalist understanding of international institutions (see Binmore and Samuelson 1994 on a related point). The complexity of the framework in regard to preference formation, and the interrelationships among the factors that this perspective views as influencing preferences, render the utility in its application minimal. While this approach is perhaps the closest we have to specifying endogenous preference change, its unwieldiness and the fact that much of the behavior it addresses is counterfactually valid makes application nearly impossible.

THE LIMITS OF RATIONAL CHOICE

Such a positive assessment begs the question of what the limits of rational choice are. There have been numerous critiques of this approach in the past years, ranging from the polemical to the nuanced and well-informed. The informed objections point out three major problems. First, experimental results indicate that people tend to violate some of the axiomatic foundations of the approach (Kahneman and Tversky 1979, Frey and Eichenberger 1989, Akerlof 1991). In this vein, scholars have noted the cognitive limits of making rational decisions, the inability to account for preference reversals, the effects of the ways in which facts are framed that affect preferences (for a discussion of such issues see Cook and Levi 1990:126). In particular, the paradigm does not provide sufficiently specific guidelines to designate preferences in advance; nearly any form of behavior may be regarded as rational in hindsight (Coleman and Fararo 1992:165). Second, the revolution in information economics has led to the innovation of some concepts that demand hyperrationality on the part of the actors concerned (Binmore 1989). Some refinements of the Nash equilibrium concept require that players evaluate actions which other actors never make. Third, as even some game theorists acknowledge, some aspects of modeling are not sufficiently concerned with social issues and the psychological foundation of the approach (Rubinstein 1991). The importance of various limitations of rational choice depend largely on one's field of inquiry. To scholars working in the field of psychology the cognitive limitations of individuals making decisions are going to be of central importance, while to the economist less so (see Hogarth and Reder 1987). Interestingly, rational choice theory is most promising when the set of options is limited, and the structure of social interactions matters (Satz and Ferejohn 1994:72).

Despite these caveats, the contributions to this volume demonstrate some areas where rational choice theory is fruitful for understanding regional integration. Most contributions to this volume directly apply a rational choice approach to questions of past, present, and future cooperation in Europe. Additionally, other formal tools are used to uncover the long-term logic of the integration process. Each chapter starts with an empirical puzzle that allevi-ates the danger of reifying methodology and of relying on unrealistic assump-

tions. The contributions focus on three central aspects of European integration
—the evolution of the process, the major institutions and rules emerging from
integration, and the main policies resulting from the cooperation of European
states.

THE EVOLUTION OF INTEGRATION

The process through which integration has evolved among states is akin to
the processes that governed the formation of states. The increasing centralization of authority as well as the transfer of domestic loyalties to the more
abstract and geographically remote government are similar to both state building and the integration process.

Ward and Lofdahl explore the large-scale mechanisms that characterize
the process of integration and disintegration in Europe. They argue that the
processes of integration in the West and disintegration in the East are different
aspects of the same cyclical process driven by elite values, social costs and
benefits, complexity, and integration. Ward and Lofdahl trace the cycle in the
geographical context in which the scale of economic exchange and political
interactions unfold.

In contrast, Cederman's analysis of the emergence of deep cooperation
among states is put in the context of converging identities and loyalties. He
argues that the viability of a political unit is a function of its scale and its
unity. As loyalties become transferred to higher authorities, the better able
those authorities are to extract resources from the domestic population and the
more coherent their external policies become. As such, integration among
states in Europe is an organic process growing out of a historical process of
changing and converging loyalties. Cederman further draws out the implications of this argument for questions concerning the widening and deepening of
European cooperation.

Hug and Sciarini explore the institutional requirements for successful
integration to emerge. In particular, they assess Deutsch's assertion that the
development of the Swiss state was a paradigmatic integration success, and the
extent to which the institutions that facilitated successful integration are still
functioning effectively. Hug and Sciarini further develop the nested game
approach that Tsebelis (1990) used in his analysis of Belgian consociationalism.

INSTITUTIONAL CHANGE AND EXPANSION

As the process of European integration has developed over the decades, the
number of member states has more than doubled. Simultaneously, the organization of the former European Community has changed significantly. In

recent years, institutional reforms embodied in treaties like the Single European Act and the Maastricht agreement have had a profound effect on the way European decisions are negotiated and implemented. The specific changes in institutional mechanisms are of central importance to the effective maintenance of the European Union, as well as to the likelihood of enhancing future cooperation among the member states. This point is illuminated by Tsebelis' examination of the conditional agenda setting power of the European Parliament. Through a formal exploration of the Cooperation Procedure, the hidden agenda setting power of the legislature becomes clear. Because the European Parliament still depends on the Council of Ministers to make policy, the agenda setting authority is only conditional. However, Tsebelis argues, integration is facilitated through the use of the Cooperation Procedure. This analysis highlights important questions concerning the decision making power of different bodies within the European Union and concerning institutional innovations embodied in the Maastricht treaty, as well as those reforms on the agenda of the EU today.

The question of increasing membership, and the effect on the level of cooperation among states, is addressed in Pahre's chapter on the widening and deepening of the European Union. Contrary to the popular notion that expansion of the EU will inhibit deepening integration, Pahre argues, through a formal model of collective goods provision, that widening the Union will facilitate enhanced cooperation among participating states. Subsidiary propositions generated from the model provide further insights as to when cooperation will become more likely, and the durability of multilateral cooperation.

Mattli's contribution focuses on the "demand side" of enlargement issues through the refinement of an integrated production frontier model. By formalizing the relationship between economic markets and governing institutions, Mattli reveals state choices concerning integration as a function of the costs associated with maintaining an unintegrated governing structure at the expense of increasing economic growth or relinquishing some sovereignty to a supranational community in exchange for enhanced economic growth. The empirical tests support the proposition; nearly all of the states applying for membership sustained several years of growth rates significantly below the Community member states.

POLICY PROBLEMS OF THE EUROPEAN UNION

Two most problematic policy issues currently facing the European Union are monetary union and progress towards unified security arrangements of the member states. These two issues are explored in separate chapters by Martin and Bernauer. The piece by Martin reveals how if the Union states form a European Central Bank, the appointed central banker will not need to be as conservative as individual central bankers in a flexible exchange rate regime.

This insight has important implications for monetary policy of the European Union if monetary union is attained.

Bernauer's chapter applies the theory of clubs to alliances. It explores the constraints that exist with regard to increasing membership of a security organization. These include for example the nature of the services provided by the alliance and the extent of external threats. The club goods model facilitates the understanding of the negotiations between NATO and some Central and Eastern European states. The argument reveals the difficulties the Union faces in arriving at unified security policy and in expanding the Union itself. Bernauer's approach challenges the indeterminacy of the traditional theories which characterize the field of international security, as well as conventional approaches concerning the optimal size of organizations. The chapter facilitates more accurate predictions concerning the architecture of Europe's future security arrangements.

It is neither possible nor desirable to address all policy questions facing the EU in one volume. In their conclusion, Bernauer, Schneider and Weitsman discuss how rational choice models may be used to illuminate the formal and informal agenda of the European Union. They also argue that sophisticated and rigorous analysis might ultimately aid policy formulation. This volume should also contribute to this end. Such suggestions need to be based on a solid analytic footing. Empirically inspired rational choice reasoning is one way for integration theory to facilitate the making of informed policy choices.

2

Towards a Political Economy of Scale: European Integration and Disintegration

Michael D. Ward and Corey L. Lofdahl

Those who consider the Devil to be a partisan of Evil and angels to be warriors for Good accept the demagogy of the angels. Things are clearly more complicated.

(Milan Kundera 1981)

The waning years of the 1980s ushered in dramatic changes in the global political and economic environment. These are simple to document, but the changes begun have not yet played themselves out. The political-economic environment will continue in flux for some time to come. The fall of the Berlin Wall has come to symbolize the political dimension: Increased democratization and declining authoritarian modes of governance around the globe. Indeed, many countries have recently begun to grapple with the issues of democratization. While it is clear that at a global level there is increased salience for "democratization," at a local level it is unclear to many what this may actually mean. Certainly, more people than ever before in the history of the globe have democratic aspirations—i.e., the expectation that they will have an important voice in the governance that affects their lives. At the same time, the globalization of market economics means that economic success for many firms has become firmly tied to growing markets in new parts of the world, particularly Asia. This in turn has meant that an increasing competitiveness has emerged. As competitiveness increases and new markets for consumption and investment blossom, we now see a larger and more articulated world market for goods and services than ever before in history.

It is a cliché that global politics and economics are changing quickly. That much we know. What is unclear is whether and how these changes implicate each other. Put simply, is economic prosperity necessary (or sufficient) for democratization? In contrast, there are important ways in which these two "trends" are not mutually reinforcing. This chapter attempts to capture the complexity of European integration by employing an approach that is in the first instance geographic. However, we do not just focus on geography as territory, but rather on geography as the terrain in which the scale of economic exchange and political interactions unfold. Our basic thesis is that *integration* is a complex process of feedback across these two arenas, and that one important implication of this characterization is that we should expect to observe that the process of integration is neither smooth nor unidirectional. Indeed, as many have noted, in Europe the process of integration is often viewed as being on an ineluctable path toward either supranationalism or subnational anarchy. These characterizations ignore the fact that integration has both political and economic aspects. These implicate each other so as to explain why we should expect integration characterized by "stops and starts" rather than by smooth, easily predictable development. We detail these processes and develop a simple model to show how these integration dynamics may be expected to play out in Europe.

Figure 2.1, discovered (during field research) on a bulletin board in an Amsterdam pub, provides a characterization of these two separate processes. On the left, we see the growing political-economic integration of Europe into an integrated whole; on the right, the fissure of previously integrated Eastern Europe into dozens of smaller units is portrayed. On the one hand, we have the economic integration of Western Europe; on the other, the political disintegration of Eastern Europe. Our thesis is that both of these processes are part and parcel of the same interconnections between political and economic life. Taken hyperbolically, increasing democratization leads to a delegitimization of central governments.

Figure 2.1
The Political Economy of Europe

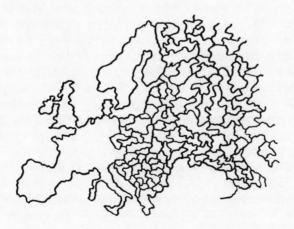

As locale becomes more salient, and as participation becomes more widespread, disintegration of state-based identities into national ones has, once again, come to pass in Europe. Not only in the former Soviet Union and the former Yugoslavia, but also in many other societies, we have seen the renaissance of national identities based on what heretofore have been denoted subnational groupings. From Serbs, Croats, and Bosnians in the Balkans, through Russians and Ukrainians, and on to Basques, Occitanians, and Quebecois, increasing democratization norms have led smaller groups to pursue a "national" agenda. One extreme conclusion is that, by the turn of the century, there may be twice as many "national" units as exist currently. A world with three hundred sovereign states (A.D. 2000) will be quite different than one with thirty (A.D. 1815). Thus, one simple effect of political integration and democratization would appear to be the reduction of scale for the political legitimacy of governance: Viable authority relations have a more localized scale in such a future.

On the other hand, the scale effects of economy cut in exactly the opposite fashion. Self-sufficiency in an era of economic integration is virtually abandoned as a strategy. In central governments, international organizations, and multinational businesses alike, it has become apparent that increasing scale of operations helps to ensure success (Arthur 1994, Buchanan and Yoon 1993). One of the major findings of the development economics literature in recent years has been that there are increasing rather than constant or decreasing returns to scale in most successful development projects. Larger markets, more diversification, and increasing strategic alliances all result from a recognition that a global market is a necessary aspect of successful economic policy today. Whether it is the local construction of an international airport or the export-oriented policies of the major development banks, there is ample evidence to suggest that major economic policy for business and society alike is predicated on a global, not a local, vision.

With regard to Western and Eastern Europe, there appear to be two cross-cutting processes at work—economic integration and national disintegration. In the West, the development of the European Community indicates an increasing unity based on economics. In the East, the breakup of the former Soviet Union and COMECON nations bespeaks of increased nationalism or political fracturing and fissuring. These seemingly opposite processes, while explanatory at the surface level, obfuscate other important considerations.

These questions are at the core of the long-standing debate about how political and economic communities are established. In this chapter, we treat politics and economics as separate but tightly coupled processes (Caporaso and Levine 1992). That is, although they are not "the same," neither can they be considered separately. Geography in terms of scale or size effects stands at the core of each, but is transparent to both. So in Western Europe, we expect economic integration to be accompanied by concomitant political integration, and in the East, increased nationalism should be accompanied by economic fracturing. We believe that in this simple question relating the scale of social activity to the implications of globalization there is much that can be learned.

In addressing the combination of politics and economics, we are working at a very high level of abstraction indeed. Moreover, politics and economics are each composed of many components interacting in many ways, far too many to explore here. To give some purchase on these issues, we turn first to a discussion of the politics of integration, building upon the work of Karl Wolfgang Deutsch. Subsequently, we examine the geography of macroeconomic relations, building on Paul Krugman's influential ideas.

POLITICAL COMMUNITY

Deutsch et al. (1957) argue that a social group is an organization, not an agglomeration. Implicit within this definition is a sense of structure and order established through communication. It is this communication, both verbal and non-verbal, that allows seeing, thinking, and acting together and that establishes intersubjectivity and integrated political communities. Economics is brought in through the definition of a country: the immediate interdependence for a wide range of goods and services. The lattice of economic interconnections is much denser in an integrated political community, i.e., country, nation state or security zone. Thus, the building of a political community requires the ordered combination of a great many items and interests, more than can possibly be enumerated (Deutsch 1966a).

These two trends—political and economic—work against one another, but how? Considered together, they lead to the following questions. What is the optimal scale for governance, or what might be called political viability? Is that scale compatible with the optimal scale for economic viability? The proliferation of political units of smaller scale, as a consequence of the globalization of democracy, may well lead to economic units that are sufficiently small to be ineffective in dealing with the global marketplace and thus are economically implausible. Conversely, as economic scale grows, it undercuts the political viability of democratic norms.

Beyond the static definition of a security or political community, Deutsch (1957) describes how previously separate peoples dynamically come together. In doing so, Deutsch differentiates between amalgamated, single government communities and pluralistic, multiple government communities. The conditions necessary to create an amalgamated security community are:

- mutual compatibility of major values;
- a distinctive way of life;
- expectations of joint rewards timed so as to come before the imposition of burdens from amalgamation;
- a marked increase in political and administrative capabilities of at least

some participating units;

• superior economic growth on the part of some participating units and the development of so-called core areas around which are grouped comparatively weaker areas;

• unbroken links of social communication, both geographically between territories and between different social strata;

• a broadening political elite;

• mobility of persons, at least among the politically relevant strata; and

• a multiplicity of communications and transactions.

In contrast, the conditions for a pluralistic community are:

• compatibility of values among decisionmakers;

• mutual predictability of behavior among decision-makers of units to be integrated; and

• mutual responsiveness.

Having pointed out the necessary conditions for integration, Deutsch does not argue that such integration is inevitable. For Deutsch, history need not necessarily repeat itself. The best we can hope to accomplish is to notice general(izable) patterns from history and apply them in analyses of the present and future. Thus, integration is "a matter of fact, not of time."

Moreover, it serves to remember that from this perspective, it is entirely possible for security communities to disintegrate. Deutsch and his collaborators suggest that the conditions behind such a process include:

• extended military commitments;

• an increase in political participation on the part of a previously passive group;

• the growth of ethnic or linguistic differentiation;

• prolonged economic decline or stagnation;

• relative closure of elites;

• excessive delay in social, economic, or political reforms; and

• failure of a privileged group to adjust to its loss of dominance.

This last laundry list may seem a little peculiar in that doing one thing may increase integration while at another time decrease it; e.g., broadening the elite can increase integration, while increasing political participation of previously passive groups can lead to disintegration. Ward (1988) addresses just such phenomena and concludes that actions that lead to beneficial consequences at one time can lead to negative ones at another. While many scholars make reference to the unintended consequences of European integration (Sandholtz and Zysman 1989, Keohane and Hoffman 1991, Garrett 1992, Moravcsik 1993, Caporaso 1993, Huelshoff 1994), a theory that fully accounts for the "stops and starts" nature of integration has not yet been developed. However, the empirical literature on European integration is littered with disagreement about the extent, speed, and direction of the process of integration. This was a shock to the policy and scholarly communities during the late 1950s (Deutsch et al. 1967) and by the 1990s had become well known and accepted. But the question remains, why?

THE GEOGRAPHY OF ECONOMICS AND POLITICS

Krugman (1991) has provided a clarion call for an analysis of economics that encompasses the geographic dimensions that are too often ignored. In Figure 2.1 we illustrate one possible geography for the Europe of the end of the twentieth century, a geography that is easy to illuminate superficially in the light of a trans-European economic and political union. Krugman's essays have pointed the way to a deeper implication of this geography of integration, and we draw upon those ideas in this section.

Three basic processes describe and prescribe the topography of integration from a geographic perspective. First, different so-called economies of scale are developed in different locales, sometime for quite curious, serendipitous reasons. Second, the cost of producing and transporting primary, intermediate, and finished goods makes these economies of scale quite robust in a geographical sense. Finally, economists have assumed that—save farmers—a mobile labor force moves to where the jobs are, and in so doing further reinforces a geographically concentrated market structure. These three basic components are mutually stimulating and reinforcing. As such they allow one to tell the story not only of economic concentration and development, but also of the creation of core and periphery areas, each organized along productivity lines.

This core-periphery model is based on a simple notion of two basic regions, generically East and West, with two basic classes of private, economic activity. One focuses on agricultural product, the other on capital-intensive manufacturing and services. If everyone, East and West, lusts after the same goodies (i.e., has identical tastes per the standard macroeconomic assumptions), then the Cobb-Douglas welfare function is largely based on manufacturing, which depends in turn on demand for manufactured goods and transportation costs. This leads quite "naturally" to a situation in which one region remains an agricultural region (with lower aggregate welfare), and the other a manufacturing sector (with higher aggregate welfare).

Doubtless, some have argued that a Northern and Southern European axis has developed along these lines. However, over the past half-century, European economic development has proceeded along other lines. It is clear that the Krugman thesis is more easily and cogently applied to the development of the manufacturing belt in the northeastern United States and that, in particular, labor mobility has been more characteristic of U.S. economic development than it has been evident in the European landscape. Europe has its long-standing tradition of Gastarbeiters, particularly in Germany, Switzerland, and France. But this shrinks in comparison to the thoroughgoing geographical disarticulation of the labor market in the United States. Not only have cultural traditions, and their attendant social institutions, served as a barrier to labor migration in Europe, but so have the ideological, political, and physical barriers between socialist governments in Western Europe and communist governments in Eastern Europe.

So the integration of Europe by the creation of a core and periphery found milder form in a North-South axis than it might have if all barriers were removed. As we witness the end of the twentieth century, by designed policy of Bruxelles and by historical torrent, these labor markets are essentially unfettered, even if some residual barriers remain. It seems most plausible that, French protestations to the contrary, agricultural activities may be pinned down in the East, while manufacturing (and service) activities will further blossom in the West. One cannot know for sure, but the broad outlines of Krugman's (1991) tale seem to delineate the likely future. It seems likely that the next decades will bring about a further concentration of manufacturing in the West and agriculture in the East. One area that might contravene this trend is arms production, for which Russian enterprises are well poised. At the same time this geographic concentration of economic activity is growing, there is a geographic deconcentration of political loyalty to smaller and smaller political units. The former Soviet Empire encompassed twenty-two million square kilometers and governed some 287 million inhabitants. Its collapse and breakup into a loose confederation, followed by the confederation's demise, led to the creation of fifteen newly independent states, including Russia. Czechoslovakia and Yugoslavia epitomize the trend. Apart from the great victory of Western ideology, it may be that the real legacy of this disarticulation is a truly democratic one that encourages people to seek smaller legitimacy associations, not larger ones. In much the same way that the Congress of Vienna in 1815 legitimized the nation-state system, the fall of the Soviet Communist party tolled loudly, not only for communist regimes, but also for state-regimes.

Thus, the geographic story is not just one of increasing pressure for large-scale political and economic activities, but it is also one in which economic concentrations work not only against but for economic integration. In a similar fashion, as states become stronger and more coordinated in matters of economics and social policy, locales become more politically relevant to citizens, not less so. Thus, we feel that the geography of integration, the erosion of political legitimacy, and the concentration of economic activity serve to explain, in part, why the ride to Bruxelles continues to be a bit bumpy. With these ideas in mind we move toward developing a model that will help us to understand the interplay of these forces in the context of European integration.

THE LOGIC OF INTEGRATION

We have already noted that current scholarship on the European Union ackowledges the multi-dimensionality and complexity of the subject matter. Understanding the European Union requires a blending of both empirical and theoretical analyses. This study uses a geographical perspective, and in doing so starts from an empirical, historical base and then uses the cybernetic methodology to create an abstract, dynamic model.

Without pinpointing the ultimate cause of the Second World War, it became clear in the 1950s that a formal federalism might be more successful than other means of holding in check German-French animosities, the list of which remains impressive, including World War I (1914-1918), the Napoleonic Wars (1799-1813), the Wars of the Spanish Succession (1702-1713), as well as the oft-contentious interwar periods.

In light of the League of Nations' failure, many concluded that closer economic and eventually political and social ties between the two traditional protagonists would almost by definition lead to a more pacific Europe (Carr 1939:235-239). On May 9, 1950, Robert Schuman, French minister for foreign affairs and "grandfather" of the European Community, proposed that Franco-German coal and steel production should be placed under the purview of a centralized authority, an institution that other European countries could join (Cole and Cole 1993). The primary mission of this institution would be to ensure peace and stability in postwar Europe.

Recounting dates, however, can only tell part of the story. The commitment to eliminate barriers to the movement of people, capital, and goods among the current European Union nations aims at increasing the economies of scale and decreasing transaction costs of interaction. Focusing solely on the material aspects of such policy ignores key aspects of the integration process. First, integration and union constitute an ideological commitment as much as a programmatic one as the European Union seeks to assure for Europe a competitive position in the world economy, especially with respect to the United States and Japan. Second, beyond the ideological components, recent structural changes in the world economy have helped to move integration along—specifically, the relative decline of the United States and rise of Japan on the world's economic stage. Third, integration has, until now, been made up of bargains among elites, CEOs, Executives, and European Commission leaders (Sandholtz and Zysman 1989).

While Europe has enjoyed a significant period of peace, an explicit goal of the European Union, the question of stability remains somewhat more problematic. This is not to discount the achievements of the organization—fifty years of peace between France and Germany given their history is a laudable success. However, there has been a significant mismatch between the expectations of stable and gradual European integration and the reality, which has been characterized by unevenness or "stops and starts." Some attribute these failures to the elites responsible for European integration or to exogenous shocks. We, however, argue that unevenness should be expected because of the endogenous structure of the system under study and the very process of integration.

The reason this explanation has been overlooked in previous studies is due in part to limitations in the analytical methodologies employed by previous scholars and in part to how humans view or explain change. Using cybernetics, we develop a different type of model that resolves some of the inconsistencies experienced by other scholars working in this field. The way in which one views a problem adds power to understanding or solving the problem, even though the information presented is the same. For instance, what is the next number in the sequence 7, 63, 511? The answer, 4,095, is not at all obvious. However, if the sequence is presented in base (8)—7, 77, 777—then the answer becomes obvious, 7,777, which translates to 4,095 in base (10). Note that no extra information is presented in the rephrasing, but the manner in which the information is presented makes understanding much easier. This, in effect, is what we attempt to do here. The method used to deliver this increased clarity is called "cybernetics." Initially developed by MIT mathematician Norbert Wiener (1961), cybernetics uses the theories of communication, control, and information originally developed in electrical engineering to study systems generally. Also important in this tradition is the biologically based work of Ludwig von Bertalanffy (1960, 1968). Although Wiener himself did apply cybernetics to social systems (1950), perhaps the best initial work on politics came from Karl W. Deutsch (1966b), in which he looked not at the raw power of politics but rather focused on the communications, "steerings," or transmissions of information that make politics possible. As useful or evocative as these balancing metaphors have proven, Deutsch did not demonstrate how institutional structures were linked with the dynamic behaviors they exhibited (Richardson 1991:277). This was accomplished by Jay Forrester (1961) in the field of management. The application of system dynamics to political questions took shape most forcefully during the now forgotten "The Limits to Growth" debate fostered by the publication of a popular book on imminent environmental collapse (Meadows et al., 1972). This popular report was based on Forrester (1971a) and explained more succinctly in Forrester (1971b). The incorporation of system dynamics and systems-based reasoning into the study of politics remains an ongoing opportunity. Thus, the key insight drawn from cybernetics—through the progression of Wiener, von Bertalanffy, Deutsch, and Forrester—is that the dynamics exhibited by a system are a consequence of the system's structure. Moreover, in political systems there is the matter of analytical scale. Collections of individuals comprise nations, and so if our analysis were truly reductionist then the analytical lens would focus on the smallest component—the individual. If our analysis were instead holistic, then we would concentrate on the higher level structures—in this case, the nation-state. Since we focus on the dynamics of national integration, the subject matter itself forces a holistic analysis.

We use a combination of resources to determine the aspects of analysis, specifically, empirically grounded news reports informed by academic theory, and begin by examining Western Europe. In April 1994, Jacques Delors, head of the European Commission, reminded European trade unions, businesses, and governments that despite the recent economic upturn, pervasive unemployment must remain a primary concern. Toward this end, in April 1994, Delors urged those addressed to use recommendations contained within a Commission white paper to develop job creation strategies. Restating this information in more general terms reveals its underlying structure. Jacques Delors represents the European Commission, which is clearly an elite body. This illustrates that *elite values* are an important variable. After all, it was the values of elites as articulated by Schuman that contributed to the creation of the European Economic Community. Delors, in making his argument, referred to two simultaneous economic processes: (1) the recent economic upturn, and (2) persistent unemployment. First, the recent economic upturn indicates that at least some members of society are "doing better," and so this represents *societal benefits*. However, others—in this case, the unemployed—continue to "do badly," which in turn necessitates the inclusion of *societal costs*.

The story of Eastern Europe can be told using the same variables but merits somewhat less optimism. Emerging from an era of centrally controlled economics, the importance of elite values is clear. The question here concerns the relative importance of societal costs and societal benefits. At this time in history, the former clearly outweighs the latter. Looking to Russia, we see one of the most direct societal costs, consumer prices, growing at a rate of 542.3 percent per year (*The Economist* of July 2, 1994). This inflation is driven by more long-term systemic factors, primarily government debt. The 1994 Russian budget deficit threatens to exceed 10 percent of GDP, and current estimates stand at 38 billion US$. Moscow owes the West more than 80 billion US$, and appeals for new loans show little sign of slowing.

While similar stories are too often repeated throughout Eastern Europe—Hungary, Poland, Slovakia, Bulgaria, and Romania all have similar problems—there are systemic reasons why societal costs outweigh societal benefits. By "systemic" we mean that the consequences were unintended, a common theme in the European integration literature. For years the Eastern Bloc, as directed by Moscow, attempted to deliver societal benefits as best it could, and initially societal benefits may have indeed outweighed costs. However, the inability to sustain this relative good is reflected in a crumbling infrastructure and ponderous debt as well as the eventual ouster of the communist leadership. Surely nobody intended for this to happen, and yet it did.

The process by which good intentions can lead to bad consequences is through *complexity*, which is simply a multiplicity of interconnected, relevant factors.

Thus, when a policy is pursued to optimize one factor or "solve" one problem, there can be side effects for other factors that escape the notice of the policymaker, and this failure can be either intentional or unintentional. If the negative consequences are delayed in time or diffused in space, which is a function of scale, then the information may not be readily accessed by the policymaker.

To politicians in both Eastern and Western Europe, inclusion of the East into the European Union appears to provide the best promise of relief for the troubled, previously communist economies. The head of the European Free Trade Association (EFTA) commented in Bucharest, "we have now different free trade areas but not one in common [in Europe] and this is damaging to all of us." He explained further that establishing free trade between Eastern and Western Europe, "will be a big step forward and a very sound basis for continuing the next phase, which should finally lead to membership of [east European states] in the Community."

European Union member states, perhaps surprisingly, appear to agree with this conclusion. Germany's Klaus Kinkel and Great Britain's Douglas Hurd wrote in a joint statement, "we must project security and stability from our part of Europe to other European countries in the East." They continued, "eventually, they should fully participate in all European institutions—in particular the EU [European Union] and NATO."

This process of unifying previously disparate entities, in this case national economies, represents the same process described by Karl Deutsch and is called *integration*. To the extent that integration unifies previously disparate factors, it increases the number of factors that leaders of the responsible institution (here the European Union) must consider when formulating policy. Thus, we see that integration contributes to complexity, and complexity contributes to unintended consequences, which can be and often are negative.

Five significant model variables have been identified in this section: (1) *elite values*, (2) *societal benefits*, (3) *societal costs*, (4) *complexity*, and (5) *integration*. They are used to explain the current state of both Western Europe (the European Union) and of Eastern Europe (the former Eastern Bloc). To develop this model further, we need to articulate the connections between these variables. This is done in the following diagram.

Figure 2.2 provides a schematic overview of the self-reinforcing and self-regulating aspects we feel are especially important in integration processes. The causal chains in this diagram link the five variables into four feedback loops—two positive and two negative. The terms "positive" and "negative" do not imply normative commitments. Instead, they refer to the type of behavior one can expect from the linkages between variables. A positive arrow means that an increase in a variable leads to an increase in the variable to which the arrow points, and a decrease leads to a decrease. A negative arrow means an increase leads to a decrease in the variable to which it points, and a decrease leads to an increase.

Figure 2.2
Linkages among Integration Components

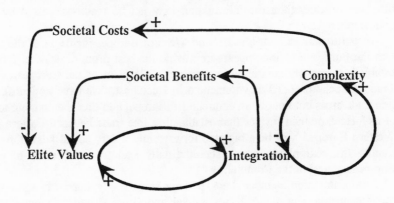

These causal connections in turn form loops, which are likewise positive and negative, the polarity being determined by the number of negative causal connections in the loop. An even number or the absence of negative connections constitutes a positive loop that tends to grow without bound. An odd number of negative connections constitutes a negative loop, which tends to seek a constant or "steady-state" value.

The first positive loop is formed by the positive connections between elite values and integration. Elites seek to bring about more integration, and the act of integration tends to benefit elites, which therefore reinforces this value.

This loop corresponds to Deutsch's observation that integration occurs when the core areas are developed. The second positive loop links elite values to integration, integration to societal benefits, and societal benefits to elite values. This can be thought of in terms of Deutsch's broadening of the political elite, although we are actually making the more general point that society as a whole benefits from integration. The two negative loops provide both the stability that keeps the positive loops from growing without bound and the capacity for the system to become less integrated over time. The first negative loop is that between integration and complexity. Integration implies that a socio-economic activity or process that had previously been pursued separately is now pursued in a connected, joint fashion. Complexity is the sum of integration, which is to say that every additional integrated economic or political process increases the possible interactions between the other previously integrated processes. In this manner, complexity works to slow integration because as more social aspects become integrated, it becomes harder to anticipate the consequences of additional integration. Moreover, the first processes to become integrated are the most obvious ones, those with the highest benefits and least cost (e.g., the production of French iron ore and

German coking coal). As integration progresses, however, the benefits become more specious while the costs become more tangible. This dynamic is captured in the second negative loop that connects elite values, integration, complexity, and societal costs. Two new causal connections are introduced here: complexity increases societal costs, which in turn decrease elite values. As we have already pointed out, the process of integration tends to deplete the most attractive candidates first. But also complexity itself contributes to societal costs in that it makes the social context more staid, more stable, and less dynamic, because an ever-increasing number of potentially undesirable interactions must be considered before an action can be undertaken. This process therefore contributes to the economic stagnation that Deutsch explains can precipitate political disintegration.

However, note that the complexity that leads to societal costs is a consequence of the integration that initially delivered societal benefits. Thus, through this model we have articulated Deutsch's observation that integration occurs when rewards are delivered before the burdens of amalgamation. Stated differently, the same actions that deliver beneficial consequences in one context can deliver undesired ones in another. This model illuminates the processes at work in Western and Eastern Europe and illustrates that they are to a large extent governed by the same social structure. However, in Western Europe, the positive loops dominate, while in Eastern Europe the negative loops do. In Western Europe, the commitment of elite values to further integration is ensured through the institution of the European Commission. Moreover, the viability of the bargains on which the Commission is based will persist so long as societal benefits continue to outweigh societal costs. However, the recent appeal by Delors to address the persistent problem of unemployment shows that societal costs in Western Europe are not negligible. Moreover, continued integration will become more problematic as it becomes harder to deliver societal benefits and forestall societal costs.

Eastern Europe provides an example of dominant negative loops. The previous purveyor of elite values, Moscow, has collapsed and now ceases to be an effective coordinator or motivator of integration. The reasons for Moscow's fall are legion, but certainly popular discontent must be included among them. In terms of the model, societal costs outweighed societal benefits for too long. Although the socioeconomic system that created such deprivations is now gone, the citizens of Eastern Europe retain the legacy of communism through high foreign debts and exorbitant interest rates. It remains to be seen just how this dire economic situation can be overcome, although integration with Western Europe is often touted as the logical solution. Integration between Eastern and Western Europe is likely to be problematic, however, just as the smaller scale unification of East and West Germany has proven (Jacoby 1994a,b).

As we look forward to the continued process of European integration, we should recall Karl Deutsch's cautionary epigram, "integration is a matter of

fact, not of time." The manner in which causal loop diagrams demonstrate
their dynamic behavior is developed in the following kinetic logic model
(Thomas 1978, 1979). In this model, the four feedback loops are expressed as
five Boolean equations, one for each of the model's five variables. Capital
letters denote variables whose values are currently being calculated. Lower-
case letters denote variables that already have values. Thus, they represent the
same variables, but the values for the lower-case variables were calculated
during the previous time period. The symbols $\wedge$, $\vee$, and $\neg$ correspond to the
logical operators *and*, *or*, and *negation*, respectively.

$$EV \quad \Leftarrow \quad (sb \vee \neg sc) \vee i_{t-2}$$
$$I \quad \Leftarrow \quad ev \wedge \neg c$$
$$C \quad \Leftarrow \quad i_{t-5}$$
$$SB \quad \Leftarrow \quad i$$
$$SC \quad \Leftarrow \quad c$$

As shown in the causal loop diagram, *elite values* (*EV*) is shown as a
function of *social benefits* (*SB*), *social costs* (*SC*), and *integration* (*I*). *I* is a
function of *EV* and *complexity* (*C*), and *C* is a function of *I*. *I* has two
subscripts, a *2* in the *EV* equation and *5* in the *C* equation. These denote time
delays of two and five time periods, and are chosen with Deutsch's observation
that integration occurs when the benefits of integration are enjoyed before the
costs come due.

Following the rules of this logic, the model changes over time, thus
revealing its dynamic behavior. One can hypothesize about a system's behavior
from the causal loop diagram, but the relationships between the feedback loops
vary over time, and so the explicit definition of a system serves to make the
analysis more rigorous and less dependent on subjectivity.

To investigate the model's possible behaviors, it is initialized with each of
its 32 (2^5) possible combinations. What is interesting is that the 32 sets of
initial conditions generate only two sets of behaviors, each a cycle of 16 time
periods and distinguishable from each other only by minor details.

Although the analysis concentrates on the more prevalent of the two cycles
(the major cycle occurs 25 times, the minor 7), the following description
applies essentially to both. Table 2.1 presents these cycles in abbreviated
format. This analysis concentrates on the cycling behavior because of its
persistence and stability. As the cycle does just that—cycles—we could begin
the analysis anywhere, but we choose to start just as the European Union
started, with elite values. (This starting point is highlighted by a ① in the
table.) Initially, *EV* is turned on after all the variables are turned off, which
denotes complete economic and political failure. In the following time period,
I is present, and in the next, economic benefits are delivered.

Table 2.1
Cycling in Integration

Time Period	Major Cycle					Minor Cycle				
	Elite Values	Integration	Complexity	Societal Benefits	Societal Costs	Elite Values	Integration	Complexity	Societal Benefits	Societal Costs
	Start of First Cycle									
1	①					①				●
2	●	●					●			
3	●	●		●		●			●	
4	●	●		●		●	●			
5	●	●		●		●	●		●	
6	●	●		●		●	●		●	
7	●	●		●		●	●		●	
8	●	●	●	●		●	●	●	●	
9	●		●	●	●	●			●	●
10	●		●		●	●	●	●		
11			●		●	●		●	●	●
12			●		●	●		●		●
13			●		●			●		●
14			●		●			●		●
15					●					●
16								●		
	End of First Cycle: Start of Second Cycle									
16 + 1	①					①				●
16 + 2	●	●					●			
16 + 3	●	●		●		●			●	
16 + 4	●	●		●		●	●			
16 + 5	●	●		●		●	●		●	
16 + 6	●	●		●		●	●		●	
16 + 7	●	●		●		●	●		●	
16 + 8	●	●	●	●		●	●	●	●	
16 + 9	●		●	●	●	●			●	●
16 +10	●		●		●	●	●	●		
16 + 11			●		●	●		●	●	●
16 + 12			●		●	●		●		●
16 + 13			●		●			●		●
16 + 14			●		●			●		●
16 + 15					●					●
16 + 16								●		
	End of Second Cycle									
	¼									

This providential period of concomitant elite values, integration, and societal benefits lasts for five time periods (3-7) but is brought to an end when the unintended consequence of continued integration, complexity, gets activated. In the next time period, integration is turned off and societal costs get turned on. After that, societal benefits disappear and remain absent for the next nine time periods. Next, elite values fails, which leaves only complexity and societal costs to dominate over the next four time periods (11-14). After that, complexity finally switches off, followed by societal costs, resulting in a period where all variables are off. Then, elite values turns on and the cycle begins anew.

From this abstract analysis, it is natural to wonder where Western and Eastern Europe fit into the described cycle. Western Europe is in the period of prosperity (cycles 3-7), but probably towards the end rather than the beginning. While there does exist an elite consensus that seeks integration, the process appears to be fraying. Unemployment, a societal cost, persists, and agricultural and immigration problems are likely to become more contentious in the years to come. Placing Eastern Europe is considerably less clear. Given that Eastern Europe's centralized authority, Moscow, only recently failed, and given the complexity of its economic problems, we might conclude that it is just now entering an extended period of high complexity and societal costs (cycles 11-14). If we instead choose to concentrate on its leaders' commitment to integration, then the outlook appears somewhat more promising. The true answer probably lies somewhere in the middle, but it is important to remember that models like the one presented here are not intended to be deterministic predictions. Instead, they present a generic pattern that helps to make understandable otherwise confusing dynamic processes. Moreover, we believe that these patterns may be fractal in the sense that the pattern we describe is evident at virtually all levels in the political landscape, ranging from the subnational, through the national, and on to the supranational (Rucker 1987:274-314).

CONCLUSION

Large-scale processes continue to rework the structure of Europe. Western Europe currently tends toward increasingly large political organizations and economies, while Eastern Europe moves toward ever-growing nationalism, i.e., smaller political organizations and economies. At first glance, these cross-cutting trends appear to be wholly independent. However, once the data is described and analyzed in a broader geographical context, we see that Western and Eastern Europe are essentially experiencing different aspects of the same cyclical process. In addition, this cycle is characterized by stops and starts, or more precisely by eras of stasis punctuated by intervals of intense change. The first is an era of integration brought about by societal benefits that outweigh costs. The second is an era of disarticulation brought about by societal costs overtaking benefits.

The "stops and starts" behavior of European integration is typical for large-scale, complex systems, although it is more often referred to as a punctuated equilibrium. The theory of punctuated equilibrium originally stems from the paleobiology work of Eldredge and Gould (1972), although it has been applied recently in the social sciences by the speculative and evocative work of Gersick (1991). Perhaps the best grounded work in the field of complex systems is in chemistry by Prigogine and Stengers (1984). In international relations, Ward (1988) addresses the phenomenon of unintended consequences, Ward (1991) addresses politics from a geographic perspective, and Lofdahl (1994) addresses chaotic cycles in transnational integration and state breakdown.

What we have shown in this chapter is that the broad, macro-level structure of political economy leads, almost ineluctably, toward periods of stability followed by periods of rapid change. The pull of integration eventually is caught by the push of downside, often unintended, consequences that bring costs to the fore. In time, the downturn is reversed again and benefits re-emerge. This is apparent in the political as well as the economic realm, where self-reinforcing mechanisms also exhibit self-defeating components. What is ineluctable is neither progress nor regress, but rather an ebb and flow of social processes. This is not to suggest a Hegelian future for Europe, but rather to broadly frame the short-term advances and setbacks in a larger context. Many past, present, and future federalists will hope for the succession of ever-increasing levels of social and political integration. Even in the face of setbacks, integration appeared to be only a "matter of time." Yet we have shown that, while the arrow of time moves in only one direction, integration and disintegration are both described by identical dynamics in the sense that they derive from the same structure. Integration, in the broad sense, can be seen not as a matter of time, but rather as a race against time, in which the accumulation of benefits must outpace the aggregation of costs.

NOTE

This research was conducted at the Program on Political and Economic Change at the Institute of Behavioral Science, University of Colorado. We would like to extend our appreciation to Jette Knudsen of MIT for her valuable suggestions during the long, slow, but fruitful ramp-up phase of this project. We also appreciate the feedback and advice of our colleagues, especially Jordin S. Cohen, Michael Shin, Ed Greenberg, John O'Loughlin, Lynn Staeheli, Tom Mayer, James Scarritt, and Walt Stone, even if we ignored many of their best suggestions. Thomas Bernauer, Dieter Ruloff, Gerald Schneider, and Patricia Weitsman were excellent stewarts of the overall project: We thank them for their efforts at keeping us pointed in the right direction. Karl W. Deutsch and Jay Forrester provided much of the inspiration for this effort.

3

Expansion or Unity? Placing the European Union in Historical Perspective

Lars-Erik Cederman

INTRODUCTION

Contemporary scholarship on European integration tends to be both ahistorical and policy-oriented. Yet the challenges facing the leaders of the European Union (EU) after the end of the Cold War are epochal. The collapse of Euro-optimism stems as much from the internal friction caused by the lingering recession and inflated aspirations associated with the Maastricht treaty as the failure to establish the Union as a coherent actor in dealing with the crises to the east. Thus, though the enormous complexity of the institutional issues call for detailed legal and economic analysis, there is also a need for a broader approach to the future of the EU. As a modest step in overcoming this formidable challenge, this chapter turns to two sources: Historical sociology and new institutional economic history. It combines the former's emphasis on community and loyalty with the latter's focus on optimization of organizational performance as a function of scale.

In essence, the model presented in this chapter conceptualizes political units' power as a combination of scale and intensity. The larger the territorial and demographic scale of a unit, the greater its international leverage. The more intense the loyalty of the population, the more effective the internal resource extraction and coherence of its foreign policy. The optimal tradeoff between these two dimensions has varied with the cultural and political conditions of the specific historical period. Whereas small city-states and large empires dominated the pre-modern era, the modern world has been dominated by the mid-sized nation-state. Although medieval history may seem a far-fetched place to start an analysis of the EU, this convergence of identities to the nation-state has important implications for European integration.

The argument is set in five sections: The first defines the dimensions of power; the second introduces the analytical framework and applies it to the emergence of the nation-state; the third extends the analysis to European integration; the fourth discusses various approaches to intensification and enlargement of the European Union; and the fifth summarizes the chapter by highlighting the contributions and limitations of the model.

THE SCALE AND INTENSITY OF POWER

In this chapter I conceive of power as a combination of scale and intensity.[1] This distinction parallels Mann's (1986:7) definition of extensive and intensive power, the former referring to "the ability to organize large numbers of people over far-flung territories in order to engage in minimally stable cooperation," and the latter to "the ability to organize tightly and command a high level of mobilization of commitment from the participants."

Here scale stands for the physical, demographic, or economic size of the unit. Ever since Adam Smith, economic theory has singled out market size as a crucial variable. The expansion of organizational size is the key to specialization and division of labor, the main sources of wealth. Drawing on microeconomic theory, economic historians have speculated about the optimal size of political organizations (Tullock 1969, Bean 1973, Friedman 1977, North 1981:138-139, Wittman 1991, see Gilpin 1981 and Scharpf 1988 for further references). Usually this literature refers to the technical and economic preconditions for efficient production of wealth and power. In an often-quoted article, Bean (1973) argues that changes in military technology and methods of taxation paved the way for the nation-state. As in the theory of the firm, this type of argument relies heavily on economies of scale up to a certain point whereafter decreasing returns set in, usually associated with problems of command and control. The result of this reasoning is a U-shaped average cost curve suggesting that there is an optimal size (or range of sizes) of organization for which the costs are minimized (Bean 1973, Gilpin 1981). No doubt there were powerful economies of scale at work in early modern history as well. What Downing (1992) refers to as the military revolution implied steadily rising costs of armaments. This fierce technological arms race eliminated scores of decentralized feudal power centers. The survivors were the much larger absolutist states who were the only units that managed to absorb the rising costs of increasingly sophisticated and expensive weaponry.

The second aspect of power, intensity, complements the economists' objective and quantitative approach to human organization with a qualitative and subjective element. Sociology offers theories of how intensive power affects organizational viability. Grappling with the fundamental transformation of European society in the nineteenth century, the founders of this discipline, Weber, Durkheim, and Marx, recognized that modernity implied a shift from the small-scale organizations of the traditional world. To conceptualize this dichotomy, they borrowed the notion of community (often referred to as *Gemeinschaft*) as a master concept from the writings of Tönnies (1957). In response to the individualistic notion of society inherent in the Enlightenment, the concept of community developed to designate "all forms of relationship which are characterized by a high degree of personal intimacy, emotional depth, moral commitment, social cohesion, and continuity in time" (Nisbet 1993:47). The puzzling fact about modern nationalism is that it is an expression of the strong feeling of community traditionally accorded to small-scale organizations—such as the tribe, village, or city-state—yet extended to entire nations stretching over vast territories (Calhoun 1991).

Preoccupied by material factors such as technology and resources, most economic explanations disregard the cognitive aspects of state formation.[2] More recently, some economists have begun to question the fruitfulness of neoclassical orthodoxy: "We simply do not have any convincing theory of the sociology of knowledge that accounts for the effectiveness (or ineffectiveness) of organized ideologies or accounts for choices made when the payoffs to honesty, integrity, working hard, or voting are negative" (North 1990:42).

This, however, is where the intensity dimension of power fits in. While coercion may elicit considerable resources from a society, in the long run such systems are prone to vast inefficiencies due to shirking and cheating. The best way to extract a maximum of resources presupposes active participation and loyalty on the part of the members of a political organization. After all, power rests not only on authority of enforcement but also on its legitimacy (Ruggie 1993, Wendt 1994).

Yet to forge such a commitment on a large scale is not easy. In the ancient world, empires usually lacked the cohesion of the modern nation-state (Gellner 1983, Poggi 1978, Gilpin 1981). In the words of Strayer (1970:11):

> The empires were militarily strong, but could enlist only a small proportion of their inhabitants in the political process or, indeed, in any activity that transcended immediate local interests. This meant a considerable waste of human resources; it also meant that loyalty to the state was lukewarm.

By contrast, city-states and tribes lacked the size of empires, but did manage to create a level of cohesion and loyalty that was vastly superior to that of the empires:

> The city-state made far more effective use of its inhabitants than the empire; all citizens participated actively in the political process and in associated community activities. Loyalty to the state was strong; at times it approached the intensity of modern nationalism. (Strayer 1970:11)

The subjective element of intensive power is evident in the emphasis on loyalty and commitment. In this predominantly sociological view of political power, control rests on the internalization of norms rather than explicit enforcement and coercion.[3]

MODELING THE EMERGENCE OF THE NATION-STATE

To analyze the influence of scale and intensity on organizational performance, it is useful to rely on a formal framework. To make the analysis easy to follow for all readers, the argument will be expounded graphically rather than algebraically. For those interested in mathematical details, the appendix provides a complete specification of the model. I start by assuming a fictitious social system of a given total size (measuring one by convention). The question is what organizational scale x will optimize power. To answer this question we need to express overall performance as a function of scale and intensity. It is convenient to postulate an intensity function $f(x)$ that measures the unit's effectiveness in mobilizing the resources for a given scale x. For simplicity, I limit the value range of this function to the unit interval.

The total amount of power wielded by the organization is the combination of its scale and its intensity, or formally: $p(x) = xf(x)$. Multiplication, rather than addition, ensures that power scale and intensity are viewed as necessary conditions. A zero-scale organization ($x=0$) produces no power, no matter how intense its power extraction. Similarly, a zero-intensity unit ($f(x)=0$) is equally ineffective even if its scope is universal.

Maximization of $p(x)$ yields the optimal size x^*. Figure 3.1 shows an arbitrary intensity function $f(x)$ indicating the intensity given any scale x. Since power is defined as the product of scale and intensity, $p(x)$ can be constructed as the area of the rectangle with the lower left corner at the origin and the upper right corner at point ($x^*, f(x^*)$). The optimal size x^* corresponds to the largest rectangle that fits under the curve. Such a rectangle has base x^* and height $f(x^*)$, implying that the area is $p(x^*) = x^*f(x^*)$. To find the optimum graphically, it is useful to draw a family of iso-power curves. In Figure 3.1, the lowest iso-power curve that intersects with $f(x)$ is $xf(x)=0.25$. The optimal size x^* occurs where this curve is parallel to the tangent of $f(x)$.

The contrast between the high intensity of power extraction in small-scale communities and the low intensity of power extraction in empires can be modeled as a decreasing function. The intensity function is assumed to depend on two components: The first one deriving from constant intensity, and the second one to size-dependent power extraction. The low level of technological innovation in ancient empires (Gilpin 1981:111) justifies partially relying on the assumption of constant intensity. Assuming that the costs of war are limited, predatory states are likely to be even more powerful after conquest, thanks to the revenues from the territorial aggrandizement. Power accumulation of this type drives massive positive returns to scale.[4]

Figure 3.1
Finding the Optimal Organizational Size

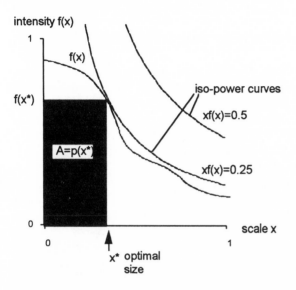

The second component of the function, corresponding to Mann's intensive power, is size-dependent. Since forging tight cultural and social communities presupposes continuous and frequent communication (Deutsch et al. 1957, Deutsch 1966a), this type of intensive power depends crucially on transportation and communication technology. In the ancient world, there was an important difference between the constraints on social surveillance and the logistical limits on military action. In his studies of ancient Asian empires, Owen Lattimore (1962) showed that whereas intensive power was restricted to interaction within village units, extensive power did not preclude military domination and raiding within vast areas (see also Mann 1986). Below the thin layer of cosmopolitan elites, the ancient world consisted of culturally diversified tribal units and city-states (Gellner 1983). Although loyalty and commitment could be considerable within these small communities, the lack of modern communications implied a sharp fall in intensity beyond the city walls or the village limit (Giddens 1985:63, Calhoun 1991:102). For example, Bean (1973:204) observes that "language, religious and racial barriers and regional particularism increase the cost of administration and control." The difficulties of intercultural communication compounded the purely administrative transaction costs associated with tax collection and resource extraction in vast territories (North 1981, Levi 1988). Thus, in trying to extend the administrative reach of intensive resource extraction, leaders in ancient times reached the point of decreasing returns after very small scales.

Figure 3.2
Intensity in the Pre-Modern World

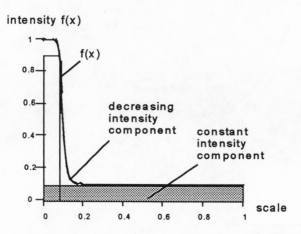

Figure 3.2 depicts a typical intensity function in the ancient world. Due to severe limits on communication and transportation technology, the intensity curve falls sharply from maximal extraction at very small scales to a much lower level for all larger organizations. The shaded area at the bottom of the diagram represents the constant intensity contribution to overall power. The unfilled area above this rectangle is the size-dependent component. The shaded area at the bottom of the diagram represents the constant intensity contribution to overall power. The unfilled area above this rectangle is the size-dependent component.

What is the optimal size in the pre-modern case? Geometric intuition suggests considerable polarization. On the one hand, a tall but thin rectangle fits under the curve for a small scale. On the other hand, there is room for a wide but low rectangle corresponding to universal empire (see the shaded area). Figure 3.3 makes this point even more clearly. In this case, we would expect large-scale empires to prevail over small-scale communities, since the local peak is lower than the imperial global maximum for $x=1$. The graph helps us to understand why city-states and other small communities were able to survive in a competitive pre-modern environment. If balance of power prevents sizes above this limit, city-states will remain among the most powerful players and might even dominate the entire geopolitical system.[5]

How does the modern world differ from the ancient one? In our simple model, the most important difference relates to the intensity function. Techno-logical and organizational innovations in early modern Europe gradually improved the extractive capacities of the emergent states.

Figure 3.3
Optimal Size in the Pre-Modern World

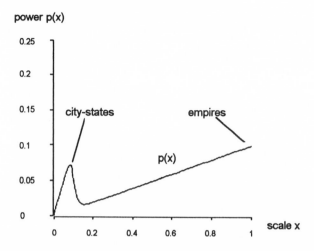

Even more importantly, new political ideas, including representative democracy, popular sovereignty, and nationalism prepared the ground for a shift from indirect to direct rule (Tilly 1990). These trends presupposed a more complex link between the rulers and the ruled. Because of the increasing scale of the emerging nation-states, these links could not be forged through direct contacts (e.g., kinship, feudal contracts, or direct democracy in city-states), but had to be mediated through abstract means requiring written communication.

Gellner (1964) explains why the shift to modernity entails a revolution in the nature of social relations. Whereas the structural inertia of traditional societies prevents culture from being used as a source of identity, in the modern world, "culture does not so much underline structure: rather, it replaces it" (Gellner 1964:155). The move toward cultural identities affects political affiliations: "Loyalty becomes linked to a high and abstract and imagined national culture rather than to structure." This is why "print capitalism" came to play such an important role in the creation of what Anderson (1983) calls "imagined communities." These national communities are imagined because they are based on abstract and categorical types of identity rather than pre-modern parochial community feelings (Calhoun 1991, Mann 1992).[6] These developments are amenable to analysis within our modeling framework. As technology and communication progress, the constraints on intensive power are likely to loosen. In terms of the diagram, this is tantamount to a rightward shift of the community threshold. Figure 3.4 depicts this change as a bold arrow pointing from the pre-modern to the modern intensity curve.

Figure 3.4
Intensity in the Modern World

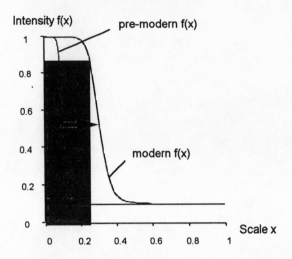

Again, geometrical intuition helps us anticipate the shape of the power function $p(x)$. As opposed to the pre-modern intensity function, the modern one has room for a large shaded rectangle that is clearly superior to the lying rectangle associated with universal empire. Figure 3.5 presents the situation explicitly.

Figure 3.5
Optimal Organizational Size in the Modern World

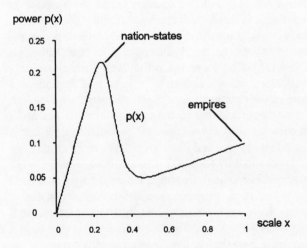

In the modern world, the equilibrium has shifted from large empire to the more compact nation-states. Moreover, the city-states have been decisively outflanked by the nation-states as well. The historical record confirms this broad outline. First, as nationalism became a serious force in the nineteenth and twentieth centuries, the old empires collapsed. World War I brought down the Habsburg, Ottoman, and Russian empires, and World War II accelerated the decline of the colonial empires (Scharpf 1988:240). With the end of the Cold War, the world has seen a continuation of this trend as the multi-cultural communist states disintegrated. Second, most of the European city-states vanished in the nineteenth century after their weakness had been demonstrated by the Napoleonic wars, the subsequent unification of Germany and Italy sealing their fate. In brief, the shift to modernity, driven by nationalism and industrialization, entails a simultaneous trend involving both integration and disintegration, each converging on the nation-state.[7] Against this historical backdrop, one might wonder where to put the process of European integration. I will devote the remainder of the chapter to this question.

MODELING EUROPEAN INTEGRATION

The technological revolution did not stop after the emergence of the modern nation-state. In an age characterized by faxes and satellites, it is natural to question the effectiveness of the "old" West-European nation-states. Indeed, the ascendancy of continent-wide superpowers suggests that the quest for larger political organization forms has not ended (Gilpin 1981:229). Regional integration, in Europe and elsewhere, can be seen as an attempt to transcend national borders in the search for internal peace and external projection of power.

It is possible to trace these developments within the formal framework. Going back to Figure 3.4, I extrapolate the trend in technological development by shifting the threshold rightward toward higher scales. Instead of a modern, or national, intensity function, the new situation could be labelled post-national. Setting the issue of world government aside, I assume that the entire system up to $x=1$ represents a regional subsystem, such as Europe (see Figure 3.6). In the new setting, the post-national organization P outflanks the nation-state N in terms of scale. The shaded square represents the power of a regional organization, the intensity of which is somewhat lower than the nation-state but whose overall power surpasses that of the smaller organization.

Before carrying the analysis any further, it is necessary to consider whether it is possible to make the leap from the Middle Ages into the contemporary era without violating the underlying assumptions of the simple framework: Are the basic categories comparable in the new post-national setting? It is well-known that power cannot always be reduced to a one-dimensional index.

Figure 3.6
The Shift from National to Post-National Intensity

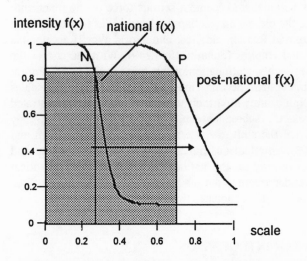

For certain analytical purposes, it is necessary to resort to an issue-specific focus and to consider issue-linkages explicitly (Keohane and Nye 1977). Nevertheless, for the study of long-term power shifts, the assumption of uni-dimensional overall power has not entirely lost its analytical bite, even though market size and foreign economic influence have tended to replace military success as the most salient power bases.

The second important difference concerns process. While military power still influences competition in many regions, much of what used to be decided in war is now ironed out in complex multilateral diplomatic negotiations. Among the developed countries, war has become virtually unthinkable (Deutsch et al. 1957, J. Mueller 1989, Kaysen 1990). Without power competition, inefficient organizations could persist indefinitely, even after important changes in the intensity function. For example, the shift from the pre-modern era to modernity presupposes selection mechanisms weeding out anachronistic entities. More than any other process, it is war that played this role until this century (Tilly 1975, 1985, 1990). For example, between 1500 and 1900, the number of European states shrunk from about 500 units to some twenty (Tilly 1975:24).

Security concerns continue to influence the optimal size of states. In particular, Hitler's near victory in Europe, as well as the perceived threat of a Soviet invasion of Western Europe, should be seen in this light. Rather than being primarily motivated by economic reasons, the creation of the European Community reflected the lessons drawn from World War II about the vulnerability of the European nation-states (Scharpf 1988:240, Milward 1992). Today, the question of small states' viability living in the shadow of the European Union and Russia, such as the members of the European Free Trade Association (EFTA) and the East European countries, focuses not only on welfare but also on political influence and military security.

Thus scale has not ceased to be a central concern in international politics. The fundamental difference between the present era and previous historical periods pertains to the processes at work. Instead of being driven mainly by a Darwinian struggle for survival, the trend toward increasing organizational scales is motivated also by learning and sometimes implemented through voluntary accession.

Few students of integration question that increased organizational scale leads to potentially enormous gains. In addition to the obvious advantages of pooling military forces, there are important economies of scale due to trade liberalization, standardization, and provision of other public goods. The superior power of the larger post-national state is not questioned. Yet the consensus breaks down over how to achieve integration and whether it is politically feasible. To date, integration theory has not been so much about the goal of integration as about how to get there.

Roughly speaking, contributions to the integration literature fall into an optimistic and a pessimistic category. The pessimistic perspective does not deny technological progress, but believes that for political purposes, the "national" intensity curve remains valid (cf. Figure 3.6). Rejecting this assumption, the optimistic schools downplay the difficulties of moving to the post-national outcome. Federalists, emphasizing the role of elites, conceive of integration as "a bargain between prospective national leaders and officials of constituent governments for the purpose of aggregating territory, the better to lay taxes and raise armies" (Riker 1964:11). In their view, high-level negotiation and the voluntary ceding of sovereignty drive the integration process. Graphically, this conception of integration corresponds to a one-step move from the nation-state to point P in Figure 3.6. The elastic intensity curve is expected to follow smoothly if it has not already assumed its post-national position.

Functionalists, also optimists, have always regarded this contractarian, top-down process with suspicion. Instead of a one-time bargain, their approach envisages a more gradual shift of loyalties from the nation-state to a web of non-territorial, functional organizations (Mitrany 1975). Realizing the impossibility of achieving welfare and solving technical problems within small-scale organizations, people demand material improvements. This need transforms itself into popular pressure on political leaders to make gradual advances toward integration (Jacobson, Reisinger, and Mathers 1986). While the move from N to P progresses more incrementally, functionalists also believe the true intensity curve to be post-national. Neofunctionalists agree on this point, but criticize the technocratic and deterministic logic of functionalism. As an alternative, they proposed a pluralist perspective that highlights the role of interest groups and elite bargains (Haas 1958b, for a pertinent comparison of the optimistic perspectives, see Taylor 1983).

Whereas all optimistic scholars predict a smooth shift of scale to post-national organizations in one way or another, the pessimists refuse to deviate from the national intensity function. According to realist orthodoxy, attempts to initiate cooperation and to expand governance beyond the nation-state clash with the "fact" of anarchy (Waltz 1979). As a result of this security dilemma, states are unwilling to relinquish their sovereignty. To do so would be to commit institutional suicide. These assumptions freeze the national intensity curve. As a corollary, wider supranational organizations will always remain powerless giants.

Having outlined the theoretical background, I now turn to a more detailed classification of various integration strategies in the context of the European Union.

GEOGRAPHICALLY AND FUNCTIONALLY SEGMENTED INTEGRATION

Although usually framed as a policy issue, the question of widening or deepening is inescapably intertwined with the theoretical debates about integration. Widening pertains to the territorial expansion of the European Union by accession of new member states. Deepening, or to use the imagery of my framework, intensification, relates to the emergence of a socio-political community that goes beyond "objective," materialistic conceptions of organizational cohesion. Although deepening requires formal and institutional machinery, the ultimate proof of intensive power depends crucially on popular loyalty, not only among the national elites but also at the grassroots level. The terms embodied in the Maastricht treaty[8] explicitly strive to increase the political penetration of the Union. As opposed to previous integration initiatives such as the Single European Act (SEA), the Maastricht treaty directly affected the very identity of the Union by introducing a formal notion of European citizenship. For the first time, albeit vaguely, the democratic nature of the Union was codified (see Article F).

Despite the ambitious agenda set by the Maastricht treaty, the Union fell well short of developing the intensive power associated with a full-fledged nation-state. Many areas indispensable for effective exercise of intensive power remain beyond the grasp of the Union, even in theory. Lacking its own military forces, the Union still has to defer to NATO in matters of defense. Moreover, the member states have retained exclusive control over the primary means of political socialization, including education and media policies.

If the institutional picture discourages inflated estimates of the Union's intensity, the Maastricht treaty's mass psychological consequences warrant even more caution. It should be recalled that intensive power depends not only on widespread support but also on identification with the institution in question. The remarkable shift from euphoria to pessimism indicates that the European Union has a long way to go before it can challenge national loyalties.[9]

As if the complexity associated with deepening were not enough, the necessity of dealing with enlargement at the same time compounds these difficulties even further. Trying to isolate the two dimensions either in theory or policy would be futile. To understand the interaction between the two dimensions, it is helpful to consult Figure 3.7. This diagram illustrates the dichotomy between the optimistic, integrationist and the pessimistic, realist intensity curves. Although analysts disagree about how easy it is to reach the post-national intensity curve, there can hardly be any doubt that the Union is located somewhere between the national and post-national intensity curves. Neither a full-fledged federation nor a powerless entity, the European Union can be depicted as resting against the intermediate intensity curve between the two extremes.

Assuming that the European Union finds itself at point *A*, what would enlargement lead to? The consequences ultimately depend on the location and shape of the intensity curve. Integration optimists believe that elite bargaining could easily push (or drag) the function rightward, clearing the way for a move from *A* to *P*. In their view, enlargement does not exclude intensification. Pessimists do not share this permissive view of identity shifts. Instead, they argue that the intermediate curve will remain stable in the foreseeable future.

Figure 3.7
The Tradeoff between Intensification and Enlargement

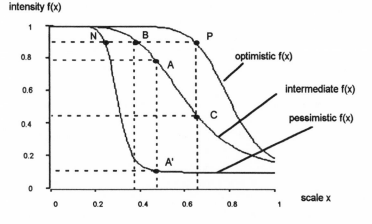

If the intermediate intensity function constrains changes in the intensity/ scale balance, enlargement can only be achieved at the price of diluting the union (a move from A to C). By the same token, intensification cannot be pursued without reducing the scale (a move from A to B). This does not necessarily imply exits from the organization, but could be tantamount to opt-outs from specific projects and issue-areas.

After the successful deepening associated with the Single European Act, many analysts thought that simultaneous enlargement and intensification were indeed feasible. Unlike the first widening, the southern expansion did not seem to slow down the pace of integration. Indeed, some commentators even saw a positive relationship between the two. Classifying this trend as "institutional spillover," Keohane and Hoffmann (1990:277) contended that "enlargement of the Community to twelve members set in motion a process that *strengthened* Community decision making institutions."

The pessimistic mood following the ratification crisis prompted a less sanguine assessment about the room for parallel deepening and widening. To see where this outlook leads us, let us assume that the intermediate intensity curve of Figure 3.7 remains fixed. Realizing the constraints placed upon further integration, pragmatic integrationists search for ways to make the desired goals of enlargement and intensification possible. Figure 3.8 illustrates a common and often effective, segmented strategy. Suppose that the regional organization attempts to enlarge and intensify its power at point A but that the constraints imposed by the intermediate intensity function frustrate these plans. Instead of abandoning the project entirely, the integration-minded politician can resort to partial solutions. Moving from A to B is possible provided that the goal of complete uniformity is abandoned. Thus the features implied by the intensification from A to B will not apply to the entire organization. The gains from this move are immediate: The organization can now add the power of Area II to its previous power of Area I. Similarly, enlargement from A to C follows the same logic by adding new members at a lower intensity (cf. Area III). Together this pragmatic type of deepening and widening yields a substantial power increase compared to the status quo (Areas I+II+III > Area I), though the gains fall short of a unified, centralized organization corresponding to point P.

Despite its obvious appeal, the power enhancement comes at a substantial price. Effective government in decentralized systems requires reasonably clear rules on how to divide authority. Failure to stipulate a clear logic of power sharing is likely to lead to decision making deadlock, reducing the power advantage (perhaps even below the level of Area I). Scharpf (1988) diagnoses the consequences of ill-defined procedures as a "joint-decision trap," and illustrates the syndrome by reference to German and European federalism. Beyond the deadlock and inertia of the joint decision trap, the possibility of less committed members "picking the raisins" and letting the more committed members foot the bill introduces a serious risk of free-riding (Olson 1965).

Figure 3.8
Segmented Intensification and Enlargement

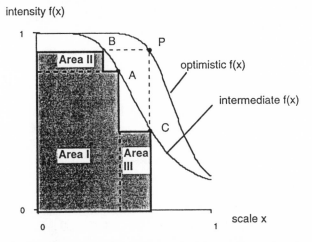

The badly needed rules of segmented power management fall into two categories. Either power is shared "vertically" or "horizontally." Vertical segmentation prescribes a geographical boundary implying domination by a more intensively committed core over a less intensive periphery.

The other approach divides power functionally by adding horizontal layers of rules. Figure 3.9 clarifies this dichotomy graphically.

Figure 3.9
Two Types of Segmented Integration

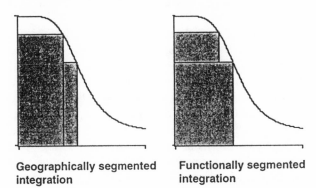

Geographically segmented
integration

Functionally segmented
integration

Given the perpetual friction of integration negotiations, it is hardly surprising that European leaders have discussed, and in some cases even implemented, various forms of both strategies. As a rule, they were all advanced as a response to the challenge of enlargement. Drawing on Wallace (1985), the next two subsections list the most important proposals.

Geographically Segmented Integration

Geographical segmentation entails accelerated integration confined to the organization's core, leaving less eager members behind. In the extreme case, the latter have to pay for their refusal to accept the proposed intensification by becoming second class members. In its more egalitarian manifestations, geographical segmentation serves as a temporary expedient before full convergence can be achieved. Fearing that the Community would dissolve "like a lump of sugar in a British cup of tea" if the United Kingdom were accepted, the French resisted enlargement throughout the 1960s (Pinder 1992:46). Shortly before resigning in 1969, General de Gaulle secretly suggested that the British adherence would be acceptable if counterbalanced by geographically segmented intensification based on a *directoire* consisting of France, Germany, and Britain. This openly asymmetric power distribution was never formalized since it predictably enough encountered fierce opposition from the marginalized members of the Community as soon as it leaked to the press (Wallace 1985:29-31). Anticipating similar difficulties, German Chancellor Willy Brandt launched an initiative in 1974. As opposed to the French plan, however, Brandt's "two-speed Europe" dealt with economic rather than political divergence.[10] Although the ultimate goal was to move toward a "single-speed" organization, the economic gap between the North and the South was thought to require longer convergence processes for the poorer countries (Wallace 1985:32-33).

More recently, the prospect of several small states, such as Iceland, Liechtenstein, Malta, Cyprus, and the Baltic states, joining the Union has also given rise to fears concerning the manageability of the organization. Although these concerns revolve around the bureaucratic capacity rather than the policies of the smaller states, they also relate to the under-representation of the larger member countries. Rather than lobbying for an explicit two-speed solution, the latter have so far chosen to counterbalance the disproportionate influence of the smaller states through adjustments of voting rules (Hösli 1993). A variation on the theme of geographical segmentation offers an alternative solution to the problem of how to deal with prospective applicants. Instead of instantly admitting the countries in question, the Union has negotiated treaties conferring associate membership before full membership can be envisaged. Fearing that they would be excluded from the internal market, the EFTA countries sought a closer form of association with the Community beyond the free trade arrangement of 1973. Signed in 1992, the European Economic Area (EEA) was initially regarded as an uncontroversial way of achieving institutional osmosis. It soon became clear, however, that there was considerable divergence in the goals of the two organizations concerning legal and institutional issues. Despite their traditional reluctance to relinquish sovereignty, the EFTA countries wanted to have a say in future decisions concerning the provisions of the EEA. To this end they suggested a separate legal body, called the EEA Court, consisting of judges from both the European Court of Justice (ECJ) and the EFTA countries. But in 1991, the European Court of Justice ruled this arrangement to be incompatible with the EC treaties (Michalski and Wallace 1992). Striking down this functionally segmented type of enlargement, the Court insisted on geographical segmentation. Unwilling to accept unilaterally the *acquis communautaire* without any direct influence over its future interpretation, the EFTA countries were left with no choice but to apply for full membership. The Europe Agreements between Czechoslovakia, Poland, and Hungary on the one hand and the Community on the other also exemplify geographical segmentation. Signed in 1991 as an attempt to promote stability in Eastern Europe and prepare these states for full membership in the future, the agreements apply to only some aspects of the internal market. Yet French agricultural protectionism and German fears of unrestricted immigration severely limited the scope of the provisions. This asymmetry suggests that geographical segmentation is even more significant than in the case of the EEA. Negotiations with other East European countries are already under way (Michalski and Wallace 1992:136-140).

Functionally Segmented Integration

The second way of managing segmentation is to divide the shared provisions into horizontal layers. Unlike geographical segmentation, these functionally defined schemes avoid territorial power asymmetries. One of the earliest proponents of functionally segmented integration was David Mitrany (1975), who promoted the notion of issue-specific cooperation, especially in technical areas. More recently, similar ideas have surfaced under various names. Responding to Community orthodoxy, Ralph Dahrendorf proposed a more flexible solution, dubbed *Europe à la carte*, by which any member government could choose freely in which policy issues it wanted to participate. Other related ways of overcoming the difficulties facing European integration in the late 1970s and early 1980s include *variable geometry, graduated integration,* and *abgestufte Integration* (Wallace 1985). In practical terms, these alternative schemes typically promoted technological cooperation projects open to non-members, the Eureka program perhaps being the best-known example. In practice, the tendency of less integration minded governments to opt in and out of certain treaty provisions also exemplifies the trend towards functional segmentation (Michalski and Wallace 1992:45-46). For example, the agreement on the European Monetary System, signed in 1979, did not encompass all governments, due to economic divergence. In signing the Maastricht treaty, the United Kingdom and Denmark chose to retain their sovereignty in monetary matters for the time being despite the other governments' wish to push ahead with the EMU. Similarly, the British refusal to join the Social Charter creates a situation of functionally segmented intensification in social matters (Michalski and Wallace 1992:45-46; see also Dinan 1994:190-193). As a response to the ratification crisis following the Maastricht summit, Jacques Delors emphasized the principle of subsidiarity, the currently most important example of functionally segmented integration (see Article 3b of the Treaty). This principle relies heavily on a functional division of authority since the locus of decision making depends on the issue area in question. Unlike *ad hoc* decisions to opt out from treaty provisions, subsidiarity serves to rationalize the choice of decision making level by appeals to utilitarian criteria. To illustrate the logic of subsidiarity, it is useful to return to the graphical presentation. Figure 3.10 shows two intensity curves pertaining to two different issue areas. Whereas Issue 1 is subject to strict popularity constraints, Issue 2 allows for a more optimistic approach to integration. Furthermore, there are two decision making levels: The national one and the federal one. The question is on which level the issues should be decided. Unlike the previous analysis, here we assume that these levels cannot be fine-tuned with respect to scale, which of course entails a certain degree of suboptimality. Again, we measure the power (or the effectiveness) as the area of the rectangle corresponding to a given institution. In issue area 1, choosing the national level fixes the institutional arrangement at point N1. Giving priority to the federal level, however, moves the institutional configuration to point F1. Comparing the corresponding power rectangles indicates a clear preference for the national level, since the rectangle associated with N1 is larger than the one defined by F1. In issue area 2, by contrast, decision making on the federal level (cf. point F2) surpasses the national level (cf. point N2). The principle of subsidiarity implies that Issue 1 should be decided by the nation-states, and Issue 2 by the federal organization. Integrationists, including the Commission itself, have embraced the principle of subsidiarity as a means of bringing the Community closer to the people (Dinan 1994:187-189). Although subsidiarity in this sense appears appealing, it has several shortcomings, the most serious being (1) how to define effectiveness in practice and (2) whom to entrust with the final choice of authority level. Not surprisingly, the term still suffers from a notorious vagueness. On the one hand, the Commission wants to retain the decision of what can be better decided on the national level. On the other hand, the national governments, especially the United Kingdom and Denmark, advance a less centralized interpretation, not unlike their preferred *à la carte* policy.[11]

Figure 3.10
An Illustration of the Principle of Subsidiarity

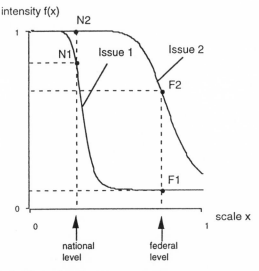

It is likely that the European Court of Justice will have to be relied upon to clarify the practical implementation of sovereignty in specific cases, a highly political task for which it is not necessarily well equipped (Hösli 1994). Although I have made a clear analytical distinction between functional and geographical segmentation, it is sometimes hard to distinguish them in practice.

Indeed, Scharpf (1988) refers to both German and European federalism for examples of poorly demarcated authority structures (see also Sbragia 1992). Such blurring is sometimes exploited by governments.

For example, integrationist governments could threaten to turn functional segmentation into geographically divided two-speed arrangements. Britain's opting out from the Social Charter's functions exposes it to the risk of being relegated to a second-rank member. While no state has ever been excluded from, or voluntarily left, the Union, exit threats play an important tacit role in high-level bargaining (Schneider and Cederman 1994).

The formal framework has highlighted the general interdependence of enlargement and intensification proposals under the assumption of popularity constraints. More specifically, governments sometimes draw on this linkage to accelerate or decelerate integration along the intensity or scale dimension. It is widely recognized that the United Kingdom promotes widening partly as a means to thwart further deepening. The integration-friendly France, by contrast, remains more skeptical of enlargement, since it fears dilution of the Union's external power (Nugent 1992:311).

Such concerns do not seem entirely misplaced, since the current applicants represent a more diversified group of countries than ever before in the Union's history (Michalski and Wallace 1992, Nugent 1992). Even the adhesion of the EFTA countries poses a serious challenge to the European integration process:

> Shared cultures, political traditions and basic commitment to liberal democratic practice are assumed to exist among the EC of fifteen or sixteen. But this overlooks the widely different evolution of the social-welfare state in the Nordic countries as well as difference in their perception as to what kind of union the EC should aspire to. (Lodge 1993:xiv)

Although the European Union has excluded exceptional treatment in foreign affairs and the end of the Cold War has made the issue partly irrelevant, the neutrality policies of Austria, Finland, and Sweden could also cause friction. Still, these complications pale in comparison with the formidable difficulties associated with a possible future East European expansion.

CONCLUSION

Conventional international relations theory tends to leave little room between the extremes of anarchy and hierarchy (Waltz 1979). Nevertheless, the value of this analytical dichotomy declines steadily with the continuous undermining of territorial sovereignty (Milner 1991, Ruggie 1993, Wendt 1994). This chapter offers an alternative framework that allows for the study of intermediate, more decentralized organization forms in addition to the nation-state.

By emphasizing the intensity of directly or indirectly mediated communal bonds, the model avoids the pitfalls of economic materialism. The power of political organizations does not depend only on scale and effective enforcement but also on their members' loyalty. The intensity function models the interaction between commitment and scale. With a small set of stylized assumptions, it is possible to conceptualize change such as that from small communities and empires in the pre-modern world to the emergence of nation-states. Most importantly, the model helps us understand various institutional arrangements falling between the extremes of the nation-state and supranational federalism.

These organizational forms differ not only in size, as suggested by neorealist theory, but also in terms of social cohesion. While there are several other pertinent differences, the current model underlines the importance of socio-psychological and national communities. It is not only neorealism that falls into the trap of elitism: both neofunctionalists and federalists pay almost no attention to the "soft" mass-psychological aspects of integration. The notion of community has got lost in the quest for deterministic theory (Taylor 1983).[12]

For all its heuristic value in historical and meta-theoretical comparisons, the framework only offers an indirect guide to historical change. It should be recalled that the intensity functions are postulated, not explained. Such an explanation requires an entirely different, dynamic theory of how political identities form and loyalties shift from one level to the other (see Cederman 1994b:chapters 7, 8). These are largely unexplored areas both in theory and practice, judging from the continued frustrations and surprises accompanying European integration.

The crucial question concerns not only the shape but also the flexibility of the intensity curve. An answer to this question requires a better understanding of political loyalty in general and nationalism in particular. As an inherently historical phenomenon, nationalism makes the intensity curve "sticky" and hard to push to higher scales. This lock-in effect is due to what could be called "vernacular closure," a tendency of political communication to crystallize into linguistically defined, self-contained national communities (cf. Gellner 1983). Failure to appreciate this dynamic leads to an ahistorical approach to integration. Implicitly or explicitly, integration enthusiasts often fall victim to the erroneous practice of using the United States as a reference point or "of employing cases of successful assimilation that were culminated prior to the eighteenth century as precedent for cases today involving self-conscious ethnic groups" (Connor 1972:171).

APPENDIX

This appendix provides a mathematical specification of the Optimal-Size Model. To formalize the distinction between scale and intensity referred to above, the model relies on three parameters: k, x_0, and c. Using these parameters, the extraction function can be written:

$$f(x) = k + (1-k)\left\{ 1 - \frac{1}{1 + (x/x_0)^{-c}} \right\} = 1 - \frac{1-k}{1 + (x/x_0)^{-c}}$$

The share of the fixed contribution $k \in (0,1)$ indicates how large a share of the maximally extractable resources can always be exploited regardless of scale. The inverse S-shaped extraction curve depends on the two remaining parameters. The location of its steepest fall is controlled by $x_0 \in (0,1)$. The last variable, $c>1$ determines how steep the decrease is. The extreme cases $c=0$ and $c \to \infty$ respectively correspond to a flat line at $(k+1)/2$ and a perfect step starting at level one that falls abruptly to k at $x=x_0$.

Having defined the extraction curve, we arrive at an expression for the power function:

$$p(x) = xf(x) = x\left\{1 - \frac{1-k}{1+(x/x_0)^{-c}}\right\}$$

What is the optimal organizational size under this specification? Propositions 1 and 2 answer this question. From a substantive standpoint, we are only interested in the optimal rather than the minimal levels of the power function. Therefore, Proposition 1 focuses on local maxima rather than all extreme points:

Proposition 1. To identify the maxima of the power function $p(x)$, let

$$k^*(c) = \left(\frac{1-c}{1+c}\right)^2$$

and

$$x_{1,2} = x_0\left\{\frac{(1+c)(1-k)-2}{2} \pm \sqrt{\frac{[(1+c)(1-k)-2]^2}{4} - k}\right\}^{-1/c}$$

There are then three cases:

1. If $k > k^*(c)$ or $x_1 > 1$, $p(x)$ has a single local (and global) maximum at $x=1$.
2. If $k \leq k^*(c)$ and $x_1 \leq 1$ but $x_2 > 1$, $p(x)$ has a local (and global) maximum at x_1.
3. If $k \leq k^*(c)$ and $x_1 \leq 1$ and $x_2 \leq 1$, $p(x)$ has two local maxima at $x=x_1$ and $x=1$.

PROOF. To find the extreme points, we start by differentiating $p(x)$:

$$p'(x) = \frac{\partial}{\partial x}xf(x) = f(x) + xf'(x) = \left\{1 - \frac{1-k}{1+(x/x_0)^{-c}}\right\} - \frac{(1-k)c(x/x_0)^{-c}}{\left\{1+(x/x_0)^{-c}\right\}^2}$$

Letting $y = (x/x_0)^{-c}$ we solve the first order condition $p'(x)=0$. Now the equation can be written:

$$1 - \frac{1-k}{1+y} - \frac{(1-k)cy}{(1+y)^2} = 0$$

After some manipulations, this expression reduces to an equation of the second degree:

$$y^2 + \{2-(1+c)(1-k)\}y + k = 0$$

with two roots:

$$y_{1,2} = \frac{(1+c)(1-k)-2}{2} \pm \sqrt{\left\{\frac{(1+c)(1-k)-2}{2}\right\}^2 - k}$$

Substituting back $x_i = x_0 y_i^{-1/c}$ we have derived two potential extreme points: x_1 and x_2. These roots are real if

$$\left\{\frac{(1+c)(1-k)-2}{2}\right\}^2 - k \geq 0$$

This condition can be simplified by factoring out $(1-k)$:

$$\left\{\frac{(1+c)(1-k)-2}{2}\right\}^2 - k = (1-k)\frac{(1-c)^2 - k(1+c)^2}{4} \geq 0$$

Since it is assumed that $0<k<1$, the first factor is always greater than zero. Thus the inequality depends entirely on the second factor, which can be rewritten as:

$$k \leq \left(\frac{1-c}{1+c}\right)^2$$

where the right hand side is $k^*(c)$ as stated in the proposition. Depending on whether the two roots are real and/or they fall within the unit interval, we get three cases:

Case 1: If $k>k^*(c)$, there are no real roots, and since $p'(0)=1>0$, it must be that $p'(x)>0$ on the interval $x \in [0,1]$. Thus $p(x)$ increases monotonously, which implies that $x=1$ is both the local and global maximum. Similarly, if $k^2k^*(c)$ but $x_1>1$ the maximum falls outside the interval so that $x=1$ is again the only maximum.

Case 2: If $k^2k^*(c)$ and x_1^21 but $x_2>1$, both roots are real but only x_1 falls within the unit interval. Since the minimum $x_2>1$, $p'(x)<0$ does not switch sign form x_1 to $x=1$, so the latter point cannot be a maximum. Therefore x_1 is the unique maximum.

Case 3: If $k^2k^*(c)$ and both x_1, x_2^21, the two roots are real and contained by the unit interval. In this case, we get two local maxima. In addition to the extreme point at x_1, the upper bound $x=1$ must also be a local maximum since $p'(x)>0$ for $x>x_2$ including $x=1$.

I have thus proven the proposition for the three cases. QED.

For substantive reasons, Case 3 is the most interesting contingency due to the shape of the extraction curve. Unlike Case 1, some combinations of k and c produce a local maximum in the interior of the unit interval. Such an optimum requires a large variable contribution (low k) and a sharp fall in extraction (high c). To see this, consider the extreme case of an entirely flat extraction function (with $k=1$ and/or $c=0$). Clearly, the absence of a "kink" on the extraction curve eliminates the room for a maximum short of universal empire, i.e., a rectangle with base $[0,1]$ and height one (if $k=1$) or $(k+1)/2$ (if $c=0$).

Case 3 in Proposition 1 fails to specify which of the two local maxima is the global maximum. As illustrated above, this question has a clear historical importance. Will city-states or empires prevail in the long run? Proposition 2 addresses this issue under simplified circumstances. It is assumed that the extraction function is a perfect step, i.e., that c goes to infinity:

Proposition 2. When $c \to \infty$ in Case 3 of Proposition 1, the power function $p(x)$ has the following global maxima:

1. $x=x_1$ if $x_0 > k$
2. $x=1$ if $x_0 < k$
3. both $x=x_1$ and $x=1$ if $x_0 = k$

PROOF. To find the global maximum, it is necessary to compute and compare the maximal levels of the two local maxima at $x=x_1$ and $x=1$ (see Case 3 of Proposition 1) while letting c go to infinity. To find the limit of the latter is straightforward:

$$\lim_{c \to \infty} p(1) = \lim_{c \to \infty} 1 \cdot \left\{ 1 - \frac{1-k}{1+x_0^c} \right\} = \left\{ 1 - \frac{1-k}{1+0} \right\} = k$$

The limit of the maximum at $x = x_1$ is somewhat more complicated.

Using the substitution $x_1 = x_0 y_1^{-1/c}$ from Proposition 1, we rewrite $p(x_1)$ as

$$p(x_1) = x_1 \left\{ 1 - \frac{1-k}{1+(x_1/x_0)^{-c}} \right\} = x_0 y_1^{-1/c} \left\{ 1 - \frac{1-k}{1+y_1} \right\}$$

Letting, $c \to \infty$ we derive the limit of y_1 and $y_1^{-1/c}$ separately:

$$\lim_{c \to \infty} y_1 = \lim_{c \to \infty} \frac{(1+c)(1-k)-2}{2} \pm \sqrt{ \left\{ \frac{(1+c)(1-k)-2}{2} \right\}^2 - k } = \lim_{c \to \infty} c(1-k) \approx \infty$$

To find the limit of $y_1^{-1/c}$ it is necessary to apply l'Hôpital's rule:

$$\lim_{c \to \infty} y_1^{-1/c} = \lim_{c \to \infty} c^{-1/c} = \lim_{c \to \infty} \exp\left(-\frac{\log c}{c} \right) = \exp\left(\lim_{c \to \infty} \frac{-1/c}{1} \right) = e^0 = 1$$

Thus, I am ready to derive the limit of the maximum at x_1:

$$\lim_{c \to \infty} p(x_1) = \lim_{c \to \infty} x_0 y_1^{-1/c} \left\{ 1 - \frac{1-k}{1+y_1} \right\} = x_0 \cdot 1 \cdot \{1-0\} = x_0$$

I can now state that $\lim_{c \to \infty} p(x_1) > \lim_{c \to \infty} p(1)$ if $x_0 > k$, which proves the proposition. QED.

NOTES

I would like to thank Robert Axelrod, Michael D. Cohen, Madeleine Hösli, Peder Olsen, Robert Phare, Gerald Schneider, Cheryl Shanks, and Patricia Weitsman for their helpful comments. Any errors and misrepresentations remain my own responsibility. I acknowledge the generous financial support from the Social Science Research Council and the John D. and Catherine T. MacArthur Foundation.

1. My definition of power is an absolute rather than relative one. For an argument for the latter type of definition, see Baldwin (1985).

2. In his analysis of the optimal size of states and nations, Wittman (1991:129) purposefully disregards both nationalism and ideology: "Economists do not use such devices to explain firm conglomeration and divestiture and they should not use them to explain nation size either." Wittman refrains from explaining what motivates this strong professional norm.

3. The emphasis on cohesion in this paper does not preclude the presence of alternative factors contributing to political survival and success. Tilly (1985:40), for example, lists six such influences: (1) availability of extractable resources, (2) the geopolitical position, (3) the skill of political leaders, (4) success in war, (5) homogeneity of the population, and (6) strong coalitions between the state leaders and the landed elite. Although Tilly relegates societal cohesion to the second rank of variables, I join Strayer in stressing its importance. As an underlying factor, cohesion has a crucial impact on Tilly's first and fourth points. Moreover, in the long run, factors (2) and (3) can be expected to partly wash out as random variations. Thus it is hard to get around the conclusion that cohesion, or the intensity, of power wielding matters as much as sheer scale.

4. Constant intensity, however, should not be confused with constant returns to scale in terms of power. Rather, this assumption implies that power extraction *per scale unit* is constant. For a discussion and further references on positive returns to scale in power accumulation, see Gilpin (1981) and Cederman (1994a).

5. Note that the power levels can be calculated graphically based on Figure 3.2. The imperial maximum corresponds to the area of the shaded rectangle: $1 \times 0.1=0.1$, and the city-state peak coincides with the area of the unfilled rectangle: $0.081 \times 0.90 \sim 0.07$. In our example, the city-states are likely to prevail against considerably larger organizations up to about size 0.7. To see this, go horizontally from the city-state "peak" to the right until $p(x)$ is intersected. The x value of this intersection is about 0.7.

6. Needless to say, these pre-modern conditions still dominate in a significant part of the world: "For most people, ethnic consciousness still lies in the future. National consciousness presupposes an awareness of other culture-groups, but, to a majority of the world's population, the meaningful world still ends with the village" (Connor 1994:18).

7. It should be recalled that Figure 3.5 represents a stylized picture of very complex historical processes. In reality, the trend toward the nation-state is less clear-cut. Most existing states remain clearly multi-ethnic. Even the old Western European nation-states contain important ethnic minorities, such as the Basques in Spain and France and Northern Ireland in the United Kingdom (Connor 1972).

8. In the following, I will refer to the Maastricht treaty, although the agreement is officially called the Treaty on European Union.

9. For a recent statistical analysis of the public support for European integration, see Eichenberg and Dalton (1993).

10. The Tindemans Report of 1975 followed the same principles as Brandt's initial proposal.

11. There is a fundamental difference between a scheme that allows for free opting in and out with respect to each issue area and one that forces each issue to be decided either on the national or the federal level but never on any intermediate level. In addition to the administrative complications resulting from interactions between functional levels, the former solution may invite free-riding. One way around this problem would be a system of "fiscal federalism"; i.e., an overlapping network of "functional federalism" that links the costs with consumption of public goods (Hösli 1994).

12. A significant exception to this materialist trend is the "old" functionalism of David Mitrany. While downplaying the difficulty of transferring popular loyalties from the nation-state to supranational bodies, this perspective treats the notion of community explicitly (Taylor 1983). See also Karl Deutsch's (1957) notion of security community.

4

Switzerland—Still a Paradigmatic Case?

Simon Hug and Pascal Sciarini

INTRODUCTION

The political institutions of Switzerland are often regarded as ideally suited to achieve the integration of a multi-cultural society in a single state. Careful balancing of different institutional features, some of them quite unique, appear to have made the peaceful resolution of conflicts possible. Several authors have argued that Switzerland represents a "paradigmatic case" (Deutsch 1976) of successful political integration. In the context of European integration this case is again being advanced as a possible example: "[Stein] Rokkan recommended that anyone wishing to study the dynamics of European Politics should immerse themselves in the study of Switzerland" (Steiner 1994:xii). But recent developments have cast some doubt on the degree to which Switzerland remains exemplary. The most significant case is the refusal of the electorate to be part of an external process of political integration, namely the European Economic Area (EEA).

In the present chapter we attempt to explore in more detail this flattering description of Switzerland and its political institutions. The nested game approach (Tsebelis 1990) is especially useful in this respect. It will allow us to explore the functioning of the political institutions of Switzerland and to show where certain strains appear. These institutions might serve both as positive and negative examples for political integration.

In the next section we describe briefly a nested game of elite interactions, which is useful to illustrate the political integration of Switzerland. We envision this political integration as the process that led to the development of the institutions in contemporary Switzerland. The main feature of these institutions is the broad inclusion of social, economic, and cultural groups and their elites into the decision making process. The nested game allows us to highlight the impact of some elements specific of the Swiss case that trouble elite interactions. The strains in the current political system are at the heart of the third section. We discuss these strains and stress the difficulties of reform that prevail in the Swiss political system. In the conclusion we summarize our main arguments and attempt to draw parallels with the current process of European integration. We illuminate the difficulties inherent in both cases for a reform, which would allow both for political integration and efficient decision making.

INTEGRATION THROUGH ACCOMMODATION

For Karl Deutsch (1976), Switzerland presented a paradigmatic case of political integration. He found the major reason for this success in the behavior of the elites. By emphasizing the importance of the "politics of accommodation" (Deutsch 1976:55), he rejoins the theory of consociationalism.

This strain of research, linked heavily to Lijphart's (1974) work, stresses the importance of elite behavior in plural societies. In such societies, particularly if they are segmented as in the Netherlands, cooperative behavior of elites can lead to stable governmental institutions. Steiner (1974) applied a very similar theoretical argument to the Swiss case, emphasizing the "amicable agreements" among Swiss elites. But Deutsch adds to this the importance of the interactions of elites have the population they represent: "One has to admit that the elite had to respect very much their people given the political conditions in Switzerland. Further the elite often had to learn a lot about perceiving and defending the interests of the people living in their canton" (Deutsch 1976:52, our translation).

Deutsch's emphasis on the way the elite considered the desires of the electorate finds an interesting parallel in Tsebelis' (1990) analysis of consociationalist politics in Belgium. This latter study is embedded in a more general approach to political situations, where actors find themselves in multiple arenas. He proposes a model where elites negotiate in a parliamentary arena, while also being involved in an electoral arena. With his model, Tsebelis attempts to explain certain features of Belgian politics, which consociational theory cannot capture.

Since the model's basic feature is the interaction among elites, and between elites and their electorate, it proves to be an interesting tool to analyze the political integration in Switzerland. Hence, in this section we will first present the game-theoretic model of Tsebelis (1990). Since the Swiss political system presents some special features, the model is not directly applicable.

We will discuss three elements which have an impact on the interaction among elites. The model enables us to synthesize the specific features of Swiss politics with the nested game and elite interaction and to take a new look at the institutions that allowed for successful political integration.

Accommodation as the Outcome of a Nested Game

Tsebelis' study of Belgian politics uses as a starting point the consociationalist assumption that elites negotiate on behalf of their electorate. According to his analysis elites find themselves in situations where they have two choices: Either they compromise with the other side, or they show themselves intransigent (Tsebelis 1990:164). Elites would prefer avoiding conflict, which implies that intransigent behavior by both actors is their least preferred outcome. If one actor compromises, while the other remains intransigent, the outcome is the most advantageous one for the second actor. The first actor, however, would prefer mutual cooperation to that outcome. Accordingly, the payoff structure of the two elites corresponds to $T > R > S > P$ in Figure 4.1.[1] Given this preference ordering of the outcomes, the elites play a game of chicken. Game theoretic analysis would predict that either one of the two elites would yield to the intransigence of the other player. She does so because of her fear of mutual intransigence. This fear is shared only partially by her followers, who are more polarized. The followers are more concerned with being exploited by their adversaries. Their preference ordering reflects the standard situations of either a prisoners' dilemma ($T > R > P > S$) or a Deadlock game ($T > P > R > S$).

The preferences of the electorate are important, since elites require electoral support in order to stay in office. Therefore, the electorate can punish elites if they do not defend the interests of the voters. To avoid such punishments the elite has to take the electorate's preferences into account each time it makes a decision. Hence, the elites consider simultaneously the payoffs from the parliamentary and the electoral arena. The total payoff matrix of the elite (POi) then becomes a mixture of their payoffs from the parliamentary ($POpi$) and the electoral arena ($POei$). The relative weight of these two types of payoffs depends on the control the electorate has over the elite.[2] If the relative weight of the electoral arena (k) is zero, the elites are playing a game of chicken amongst themselves. In that case, the elite does not consider the preferences of the electorate.

Figure 4.1
A Game of Elite Interaction

		Actor B	
		C(ompromise)	I(ntransigence)
Actor A	C	R, R	S, T
	I	T, S	P, P

Otherwise, if the electoral arena takes predominance $(k=1)$ the elites play either a game of prisoner's dilemma or of deadlock. Hence, the preferences of the electorate take precedence.

$$PO_i = k\,PO_{ei} + (1-k)\,PO_{pi}$$

In the first case, politics becomes pragmatic, since the best action of one elite is contingent on the other player's behavior. In the second case, dominant strategies exist that lead to mutual intransigence. Between these two extreme values of k, the payoff structure becomes a mixture of the two games. The value of k depends, according to Tsebelis (1990:168), on two elements: The difficulty of forming new elites, and the degree to which information on elite negotiations is available. If it is difficult for new elites to emerge or information is scarce, the electorate will be less reluctant to follow its elites. This means that k becomes smaller. In the opposite situation, k increases and renders the elites more dependent on their respective electorates. As a consequence, if the electoral arena is important, the likelihood of compromise between elites diminishes. On the other hand, if elites do not have to take the preferences of their electorate into consideration, compromises become more likely.

In addition to this feature of nested games, an important factor concerns whether the game is played a single time or repeatedly. In the first case, standard equilibria appear, as, for instance, mutual intransigence in a prisoners' dilemma game. The repetition of the same game allows for contingent strategies, which can improve on standard equilibrium payoffs (Axelrod 1984, Fudenberg and Maskin 1986). This framework allows Tsebelis to arrive at several interesting deductions, which explain some features of Belgian politics. First, from the very structure of the game it appears that elite-initiated conflict is very likely when issues are important. This is in stark contrast to consociationalist theory, which emphasizes the compromising nature of decision making. But when issues are important the stakes are so high that elites are unlikely to make package deals that include other issues. Such cases are best represented by a single iteration of the game. In that situation, the only possible equilibria of the game have at least one elite remaining intransigent, while the other either compromises or is also intransigent.

Second, in repeated interactions two possibilities appear. If mutual cooperation provides important benefits compared to the other outcomes, cooperative behavior can be sustained. If this is not the case, the sequence of outcomes can be characterized as switching compromises. In one interaction one elite is yielding, while in the next the other one compromises. This corresponds largely to agreements where one elite is decisive on certain issues, while another one has predominance on others. Tsebelis (1990:179) associates these with liberal or federal arrangements. In that case, some decisions are delegated either to specific groups or territorial authorities. A danger exists, however, when issues are important to both elites: in such a situation mutual intransigence might result. In Belgium it appears that the solution is to postpone making the decision under such circumstances.

Nested Games and Swiss Political Integration

Although Switzerland often appears as an example of consociationalist politics in the literature, various scholars have expressed doubts about the applicability of the model to Swiss politics. In particular, three features of the Swiss case raise problems for consociationalist theory. They concern the absence of strong cultural segmentation, the presence of direct democracy, and the particular coalitional government that has relied on the same coalition partners since 1959. These three elements also raise the question of the applicability of Tsebelis' model to Switzerland. We will show below that the second and third elements can easily be synthesized into a nested game of elite interaction. The absence of strong segmentation, however, requires a different kind of treatment because it is a prerequisite for the definition of the elites. Since Tsebelis' model tries to explain the interactions between two elites, we will first discuss the problems of cultural segmentation. We will then show that direct democracy and the special features of the Swiss executive can be readily enveloped into the nested game framework.

It is true that, Switzerland is a pluralistic society, the different cultural groups are not significantly segmented or isolated from each other. Rather, Switzerland is characterized by cross-cutting cultural cleavages that give way to various combinations and, consequently, to various political configurations from one canton (state) to another (Steiner 1983). Nor are strongly segmented sub-cultures present—and therefore represented—at the national level of the political system.[3] However, one may consider Swiss federalism as a "functional equivalent" of the formation of pillars in the Netherlands or in Belgium (Kriesi 1990). This feature did not lead to a vertical segmentation, but to a territorial segmentation shaping several sub-societies at the regional level.

The creation of the Swiss federation was an institutional compromise between the conservative Catholic cantons hostile to centralization and the radical Protestants who favored national centralization or at least a federal government strong enough to make the necessary decisions in the common interest. The radicals, winners of the short civil war that gave birth to modern Switzerland, were ready to share power with the losers (the conservatives). Adopting a federalist solution, the radicals conceded control over their subculture to the Catholics. More generally, these institutional arrangements allowed traditional elites to preserve most of their social control on citizens of their own regions. The cantons, in their determination to maintain a large degree of political autonomy, retained most of their powers and assured themselves participation in the future decision making in the new federation (Linder

1994:39). Thus, contrary to the Belgian case, federalism was present from the very beginning of the Swiss state; while in Belgium federalist arrangements were introduced to diffuse conflict, Switzerland used the existing federalist institutions both to solve conflicts and as a means for integration. Linder (1994:xvii), for instance, considers federalism as the main institutional arrangement of consociational democracy and, therefore, as one of the most important ingredients of successful Swiss political integration.

Despite the continuous process of transfer of authority to the Confederation, considerable power is still retained by the cantons. Federalism remains a crucial element of the functioning of the Swiss political system, both in the decision making process and in the implementation of policy. For example, the cantons are allowed to participate in the central government's decision making process through the presence of one assembly representing the cantons (the Council of the States). This chamber, in which each canton has two deputies regardless of the size of its population, has equal power as the other assembly which represents the people (the National Council). The mutual neutralization of the veto power that both councils have at their disposal makes consensus necessary. Moreover, the votes of cantons are decisive for constitutional referendums; in addition to the majority of the citizens' votes, a majority of the cantons have to agree for a constitutional amendment to be accepted.[4]

Federalism thus fosters elites who represent different sub-cultures. The various elites present in parliament may reflect interests that differ from one canton to another, as Deutsch (1976:53) notes, but may also be based on other cleavages. We define elites as the relevant actors in the national parliament. They attempt to negotiate among themselves to arrive at compromises. While the presence of federalism is essential for the pertinent application of the consociational model and the nested game, the presence of direct democratic institutions raise more significant questions concerning the application of consociationalist theory to Switzerland. But setting direct democracy within the nested game will help us understand the impact of referendums and initiatives on the interactions between elites and their electorates. Referendums and initiatives trouble the elite interaction, but can be readily included in a nested game by modifying the model. The presence of direct democracy basically implies that some decisions are made by the electorate. One can distinguish between the popular initiative[5] and the so-called referendum, which exists in a compulsory and in an optional form. A referendum has to take place for all constitutional amendments decided by the parliament, and can be invoked for all laws voted by parliament.[6] The consequences of these direct democratic institutions for the application of the nested games model are mainly two-fold. First, these institutions create for some decisions an addi-tional arena where the electorate intervenes in a direct way. If the elites had perfect control over their respective electorates, this additional arena would not have much influence. But empirical evidence suggests that political parties have only partial control over their voters in referendums. A proposal has to find the support of all or almost all parties present in the parliament to be assured of certain acceptance in the popular vote. Proposals supported by fewer parties, for instance only by those represented in government, were defeated on average every fifth time between 1970 and 1987 (Hug 1994:176). This limited control introduces uncertainty into the interactions between elites. The elite might arrive at an agreement, but the electorate could refuse to follow its leaders. While elites are able to make package deals and compromises across different issues by their involvement in iterated games, this is very unlikely for the electorate. Here every decision is isolated from the next, since voters cannot make credible commitments among themselves on the way they will vote. Hence, decisions are made at the end of the process by a final majoritarian popular vote, preventing further appeal or bargaining (Papadopoulos 1991:10).[7] In other words, Swiss citizens have at their disposal additional resources to withdraw from choices made by their elite, that is, by punishing them in a referendum.[8] In the case of a referendum, since the options open to the electorate consist only of either accepting or rejecting a proposal, the choice is between a compromise developed by the elite, or at least part of it, and the status quo. For the elites who put together the compromise, the latter option is, however, their least preferred outcome since it corresponds to the outcome of mutual intransigence. Hence, for each compromise there is a certain probability that a referendum is demanded and that the official proposal is defeated by the electorate.[9] This probability can take two values.

In Figure 4.2 *pcc* represents the probability of an unsuccessful referendum in a case where both elites compromise; *pnc* corresponds to the probability of an unsuccessful referendum where only one elite compromises. As a consequence of direct democracy, each payoff resulting from an outcome of the elite interaction becomes a mixture between the original payoff of the game without direct democracy (Figure 4.1) and the payoff of the status quo. This is so since a referendum that leads to the rejection of the official proposal automatically results in the status quo. It is likely that the probability of a defeat for the government in a referendum is higher if only one elite compromised while the other remained intransigent.[10] Elements of the elite that compromised might feel exploited and demand a referendum.

Additionally, since the proposal is supported by only a part of the elite, rejection of the proposal in a referendum is more likely. If it is true that these two probabilities differ, it is easy to show that the presence of direct democratic institutions lead to a relative increase of the payoff from mutual compromise, compared to all other outcomes. This increase is a direct function of the probability that a proposal suffers defeat. Tsebelis (1990:71) shows that an increase in the relative payoff for mutual compromise leads to more cooperative behavior of the elites. Consequently, when referendum campaigns by opposing elites become more successful, the elites' strategy is often to become more compromising. They attempt to rally behind their proposals as big a coalition as possible.

Figure 4.2
A Game of Elite Interaction with Direct Democracy

| | | Actor B | |
		C(ompromise)	I(ntransigence)
Actor A	C	pccP + (1-pcc) R, pccP + (1-pcc) R	pncP + (1-pnc) S, pncP + (1-pnc) T
	I	pncP + (1-pnc) T, pncP + (1-pnc) S	P, P

This largely explains the second effect of the presence of referendums. Several scholars (Neidhart 1970) have noted that direct democracy has indirect effects of great significance for the functioning of the Swiss political system. As we noted earlier, by occurring at the end of the political process, the optional referendum has a veto function, allowing the electorate to reject unsatisfactory laws. The same is true for the compulsory referendum. To avoid the threat of referendums, elites must compromise during the initial phase of the legislative process—the so-called pre-parliamentary phase. This fourth arena is one in which elites test the grounds of their proposals. Every group able to threaten in a credible way the whole process is invited to take part in the pre-parliamentary phase. Participation takes the form of either "expert" commissions which are supposed to elaborate a first "embryo" of consensus or consultative procedures aimed at analyzing and compiling positions of all concerned parties, interest groups, or cantons.

Historically, the integration of oppositional forces leads to the expansion of a political culture emphasizing compromise at the elite level. This political culture tries to resolve economic, social, and cultural conflicts through concerted action. Given the importance attributed to the search of compromise in the pre-parliamentary phase, it is no surprise that less than one proposal out of ten is actually contested and voted on in a referendum (Papadopoulos 1991:14). In this fourth arena, political actors try to avoid rejection of an issue, by bringing all groups that might be able to launch a referendum or to campaign against a constitutional law into the decision making process. The pre-parliamentary phase has transformed the Swiss "plebiscitarian democracy" into a "bargaining democracy" (Neidhart 1970). The process of negotiating and compromising are the basis of the peaceful resolution of conflicts in Switzerland and successful internal political integration. Furthermore, this process has shaped a "democracy of concordance" (Lehmbruch 1967); namely, the integration of all important political forces into the central government. Again, this fourth arena allows for enhanced electoral control over the elite.

While referendums provide for the possibility of a final decision by the electorate and push the elites to more compromising behavior, initiatives introduce a real openness into the Swiss political system. Political groups that otherwise would remain excluded from gaining access to the political system can submit new proposals.[11] This allows for the co-opting of opposition, which, in the absence of initiatives, would attempt to find other means of expression. Simultaneously, it may provide the group that launched the initiative more power and legitimacy. This also implies that new elites can emerge easily. As Tsebelis' model shows, this increases the importance elites have to give to the electoral arena since k increases. To avoid seeing new political forces emerging, the established elites will pay tribute more often to the preferences of their electorate. Hence, the presence of initiatives strengthens the control of the electorate over the elite.

In brief, direct democracy induces elites to forge compromises in the pre-parliamentary and parliamentary phase. Contentious issues, by being decided by the electorate, risk yielding the outcome of mutual intransigence, namely, the status quo. In addition, direct democracy limits the control of the elite and increases the power of the electorate. Contrary to this effect is the absence of government responsibility toward the parliament or the people in terms of changing representation. The influence the citizens have through national elections is minimal.

First, the federal executive is not elected by the people, but by the parliament. Yet, ministers cannot be revoked by the parliament. After each mandate in office the ministers have to be reelected by parliament. But these elections are almost always purely routine, since former members of the executive are always re-elected. Second, the electorate has very little influence on the composition of the government. The division of government seats between parties has remained fixed for several decades (since the creation of the so-called "magic formula" in 1959). Election outcomes do not affect this composition (Steiner 1982). The electorate loses, therefore, an important instrument to punish elites. It can punish parties individually, but not the government for its policies. A consequence of this is a lower k, which implies that the preferences of the electorate become less important. It diminishes also the importance of elections: "Under the constraints of an all-party government, voters dissatisfied with the government have no chance to bring an opposition party to power" (Linder 1994:131).

Again, as Germann (1994:200) correctly observes, the fact that the government remains almost untouchable is an effect of the institutions of direct democracy: the integration of wider circles of elites into the government is dictated by the threat of repeated initiatives or referendums against government policy. This balance between a stronger influence of the electorate through the instruments of direct democracy, and a weaker one through the instruments of representative democracy, appears to be at the heart of the Swiss model (Linder 1994:132-133). But as we will see below, this balance is difficult to maintain, and might be the source of strains that the Swiss political system is experiencing.

Table 4.1
Elite Behavior in a Nested Game with Direct Democracy

increases in	lead to
k	less compromising behavior of the elite
pnc	less compromising behavior of the elite
pcc	more compromising behavior of the elite

In summary, the consociational mechanisms developed in Switzerland should be viewed as the consequence of the functioning of federalist and direct democracy institutions; as a result of cultural and sociological complexity, the intricacies of the Swiss institutions could only be managed by the cooperation of the elites. In that sense the political institutions of Switzerland have effectively allowed for successful political integration.

We summarize in Table 4.1 the three key variables of the nested game with direct democracy. While the influence of k on the likelihood of compromise is the same as in Tsebelis' model, the other variables are specific to this game. As pnc increases, compromising behavior of the elites decreases. If pcc increases, the likelihood of a compromise increases. In the next section we will use these elements to look at the current strains in the internal political integration of Switzerland.

STRAINS IN SWISS INTEGRATION

During the last two decades, Switzerland has experienced difficulties that have put into question the success of its internal political integration. Exogenous changes, caused either by economic crisis or by transformations in the international environment, seem to endanger the functioning of the Swiss political system. Our argument is that the two main institutions that facilitated internal political integration—direct democracy and federalism—are paradoxically at the heart of the most important difficulty of external integration for modern Switzerland. In this section, we will present some indicators of a process of deterioration that takes place at three different levels: Among the political elite, between the elite and the basis, and among the population. With the example of the EEA, we will show that these strains are particularly salient on issues concerning foreign policy. We will also try to sketch some plausible explanations for this negative revolution.

In domestic policies, the growing number of optional referendums demanded for various important issues provides a first indicator of the integration deficit at the level of the elite.[12] Already during the second half of the seventies, optional referendums experienced an important revival. This is linked to the fact that in times of economic difficulty conflicts become more salient, which makes compromise more difficult to achieve (Delley 1987:107), as we have shown in the previous sections with our model. This explanation has been confirmed by developments in the early nineties: optional referendums were demanded increasingly against central projects like country planning, professional education, the revision of pension, and health insurance. After thirty years of concordance, the parties forming the government coalition experience considerable difficulties in finding a common denominator (Linder 1994:115). Evidence that direct democracy has lost part of its capacity to pressure for consensus ("Konkordanzzwang") is manifest in the growing polarization of votes in the parliamentary arena (Lüthi et al. 1991). But in our framework this is not surprising, since important projects prohibit package deals. Each issue is dealt with separately and intransigence by at least one elite becomes more likely. As a consequence, the elite's capacity to control the referendum, that is, to avoid a referendum being demanded, has decreased markedly (Germann 1994).

The same is true in foreign policy, where the most significant challenges for the Swiss internal political integration arise today. Both European integration and the GATT-negotiations (Sciarini 1992, 1994) illustrate the pressures arising from the international environment, especially due to the presence of direct democracy. First, international negotiations concern increasingly topics that previously fell under national jurisdiction. Since these issues touch the established domestic order, they are unlikely to foster the elite's consensual support. But, contrary to the Belgian case discussed by Tsebelis where the elite often chooses to delay a decision when they cannot find an agreement amongst themselves, this is impossible when the issues are grounded in international negotiations. Agreements have to be ratified within a fixed time period and amendments are difficult or even impossible to add. Hence, these issues often reflect the case where one elite compromises, while the other's viewpoint is only partially respected. This increases the likelihood of a challenge in the arena of direct democracy, since pnc exceeds pcc.[13]

Second, this increasing inter-penetration of international and domestic politics influences the jurisidiction of direct democracy. Historically, foreign politics almost totally escaped the mechanisms of direct democracy. The partial revision of the Swiss constitution in 1977 enlarged the judicial domain in foreign politics, where direct democracy applies. Still, the scope remains significantly larger for domestic than for foreign politics. But this difference is slowly diminishing, because of the dissolving frontiers between domestic and foreign politics. Consequently, Swiss diplomacy is becoming increasingly subject to both layers of direct democracy (Germann 1994:178); in addition to the ratification of an international agreement, partial revisions of the federal constitution or laws are also necessary and must be accepted by the electorate. Consequently, the electorate's influence on the elite via the instruments of direct democracy increases. As the number of referendums concerning important matters increases, the influence of the voters increases. This evolution is reinforced by the growing number of compulsory referendums,[14] where citizens automatically have the last word.

In observing the relationship between elites and the electorate one notes other forms of integration deficits. Particularly in foreign policy there appears to be a growing gap between the elite and the people. Indeed, Papadopoulos (1994:146f) shows that proposals in the field of foreign policy are those that face the highest risk of being rejected by the electorate. Between 1970 and 1987, three out of five proposals in this category suffered defeat in a referendum. In the same period the average acceptance of governmental proposals was above 75 percent, a percentage that persists up to the present time. Consequently, in the field of foreign politics the control of the voters over the elite, captured by k, is consistently higher than in other fields. This leads, according to Table 4.1, to less compromising behavior among the elite.

We see two main reasons for this gap between the elite and the population in foreign politics. The first lies in the clash between the logic governing international negotiations and the logic governing direct democracy; the second lies in the opposition between the elite and the citizens concerning the definition of foreign policy. We will briefly develop these two points. First, while international negotiations are characterized by iterated games and issue linkages, direct democracy is characterized by single shot games and isolated decisions. Moreover, the issue-linkages become increasingly important at the international level, due to the globalization of negotiations. This is particularly clear in European integration, the essence of which postulates the interdependence of public policy. The connection that negotiators establish between different unrelated issues to avoid zero-sum-games and to increase the chance of a compromise upset the logic of referendums (Germann 1994:170). Indeed, in the arena of direct democracy the voter may reject the whole package because of one unacceptable component. Still worse, the vote on package deals increases the risk of accumulating oppositions. For instance, the EEA agreement was a package deal and was directly linked to the agreement on alpine transit. The Swiss electorate followed the authorities in accepting the construction of rail tunnels through the Alps, but refused to do the same three months later, and the EEA agreement was rejected.

The EEA vote also illustrates strikingly the gap between the elite and the electorate concerning the definition of foreign policy. This is particularly salient in the German-speaking regions; while the EEA Treaty had been approved by a large majority of the Swiss German political elites, be it in the parliamentary arena (55 percent yes in the National Council, 91 percent in the Council of the States) or at the canton executives level (all governments in favor), only 44 percent of the Swiss German electorate and one canton out of 16 supported the EEA. Moreover, a poll indicated that this vote may be seen as a signal of mistrust vis-à-vis the government: 70 percent of the citizens who trusted the government accepted the EEA, while only 27 percent of those who did not trust the government voted for that treaty (Kriesi et al. 1993:33-34).

More generally, periodic surveys show a growing mistrust towards the political elite since the beginning of the eighties, particularly towards the federal government (Longchamp and Kraut 1994).

Direct democracy makes a "crisis of representation" perceptible. A sanctioning vote allows the electorate to have an effect on the specific issues, and also—though indirectly—on the elite. More precisely, if elites are afraid of being punished in the electoral arena after a negative vote on a given issue, elites will take the electorate's preferences in the parliamentary arena into account. An example of this is given by the refusal of the elite to talk about a new vote on the EEA, or even more contentious, on membership to the European Union, before the 1995 national elections. Elites fear losing votes in favor of the nationalist or populist parties. Thus, the increasing influence in the arena of the referendums has an effect on the parliamentary arena. Further, the electoral arena contributes to strengthening the control the citizens have over the elite through votes and therefore reinforces the disequilibrium mentioned above.

Finally, we need to look at the cleavages within the population. Indeed, it would be a mistake to consider Swiss citizens as a homogeneous group, i.e., as if there were political consensus. On the contrary, political attitudes are strongly polarized in Swiss society on fundamental issues, as in the management of economic crises or the position of Switzerland in its international environment. While the first set of issues divides mainly the citizens on a classic left-right axis, the second divides the Swiss electorate along a different dimension. The process of opening the country to the impulses of regional integration or international cooperation influences the jurisdiction of direct democracy, and also the substance of the issues involved. Indeed, this phenomenon challenges the Swiss political culture, strongly marked by neutrality and the desire to preserve national sovereignty.

The analysis of the structural and cultural cleavages of Swiss politics that emerged on national referendums during the eighties reveals a conflict on issues relating to the most important myths of the Swiss identity (Sardi and Widmer 1993). This division is apparent on three primary topics—army, labor, and foreigners. The conflict concerns values on a dimension of the desired level of openness versus closedness. It separates the traditional and rural Switzerland on one side, from the modern and urban Switzerland on the other (Kriesi 1993:285).

The EEA vote illustrates the importance of this cultural opposition on a openness-closedness dimension for the current deficit of Swiss political integration. Indeed, Kriesi et al. (1993:42-50) show that this cultural cleavage was largely responsible for the rejection of the EEA by the Swiss electorate. Beyond the economic considerations, it appears that two images envisioned for the future of Switzerland clashed on December 6, 1992. While supporters of the EEA wanted to promote an open and audacious Switzerland, opponents wanted to defend the traditional Switzerland that stands for its myths and venerates the courage of remaining alone. Furthermore, the results and analysis of the vote (Kriesi et al. 1993) revealed a deep cleavage between the German and the French part of Switzerland on this cultural dimension. Although the political and economic elite have attempted to downplay the linguistic cleavage, these two regions are without question on opposing sides of this central issue.

The EEA vote also illuminated another force threatening the political integration of Switzerland: the discrepancy between the popular vote—almost equally distributed between acceptance and refusal—and the vote of the cantons—largely against the proposal.[15] Due to the combination of the two decision making principles, namely direct democracy ("one man, one vote") and federalism ("one canton, one vote") that characterize a constitutional referendum, a majority of the cantons can block the solution preferred by a majority of the citizens. Since differences in population size have markedly increased due to migrations from rural to urban regions, the weight of federalism—i.e., the weight of small cantons—has increased.[16] This demographic evolution, added to the growing number of compulsory referendums, has increased the risk of a clash between the "two majorities" (Germann 1994:135). Six out of the seven clashes that have taken place since the beginning of the century occurred after 1970,[17] the last two on June 6, 1994.[18] These most recent cases have given rise to serious criticism of the majority rule applied to cantons.[19]

Finally, the lack of integration within Switzerland has a negative effect on the efficiency of the decision making system. In Switzerland, innovation historically followed a parallel evolution in political integration: "The policy of integration, and of conservative adaptation rather than risky innovation, was important, and it worked" (Linder 1994:136). But Deutsch (1976:56f) stressed in his conclusion the increasing difficulty in maintaining innovation in the Swiss system of accommodation. It seems intuitive that a political system emphasizing both accommodation and political stability would tend to protect its existing structures and slow down processes of adaptation.[20] Today, most authors agree that one of the main weaknesses of the Swiss political system lies in its lack of efficiency (Kriesi 1980, Borner, Brunetti and Straubhaar 1990, 1994, Germann 1994, Linder 1987, 1994). Direct democracy, and more precisely the referendum, contributes to the inefficiency in decision making. On the one hand, constitutional reforms are not easy to introduce, since the compulsory referendum requires both a majority in the electorate and among the cantons. One could say that Switzerland, though not directly facing the "joint-decision trap" described by Scharpf (1988) for the German and EC case,[21] experiences a variant of this trap due to the influence of federalism in constitutional referendums (Kriesi 1990). The requirement of two majorities, one of the electorate, the other of the cantons, might lead to sub-optimal decisions.[22] On the other hand, optional referendums mean that frequently the status quo will be maintained, the least preferred outcome for the elite. When the government is unsuccessful (referendum demand is made and proposal of the parliament is rejected by the electorate), the effect is to perpetuate pre-existing legislation. When the government succeeds (either not demanded or proposal of the parliament accepted by the electorate), frequently partial solutions or compromises of limited scope are the result, since the principal actors succeed in attaining their goals in the pre-parliamentary or even parliamentary phases.[23] In the Swiss political system radical innovations are less likely to occur than incremental changes.

Furthermore, the problems of inefficiency that Switzerland encounters are worsened when the internal integration is no longer guaranteed. Given the particularities of the Swiss political system, its efficiency, even minimal as it might appear, depends on its integrative capacity. For instance, to consider the rejection of the EEA as a problem of efficiency seems erroneous. This rejection constitutes, first of all, a failure in terms of internal integration. Indeed, when dealing with the important challenge of integrating into the single market of the EC, the Swiss political system was largely rigid in the first phase. But the EEA negotiations allowed the elite to show some capability to react, as a consequence of a learning process by the administrative, economic, and political elite (Sciarini 1992). This learning, however, was voided by the refusal of the electorate and the cantons to accept the EEA treaty. From this point of view, the question of whether or not Switzerland is still a "paradigmatic case of political integration" arises.

Our interpretation contrasts with the mainstream literature, which assumes the existence of a tradeoff between innovation and integration (Linder 1994). Such a tradeoff suggests implicitly that it is possible to alter or modify political institutions at will. In the Swiss case, such an assumption implies a complete revision of the constitution. Since the four arenas of Swiss politics are closely linked, altering one element might have unexpected consequences on the institutional balance. Such reform seems highly unlikely, at least in the short- or medium-term. Even substantial amendments to the constitution, entailing abandoning or even relaxing the "second" majority (of cantons) prerequisite in a constitutional referendum, or limiting the instruments of direct democracy in foreign politics, is extremely difficult to imagine. Indeed, it is highly unlikely that citizens and cantons that would naturally vote on such proposals would accept relinquishing elements of their control.[24] In that sense, there is no tradeoff between integration and innovation; the former is a causal factor of the latter.

CONCLUSION

We argue in this chapter that Switzerland successfully achieved political integration through a careful balancing of institutional features, like federalism, direct democracy, and the particular government system. This institutional mix increases on the one hand the control the electorate has over the elite through the instruments of direct democracy, while on the other it decreases their control traditionally experienced via the representative democracy. But this careful balancing seems to move more and more towards enhancing the power of the electorate. As a result of the difficulty the elites have in attaining compromise, the growing number of referendums held on domestic and on foreign policy issues has enhanced the electorate's power. Similarly, the growing number of compulsory referendums has given an ever smaller part of the population a veto right on constitutional changes, due to the federalist element in direct democracy. As such, the institutions of direct democracy and federalism increasingly reveal strains among the elite, between the elite and the electorate, and among the electorate. In other words, the same institutions that presumably were at the core of the integration success are nowadays vectors of the main integration deficit of modern Switzerland. Moreover, this integration deficit lowered the already minimal efficiency of the political system. Given the very low probability of a radical institutional reform, we suggest that the only way to give the system a minimum of efficiency is to rebuild consensus.

Despite big differences between Switzerland and the European Union (EU), one can trace some parallels between the Swiss experience concerning political integration and the history of the EU. First, the European Union has also developed a series of institutions (Committee of Permanent Representatives, Economic and Social Committee, expert committees, etc.) that allow for the integration of public and private actors (member states and lobbies) in the initial phase of the decision making in order to facilitate consensual solutions. In the EU it is mostly the demanding decision making rule (unanimity or qualified majority) at the level of the Council that created the incentives to elaborate several consultative and collaborative mechanisms. These allow the commission to develop a first "embryo" of compromise. In Switzerland, we have seen that the presence of referendums explains to a large degree the creation of a fourth arena, where actors are integrated into the search for a compromise in the pre-parliamentary phase.

Another parallel between Switzerland and the European Union concerns federalism. In Switzerland, the consideration of the cantons through the principles of subsidarity, and made concrete by federalist institutions in the elaboration and the application of policies, has historically favored political integration. The European Union seems for its part also to follow a federalist path (Sidjanski 1992). The federalist elements present since the beginning are manifest in the overrepresentation in seats and votes of small and medium states in the Commission and the Council, others added with the Single European Act, and even more with the Maastricht treaty through the principle of subsidarity. As in the Swiss case, federalist institutions might allow for more successful integration and at the same time help diffuse conflicts.

Finally, what distinguishes the political institutions of Switzerland from those of the European Union the most is direct democracy in the former and its absence in the latter. Direct democratic experiences in the history of European integration have shown the risk of blocking, which is inherent in the instrument of referendums. The first Danish vote on Maastricht demonstrated that treaties make it necessary for the European Union to respect the will of small countries. Danish rejection also jeopardized the whole process of regional integration for several months. This unhappy experience with referendums, linked together with an increased need to find unanimity at the elite level, both in Switzerland and the EU, illustrates the dilemma between integration and efficiency, which is inevitably present in every political entity, be it national, supranational, or international.

In the aftermath of the ratification process of the Maastricht treaty, it seems certain that the European Union will remain a hybrid form for some time, mixing elements of intergovernmentalism, still heavily dominant, and certain supranational elements. From the supranationalists' perspective, the "deepening" of European integration by strengthening supranationalist institutions simultaneously allows for enhanced political efficiency. This assertion assumes that either the unanimity rule in the intergovernmental decision making (European Council and Council of Ministers) can be dropped, or, more fundamentally, supranationalist institutions (Commission and European Parliament) can be strengthened at the expense of the intergovernmental institutions. Both the Single European Act and the Maastricht treaty suggested some movement in that direction. Some new capabilities have been transferred to the level of the Union, and the fields in which the Council decides by qualified majority have also been enlarged. Further, the cooperative decision making procedure from the Single European Act (Tsebelis 1994, and this volume), and even more the codecision procedure of the Maastricht treaty, have turned the European Parliament into a more powerful actor.

Intergovernmentalism, however, is still dominant in the Union. Decisions on reforms of treaties ("high politics") still require unanimity. The intervention of supranational actors and qualified majorities in the Council have only been enhanced in the legislative procedures ("low politics"). The co-existence of these two channels of decision making creates incentives in the arena of "low politics" to provoke negative spillovers: After a defeat a country might ask for compensation at summit meetings where unanimity rules, or even to make contingent threats (Schneider 1994a, 1994b). In other words, the coexistence of these two decision modes reproduces a "joint-decision trap" and, consequently, also an impulse to find a compromise solution for each issue among all or almost all actors involved (mostly the member states).

While the European Union has already put a revision of its decision making procedures on the agenda for 1996, Switzerland has made several attempts to revise fundamentally its constitution. Recently, scholars proposed a radical change in the Swiss political system to regain its efficiency (Germann 1994, Borner, Brunetti, and Straubhaar 1990, 1994). However, in Switzerland as well as in the European Union, radical changes all presuppose an inevitable tradeoff between efficiency and integration. As we have seen, however, this tradeoff appears only if institutions can be redesigned essentially from scratch. In the case of the EU, 1996 will show whether or not reform is possible, while in Switzerland the continuing debate on revision of the constitution might still drag on for some time.[25] Given the institutional features of the two entities, an improvement of the political integration might be, in Switzerland as well as in the EU, a necessary condition to improve the efficiency of the political system.

NOTES

A first version of this paper was presented in the staff seminar of the Department of Political Science at the University of Geneva. We are indebted to its participants, especially Hanspeter Kriesi, for their helpful remarks. Thanks are also due to Cédric Dupont, Yannis Papadopoulos, Gerald Schneider, and Patricia Weitsman, who provided us with extensive comments on the first draft of this chapter.

1. The symbols of the payoffs have the following meanings: T stands for temptation, R for reward, S for sucker, and P for penalty.

2. As Tsebelis (1990:160) correctly notes, considering elites either as independent, as the consociational literature does, or as simple representatives of the masses, provides a poor description of the interaction among elites, as well as of the interaction between elites and masses. By considering the link between the electoral and the parliamentary arena, Tsebelis corrects one of the principal shortcomings of the consociationalist theory, which assumes implicitly the independence of the elites and the docility of the masses. These are necessary conditions for the elaboration and implementation of consociationalist decisions.

3. For instance, contrary to the Belgium case, the linguistic cleavage in Switzerland did not give birth to specific political parties.

4. Cantons take part in other levels of the political process. For instance, each canton can address proposals (initiatives) to the Federal Assembly. Moreover, each canton is consulted in cases of new federal laws. Federalism is also crucial during the implementation phase: Switzerland is characterized by so-called "federalism of implementation," each canton being responsible for the implementation of federal laws.

5. To launch a popular initiative, 100,000 signatures of citizens are required. Any group can ask the Swiss electorate to vote to amend the constitution, whatever the subject. As with all constitutional modifications, a majority of the voters and a majority of the cantons have to vote in favor of the initiative.

6. By collecting 50,000 signatures against a law voted by the parliament, any group may call for a final decision by the electorate on the project.

7. The elite counters this by making a number of attempts. For example, the introduction of women's voting rights, and the value-added tax (VAT) appeared several times on the ballot before being accepted by the electorate.

8. Again, one can note that the popular initiative also provides an opportunity to express demands without involving the elites.

9. This only holds for optional referendums. In the case of compulsory referen-

dums, the probability corresponds to the likelihood of the proposal's defeat.

10. This implies that $pnc > pcc$. It is easy to show that if the two probabilities are equal, the strategic interaction between the two elites is not changed. More precisely, in that case the utility function undergoes a monotonic transformation, which leaves its ordinal properties unchanged.

11. We should add that initiatives are rarely successful. Between 1891 and 1990, 105 have been put on the ballot, of which only 10 have been accepted. However, one should not underestimate the indirect effects of the initiatives. In spite of being rejected they can be partially successful. For example, the initiative may stimulate the creation of a new law which introduces some part of the proposals found in the initiative (Delley 1978, App 1987).

12. This increase concerns mostly projects that are of crucial importance for the country. We cannot agree, however, with authors who use the increasing number of optional referendums as a proof of a diminishing consensus. In fact, this increase (Kriesi 1991, Linder 1994) of the number of optional referendums voted on by the electorate is largely due to an increased legislative activity of the parliament. The referendums demanded as a proportion of all proposals subject to a demand remains relatively stable.

13. One can draw a parallel between this feature and the effect of the popular initiatives. In both cases, the agenda setting is partially beyond elite control.

14. The number of votes on constitutional amendments has increased by approximately 100 percent every 20 years since 1930 (Germann 1994:138-139).

15. The small rural Swiss German cantons, which have a more important weight due to the requirement of a majority of cantons for the passage of certain laws, are simultaneously the most conservative on the dimension discussed above (i.e., the most devoted to tradition and to isolationism). The stabilization of the attitudes, combined with the "double majority" rule, leaves little hope for a rapid change in the Swiss voters' attitude towards European integration.

16. Germann's (1994:141) calculations show that due to this second majority (of the cantons) about 20 to 25 percent of the population have an effective "minimal veto power."

17. In comparison, the inverse clash (a majority of the people blocking a majority of the cantons) occurred much more seldomly (two cases since the beginning of the twentiest century, the latest in 1957).

18. Of the voters, 52.9 and 51 percent, respectively, accepted to facilitate the naturalization for immigrants' children and the introduction of a constitutional article supporting culture, but were defeated by a majority of the cantons (thirteen cantons against ten and twelve cantons against eleven, respectively).

19. For the first time, some politicians suggested a revision of this rule, either by reducing the weight of the small cantons or by introducing a qualified majority.

20. Various authors addressed this dilemma in the Swiss case by stressing the tradeoff between a system's rigidity and its flexibility (Brunetti 1992), or by stressing the ambigious nature of political stability (Sciarini 1994).

21. In Switzerland, as in the United States, the governments of the member states (cantons) do not directly participate in the decision making at the federal level. Further, the decision making does not require unanimity.

22. One might add that the veto power held by actors present in the fourth (pre-parliamentary) arena (not only the cantons, but all actors with the capability to launch a

successful referendum campaign) gives rise to another form of the "joint-decision trap."

23. In a book presenting the main results of research on decision processes, Linder (1987:202f) notes that substantial proposals with a relatively long duration have little chance of succeeding in Switzerland. On the contrary, in practice one observes mostly changes of limited scope and short duration, which carry the imprint of special interests.

24. Scharpf (1988:269) argues that decision making according to "joint-decisions" is also a "trap" in the sense that they can block the further evolution of decision making mechanisms.

25. Although the Swiss government recently re-launched the project for a total revision of the constitution, it seems unlikely that spectacular changes will result from this undertaking.

II

INSTITUTIONAL CHANGE AND

EXPANSION

5

Power of the European Parliament as a Conditional Agenda Setter

George Tsebelis

INTRODUCTION

The European Parliament is widely considered a weak parliament (Lodge 1989, Edward 1987, Fitzmaurice 1988, Lenaerts 1991, Wessels 1991). Moreover, discussions are frequently advanced about the "democratic deficit" of European institutions, which, among other things, implies weakness of the European Parliament. (Bogdanor 1989, Thomas 1988, Williams 1991, Bowler and Farrell 1993).

Yet in 1989, the European Parliament, when confronted with the common position of the Council of Ministers specifying low standards on exhaust emission of small cars, raised the standards, and was able to impose its decision on both the Commission and a "reluctant majority" in the Council of Ministers (Jacobs and Corbett 1990:170). According to the Cooperation Procedure, the Council of Ministers can modify the position of the Parliament by a unanimous vote, but in this case it could not agree on any alternative. The legislation in question is far from trivial, since it affects around 60 percent of all passenger cars in the EU (Kim 1992). Moreover, the difference in positions between the Parliament and the Council was significant: Compared to the Council's position the adopted legislation raised the price of small cars by more than $500 apiece and significantly improved the environment.

To place this story in a comparative perspective, the reader is reminded that the American president has been known to veto legislation when his disagreements with Congress are of equal or even less importance. For example, President Bush vetoed legislation regarding parental and medical leave (June 29, 1990), legislation regarding "orphan drugs" allowing marketing rights for drugs developed to combat rare diseases to be shared (November 8, 1990), and the Indian Preference Act (November 16, 1990), which provides preference to qualifying Indian enterprises in the award of federal funds

(Congressional Quarterly Almanac 1991).

How did the weak European Parliament impose its will on both the Commission and the Council? In comparative perspective, why did the Council—formally empowered with the right to modify proposals sent to it—accept a weak Parliament's positions, while in similar circumstances the American president—who cannot modify legislation—resisted successfully the most powerful legislature in the world?

This chapter explains this surprising power of the European Parliament. I argue that the Parliament under the current "Cooperation Procedure" has an important power: It can make proposals which, if accepted by the Commission, are easier for the Council of Ministers to accept (qualified majority is required for acceptance) than to modify (unanimity is necessary for modification). I call this "the power of the conditional agenda setter" and study its properties.

My answer generates a second question: If Parliament is able to influence the legislative process significantly, why doesn't it do so all the time? Alternatively, if the conditional agenda setting power is significant, Parliament should have been recognized in the literature as a strong parliament. To address these issues the chapter specifies the conditions under which the Parliament can make use of its agenda setting power.

The study of the power of the European Parliament vis-à-vis the Council of Ministers is important in order to understand the pace and the extent of European integration. Indeed, the Parliament is a supranational institution while the Council of Ministers constitutes the expression of national governments. Understanding the relationship between these two institutions (and the corresponding role of the European Commission) will shed light on the major theoretical controversy surrounding European Union: Whether it is a product of supranational forces (spillover theories) or of the will of national governments (intergovernmentalism). Other studies have tried to answer this question by investigating historically important steps of the process of integration, such as the Single European Act of 1986, the European Economic Area of 1991, and the Maastricht agreement. This chapter adopts a different strategy and studies the outcomes produced by one existing institution.

There are two ways of undertaking such an institutional investigation. The first is empirical: Study the universe of existing outcomes and assess the relative contribution of each of the three institutional actors (the Parliament, the Commission, and the Council) to the legislative outcome. Such studies are currently under way and come to the preliminary conclusion that "the impact of the EP on crucial issues of the Council's deliberations is rather limited" (Wessels 1991:145). The second, which I will undertake in this study, is theoretical: I will examine the logic of compromise among the three institutional actors generated by the Cooperation Procedure. In this sense, my approach is part of a series of studies (Scharpf 1988, Weber and Wiesmeth 1991, Garrett 1992, Garrett and Weingast 1992) that attempt to apply the institutional approach developed in the study of American politics to the institutions of the community.[1] My results complement empirical studies. I explain why little influence of the Parliament is found in most cases; I explain why the Parliament in rare instances such as the automobile emission standards was so influential; finally, my analysis clarifies why cases involving high parliamentary influence are likely to multiply in the future. The chapter is organized into four sections. The first section presents the Cooperation Procedure and some of its outcomes. The second section analyzes formally the interaction among the three institutional actors according to the Cooperation Procedure. The third section explores the implications of the analysis for the role of the European Parliament. The final section discusses the theoretical problem of specifying the driving forces of European integration in light of the results of my model.

AN INSTITUTIONAL FRAMEWORK, A STORY, AND SOME RELATED STATISTICS

The Cooperation Procedure did not cover all areas of Community legislation (Lodge 1989:69, Jacobs and Corbett 1990:169).[2] It applied to some nine articles of the Rome Treaty: Prohibition of discrimination on the grounds of nationality (art. 7); freedom of movement of workers (art. 49); freedom of establishment (art. 54(2)); coordination of provisions providing special treatment of foreign nationals on grounds of public policy, public security, or public health (art. 56(2)); mutual recognition of diplomas, etc., and coordination of provisions on activities of self-employed persons (art. 57(1) and 57(2)); harmonization of measures for the establishment and functioning of the internal market (art. 100a and 100b); the working environment and the health and safety of workers (art. 118a(2)); economic and social cohesion (art. 130e); and research and development (art. 130q). Of all these issues, the most important are the harmonization of the internal market, social policies, research programs, and regional fund decisions. Legislation examined under the Cooperation Procedure constituted between a third and a half of parliamentary decisions (Jacobs and Corbett 1990:169).

Alternative legislative procedures applicable to other areas of the Rome Treaty were the *assent procedure* and the *consultation procedure*. Each of these procedures attributed different powers to the three institutional actors, the Parliament, the Commission, and the Council. This is the reason why several times before the discussion of particular pieces of legislation a political and legal battle among the three actors takes place (Garrett 1991, Lodge 1987, 1989) in order to decide which procedure will be followed. I will not discuss these institutional battles here.[3] Instead, I will focus on presenting the Cooperation Procedure and describing its implications by using a case study and some relevant statistics.

The Cooperation Procedure

The Cooperation Procedure entails two readings of each piece of legislation (which is introduced by the Commission) by the European Parliament and the Council of Ministers. The Council makes the final decision either by qualified majority or by unanimity. In the abstract, the procedure is reminiscent of a navette system between two houses of a bicameral legislature where the upper house (the Council) has the final word.[4] However, the European case of navette presents interesting, special features that require detailed description and analysis. The procedure is presented schematically in Table 5.1.

The legislative process begins with the submission of a Commission proposal to the European Parliament. At the same time, the Council may begin deliberating but cannot reach a decision until it receives the position of the Parliament. The Parliament in the first reading may accept, amend, or reject the proposal; it may also withhold its opinion by referring the legislation back to committee, thereby effectively aborting the proposal. Once Parliament decides, the proposal goes back to the Commission which may revise the initial proposal to accommodate Parliament. The Commission presents the proposal as amended to the Council, which adopts a "common position" by qualified majority (fifty-four out of seventy-six votes).[5] No time limits on deliberation exist in this first reading of the proposal. It is therefore obvious that any of the institutions can effectively abort legislation at this stage of the process.

Once the Council adopts its common position, the second reading of the proposal begins. The Council sends its common position back to the Parliament, along with a full justification of the reasons why it adopted this position. The full justification of the Council's and the Commission's positions is required by article 149(2b) of the Single European Act. However, in the early phase of application of the procedure the Council provided extremely sketchy reasons or no reasons at all. In one case it even apparently failed to notice that the Parliament had tabled amendments to the Commission proposal (Bieber 1988:720). The Parliament formally protested, its President declaring on October 28, 1987 that "as a minimum, the Council should provide a specific and explained reaction to each of Parliament's amendments" (Jacobs and Corbett 1990:173). On November 18, 1987 the Parliament, in two resolutions, threatened the Council with legal action (Bieber 1988:720). As a result, the Council altered its approach, and now provides an account of its point of view on each of the substantive issues raised by draft legislation (Jacobs and Corbett 1990:173). The Parliament has three months to select one of three options: Either to approve the common position of the Council (or take no action),[6] in which case the Council adopts the proposal; to reject the common position by an absolute majority of its members (currently 260 votes); or to amend the common position again by absolute majority of its members. In this second round, time is of essence.

Table 5.1
Outline of the Cooperation Procedure

I Commission Initiative	II European Parliament 1st reading	III Council 1st reading	IV European Parliament 2nd reading	V Commission	VI Council 2nd reading
Proposal of the Commission	Parliament's opinion (no time limit)	Council's common position – without modification of the proposal: qualified majority – modification of the proposal: unanimously (no time limit)	– Parliament approves Council's common position or has not taken a decision within 3 months (1)		– Council adopts the decision, by qualified majority or unanimously (cf. column III)
			– Parliament rejects Council's common position by an absolute majority (260 MEP), within 3 months (1)	Re-examination (1 month)	– Council has unanimously taken a decision within 3 months (1) (adopts Council's common position) – Council has not taken a decision within 3 months (1): the Commission's proposal is rejected
			– Parliament proposes amendments to the Council's common position by an absolute majority (260 MEP), within 3 months (1)	Re-examination (1 month) – Commission adopts a reexamined proposal with the amendments of the Parliament – Commission adopts a reexamined proposal without the (or certain) amendments of Parliament	– Council approves reexamined proposal by a qualified majority within 3 months (1) – Council modifies reexamined proposal unanimously within 3 months (1) – Council has not taken a decision within 3 months (1): Commission's proposal is rejected.

Source: Van Hamme (1989:312).

(1) the time limit of 3 months may be extended to 4 months by common accord between Council and the Parliament.

The clock starts when the President of the Parliament announces that he or she has received all relevant documents in all nine official languages.[7] The Commission may or may not introduce to the Council legislation rejected by Parliament; if such legislation is introduced, the Council can overrule the rejection by voting unanimously in favor. Amended legislation is presented to the Commission; which has to revise the proposal within a month. Parliamentary amendments that are accepted by the Commission can be adopted by the Council by qualified majority (54/76); whereas any other version requires unanimity in the Council (Nugent 1989:248). If the Council fails to act within three months (four with the agreement of the Parliament) the proposal lapses.

This account makes the Commission appear to be the agenda setter. Indeed, a proposal by the Commission is required to initiate the legislative process, and it is the Commission's proposal that the Council accepts by qualified majority or modifies by unanimity. Neither the Parliament nor the Council have the right to initiate legislation.[8] However, the Council was given the right under article 152 of the EEC treaty to request that the Commission undertake studies and submit to it the appropriate proposals. Similarly, the Parliament on its own initiative has several times adopted resolutions calling for new legislative proposals (for example, those concerning the ban on imports of baby seal skins to the Community, or trans-frontier television broadcasts) (Jacobs and Corbett 1990:181). In 1982 the Commission agreed in principle to take up any Parliamentary proposals to which it does not have major objections; if it has objections, it undertakes to explain its reasons in detail to the Parliament (Jacobs and Corbett 1990:181). Nugent (1989:240) argues that it is difficult to establish the initial impetus for legislation, and that even resolutions from Parliament may have in fact originated from the Commission, the latter wanting to reinforce its own position vis-à-vis the Council. In any case, all three institutional actors can in fact place items on the legislative agenda. Once discussion is initiated by a Commission proposal, there are no restrictions on the amendments that Parliament can introduce in its first reading. There are, however, restrictions on its second reading. Parliamentary amendments in the second reading are restricted not by the Single European Act, but *by the parliamentary rules themselves*. According to article 51(2), only amendments concerning those parts of the text that have been modified by the Council and that seek to adopt a compromise with the Council or which restore Parliament's position from the first reading are acceptable during the second reading (Bieber 1988:722). Further, only a committee, a group of at least twenty-three Members of Parliament (MEPs), may present amendments (Fitzmaurice 1988:397). Did the Parliament tie its own hands? Nothing of the sort. These restrictions simply increase the efficiency of Parliament during its second reading, since substantively they permit the adoption of any position in the interval between (and including) Parliament's initial position and the adoption of the Council's common position.

There is, however, a very important restriction on Parliament's second reading amendment power. Amendments require absolute majorities to be adopted. In practice the 260 required votes constituted a two-thirds majority of members present. Moreover, given that the 518 MEPs of the 12 countries were organized into more than 10 (crossnational) parliamentary groups, and that voting alignments occur more frequently by political group and less frequently by country, and given that voting discipline is weak, 260 votes is a stringent requirement. The most likely combination to achieve an absolute majority is a coalition of Socialists and Christian Democrats (European People's Party —EPP), who together controlled 301 seats.

To summarize, according to the Cooperation Procedure, in its second reading Parliament can by an absolute majority of its members make a proposal, which, if adopted by the Commission, can be accepted by a qualified majority (54/76) of the Council, but requires unanimity of the Council to be modified. This proposal can be anywhere between the Parliament's and the Council's first reading of initial legislation, including a reiteration of the Parliament's previous position. Consequently, if the Parliament manages to make a proposal that makes the Commission and a qualified majority of the Council better off than legislation which can be voted on unanimously, this proposal will be adopted by all institutional actors. If, however, such a proposal does not exist, or if the Parliament cannot adopt one by an absolute majority of its members, or if it makes the wrong choice, then the agenda is transferred into the hands of the Council, which can modify the Parliament's proposal by unanimity. These conditions describe the "power of the conditional agenda setter," which is attributed to the Parliament by the Cooperation Procedure. In the remainder of this section, we will examine how this power has been used, and in the next section, we focus on its theoretical properties.

The Car Emission Story

Some background to the legislative story[9] may be necessary: automobile density is much higher in Europe than in the United States. For example, there are 72 autos/km^2 in Germany, and 128 autos/km^2 in the Netherlands, while only 12 autos/km^2 in the US. Small cars represent 60 percent of the total number of passenger cars in EC countries, but they are prevalent in France (60 percent) and Italy (84 percent), while less common in Germany (37 percent). So, adoption of car emission standards would affect differently both the car industries and the environment of different countries. Lower standards could be met by lean-burn engines, while higher standards require catalytic converters. Technically speaking, catalytic converters reduce emissions by 90 percent, are costly, require unleaded gas, and have to be replaced every four years; lean-burn engines reduce emissions by about 50 percent, are less costly, improve fuel efficiency, and are still in the research and development stage.

On February 15, 1988, the Commission introduced legislation concerning small car emission standards to the Council (composed of the twelve Ministers of the Environment). The proposal would reduce emissions from small cars by 58 percent by 1992 to 1993 and could be met either by catalytic converters or by lean-burn engines. The Council commenced discussion and found the positions of the 12 ministers to be divergent: Luxembourg, Ireland, and Belgium agreed with the proposal; France, Britain, Italy, Spain, and Portugal found the standards too strict; and Holland, Denmark, Greece, and Germany found the standards too lax. Before the Parliament's first reading, several countries modified their positions (notably France and Germany), allowing the Environmental Council to approve the Commission's proposal by qualified majority.[10]

The Parliament, in its first reading (September 1988), voted overwhelmingly (243 for, 63 against, 14 abstentions) for U.S. 83 standards (19 grams of CO and 5 grams of $HC+NO_x$). The Commission rejected Parliament's amendments. The Council, after a series of compromises, adopted the Commission's proposal as a common position by qualified majority. In April 1989, the common position came before Parliament for a second reading. Parliament insisted on its previous set of U.S. 83 standards. This renewed (but not new) proposal met the agreement of the Commission this time around. At this point, accounts diverge: One account has it that the Commission was forced to make a U-turn, a second argues that it changed its mind, and a third argues that it did not have a firm position anyhow. Jacobs and Corbett (1990:170) claim that the Parliament threatened the Commission, stating that unless the Commission accepted its version, it would reject the Council's common position, which, given the absence of unanimity in the Council, would be equivalent to aborting the legislation. This threat was credible because European public opinion is very sensitive on environmental issues, and the election date of the European Parliament was approaching. Kim (1992) considers that the replacement of the Environment Commissioner, Stanley Clinton Davis, with Carlo Ripa di Meana on January 1, 1989 was instrumental in the Commission's U-turn. Finally, Stephen (1992) argues that the Commission is usually swayed by the industry, so in this case it did not have a strong preference, since the automobile industry was divided on the issue. Once the Council was faced with the proposal incorporating higher standards, knowing that it could not come to a unanimous decision, it adopted the Parliament's position by a qualified majority. Kim's (1992) account of the Council's acceptance of Parliament's proposal involves discussion of a series of bilateral negotiations between members of the Council and the instrumental role played by small countries (particularly Holland). However, once the Commission's U-turn is explained the U-turn of the Council does not require explanation. Indeed, once the Parliament's second reading proposal is accepted by the Commission, and since there is no unanimity in the Council, the real choice for the Council is either to accept the proposal or to revert to the status quo. Consequently, if the proposal is marginally better than the status quo for the Council, it will be adopted. In this case, Parliament forced the other two actors to make policy U-turns and imposed its own position on the other actors *because* it was able to make a take it or leave it offer to them, that is, because of the power of the conditional agenda setter. Can Parliament use this strategy often? The following statistics provide the answer.

Cooperation Procedure Statistics

During the period from July 1987 to June 1989 the Parliament dealt with 68 Commission proposals under the Cooperation Procedure and amended 57 of them (accepting 11).[11] The Commission accepted 473 out of the 712 parliamentary amendments, and the Council accepted 47 percent of Parliament's first reading amendments. In the second reading, Parliament approved without amendment 35 of the 68 Council common positions it considered. In 32 cases, Parliament adopted 132 amendments, 70 of which were adopted by the Commission and only 30 by the Council. In one case the Parliament rejected the common position and the Council was not able to overrule.

Using similar figures Lodge (1989:75) points out that "the EP's second-reading amendments stand a far slimmer chance of survival," while Bogdanor (1989:208) comes to the conclusion that "the main effect of the second reading of Community legislation is to increase the importance of the first reading as a point of leverage for Parliament." Similarly Fitzmaurice (1988:390) argues that "the second reading 'navette' will have little real purpose." Little can be made of these first versus second reading statistics because, without further investigation, we cannot assess the importance of Parliament's amendments. Consequently, we cannot tell whether amendments were accepted in the first reading because they would have been accepted in the second, or whether the Council accepted some amendments in order to weaken the Parliamentary majority. This would make Parliament unable to offer amendments in the second reading. Finally, we cannot tell whether these or some competing explanation could be advanced. What is clear, however, is that the majority of the Council's common positions go unchallenged by Parliament and that a large percentage (77 percent) of Parliamentary amendments eventually fail.

How can these poor quantitative results be reconciled with the image of a powerful European Parliament generated by the car emission case study and others like it?[12] The next section analyzes formally the conditional agenda setting aspect of the Cooperation Procedure to provide the answer.

CONDITIONAL AGENDA SETTING

Agenda setting players have power when it is impossible, difficult, or costly for decision makers to modify their proposals. Modifications of proposals may be precluded by the prevailing institutions. For example, when the President of the United States nominates a candidate for the Supreme Court, the Senate cannot modify the proposal. In the first theoretical paper analyzing the power of agenda control (McKelvey 1976), the agenda setter could make a series of proposals that would be voted under "closed rule," that is, without amendments. This agenda setter had quasi-dictatorial powers: He could drive a society through a series of successive votes to select his ideal point. However, an agenda setter loses his power under open rule, because his proposals can subsequently be modified by amendments of the deciding body (Shepsle and Weingast 1987a, 1987b, Krehbiel 1987). Another way that agenda setters have power is if the deciding body is impatient, that is, it pays a price as long as there is no agreement. Impatience creates an asymmetry between the proposal of the agenda setter and its modifications (Baron and Ferejohn 1989, Tsebelis and Money forthcoming).

The Cooperation Procedure presents a different mechanism for agenda setting power. Regardless of impatience, it is more difficult for the Council to modify a proposal of the Parliament (provided this proposal is accepted by the Commission) than it is to accept it. Indeed, a qualified majority is needed for acceptance, but unanimity is required for modification. This procedure *may* enable the Parliament to make a proposal that makes a qualified majority of the Council better off than any unanimous decision. *If* such a proposal exists,[13] *if* the Parliament is able to make it, and *if* the Commission adopts it, then the Parliament has agenda setting powers. If, however, these conditions are not met, the Parliament loses its agenda setting power. This is why I say that the Parliament, under the Cooperation Procedure, has conditional agenda setting power. This section studies the last reading of the Cooperation Procedure, first in one and then in two dimensions or more. I will provide necessary conditions for the existence of a winning EP proposal (that is, a proposal that will be accepted by the Commission and a qualified majority of the Council). I will call such a proposal X and show that it exists only some of the time, thus explaining why most of the time Parliament accepts the common position of the Council and why quite frequently Parliamentary amendments fail. Consider that the twelve EC countries are arranged along a one-dimensional continuum. Garrett (1992) presents a one-dimensional representation of the Council of Ministers, arguing that the interpretation of this dimension is European integration. He positions the different countries in the following way: At the lowest end, least integrationist, are the United Kingdom and Denmark; in the middle, France, Germany, and the Benelux countries; and at the highest end, the most integrationist, the "south," that is, Italy, Spain, Portugal, Greece, and Ireland. The positions of the Commission and the Parliament on the integration axis are even higher than those of the south. I will follow this spatial representation and study the power of the Parliament as a function of the position of the status quo along the integration dimension. Figure 5.1 replicates Garrett's argument.

Figure 5.1
Position of Status Quo, Countries, Council, Commission, and Parliament in One-Dimension (Integration)

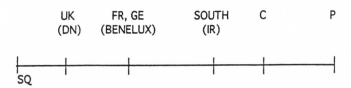

Source: Garrett (1992)

Assuming that countries have symmetric indifference curves, that is, that they prefer their ideal point on the continuum and they are indifferent between two points with the same distance from their ideal point (one above and one below their ideal level of integration), we can study the properties of the successful proposals that the Parliament can make.

We will proceed from the simple to the more complicated cases and study the properties of different institutional arrangements. In particular, I will start with the study of the process in one dimension, and in order to explain the powers of the "conditional agenda setter" I will present the outcomes of an unconditional and a conditional agenda setting process. This presentation will help explain the logic of Parliament's calculations. Once this logic is understood, I will present the argument in the more realistic two-dimensional and more-than-two-dimensional settings.

Unconditional Agenda Setting

Suppose that the Parliament can make a take it or leave it offer to the other institutional actors. In Figure 5.2 I have replaced the twelve countries of the European Council of Ministers by a seven-member body, in the interest of graphic simplification. I have selected seven voters because the qualified majority of five out of seven voters is approximately the same as the actual qualified majority in the Council of Ministers (fifty-four out of seventy-six).[14]

Figure 5.2
Unconditional Agenda Setting Power (One Dimension)

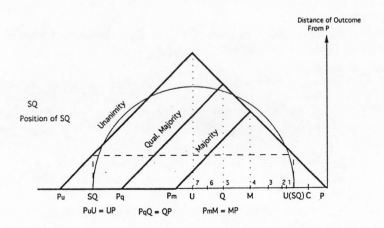

In order to understand the importance of the decision rule in the Council of Ministers, I will consider three cases: The cases in which Parliamentary proposals require unanimity, qualified majority, and simple majority to be accepted.

A. *Unanimity*. Suppose now that the Parliament can make a take it or leave it proposal to the Commission and the Council. This proposal has to be accepted by the Commission and a unanimous Council, otherwise the status quo remains unchanged. In this case, Parliament can make a proposal that will make the least integrationist member of the Council indifferent (indicated by 7 or U in the figure) between the proposal and the status quo. This is the point U(sq) in Figure 5.2.

B. *Qualified majority*. If the Parliament can make a take it or leave it proposal to the Commission and the Council, and if this proposal requires acceptance by the Commission and a qualified majority of 5/7 in the Council, otherwise leaving the status quo unchanged, then the Parliament can make a proposal that will make the fifth least integrationist member of the Council (indicated by 5 or Q in the figure) indifferent between the proposal and the status quo. In Figure 5.2, this point is to the right of the ideal position of the Parliament, so the Parliament can propose its own ideal point and it will be accepted.

C. *Simple majority*. If simple instead of qualified majority is required in the Council, Parliament can make a proposal that will leave the median voter of the Council (indicated by M or 4 in the figure) indifferent between the proposal and the status quo. Since this point is to the right of the ideal position of the Parliament, the Parliament can once more have its own ideal position adopted.

From the figure it is easy to see that under the (realistic) assumptions that the status quo is less integrationist than the positions of the countries and that the positions of the Parliament and the Commission are more integrationist, the final outcome of the process is closer to the position of the Parliament the smaller the required majority for the decision of the Council. Indeed, the Parliament has to consider the least integrationist member in case of unanimity, the fifth least integrationist in case of qualified majority of five-seventh, and the fourth least integrationist (the median) in case of simple majority.

Figure 5.2 also offers a graphic representation of the position of the final outcome of an unconditional agenda setting process as a function of the position of the status quo and the decision rule required in the Council. In all cases, the outcome will be between the position of the pivotal member (U for unanimity, Q for qualified majority, and M for simple majority) and the position P of the Parliament.

In order to find the exact outcome, we must use the diagram in the following way. First, note that Pu is the symmetric of P (the ideal position of the Parliament) with respect to the least integrationist member of the Council (U or 7).[15] If the status quo is to the left of Pu the Parliament will successfully propose its own position. If the status quo is between Pu and U, then the final outcome will be U(SQ), which is symmetric to SQ with respect to U. U(SQ) can be found by following the dotted line from SQ up to the line called unanimity, then horizontally until it intersects the other side of the triangle, and then back down until it intersects the horizontal axis. If the status quo is to the right of U, then there is no Parliamentary proposal that can defeat it. So, the distance of the final outcome as a function of the status quo can be seen by following the sides of the triangle named "unanimity" in Figure 5.2. Similarly, the distance of the final outcome as a function of the position of the status quo when qualified (simple) majority is the decision rule in the Council can be found by following the sides of the triangle called "qualified (simple) majority." It is easy to observe that the distance of the final outcome from Parliament's position is smaller the smaller the required majority (the majority triangle is included in the qualified majority triangle, which is included in the unanimity triangle). In all cases, the final outcome will be between the position of the pivotal voter (U, Q, or M) and the position of the Parliament. The Parliament can attain its own ideal point when the status quo is "far enough" (further than Pu, Pq, or Pm depending on the decision rule). Finally, if the status quo is between the position of the Parliament and the pivotal voter in the Council, it cannot be changed.

Summary 1

In an unconditional agenda setting procedure in one dimension the final outcome is always between the position of the Parliament and the position of the pivotal voter in the Council; it is closer to the position of the Parliament the smaller the required majority in the Council; if the status quo is between the position of the pivotal voter (U, Q, or M) and the Parliament it cannot be changed; and if the pivotal voter in the Council is between the status quo and the position of the Parliament, the further away the status quo, the more powerful the Parliament.

Conditional Agenda Setting

Consider now a set of rules that better approximates the actual Cooperation Procedure: The Parliament makes an offer, that if accepted by the Commission, can be accepted by a qualified majority of the Council and can be modified by unanimity in the Council. In the case of conditional agenda setting, the strategic calculations of the Parliament become more complicated. The winning proposal has to be better for a qualified majority of the Council, not only from the status quo, but also from what the Council could achieve on its own by unanimity.

From Figure 5.2, we can see that any point in the SQ,U(SQ) segment is unanimously preferred to the status quo. We have no way of knowing *a priori* which one of these points would be selected by the Council. At this point I will simplify matters by assuming that a unanimous Council would select the least common denominator, that is, the position of the least integrationist state. This assumption is reasonable for a one-dimensional space, and is frequently made in the empirical literature. I will call this assumption the *minimalist assumption*. It is not at all an innocuous assumption. I will discuss its consequences and relax it when turning to multi-dimensional issue spaces. The minimalist assumption relies on the argument that the least integrationist member of the Council can make a credible threat that it will not vote for any proposal offering more integration than it wants.

According to the minimalist assumption, if the status quo is less integrationist than the least integrationist member, the Council will unanimously vote for the position of the least integrationist state (U or 7), while if it is more integrationist than the position of the most integrationist member (1 in Figure 5.3), the Council will unanimously vote for 1.

So the Parliament has to make an offer that makes the qualified majority better off than the status quo or the position that the Council can unanimously adopt (1 or U depending on the position of the status quo).

Figure 5.3

Conditional Agenda Setting Power: Approval by Majority, m, or Qualified Majority, q, Modification by Unanimity, u (One Dimension; Minimalist Assumption)

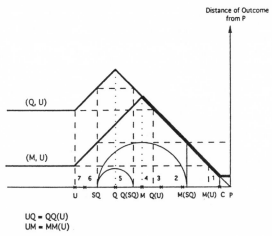

There are four cases:

• If the status quo is less integrationist than U (to the left of U in the figure), the winning proposal is Q(U), which is symmetric to U with respect to Q.
• If the status quo is more integrationist than U, but less than Q, as in Figure 5.3, the winning proposal of the Parliament is Q(SQ), which is symmetric to SQ with respect to Q.
• If the status quo is between Q and the most integrationist member (which I have called 1), there is no proposal that would upset it.
• If the status quo is between the position of the most integrationist member of the Council and the position of the Parliament, the outcome will be located at the position of the most integrationist state.

The line called (Q,U) shows the outcomes as a function of the position of the status quo when acceptance requires qualified majority q, and when modification requires unanimity. It is easy to observe that the final outcome will always be inside the segment covered by the positions of the pivotal member of Council and the member of Council closest to the Parliament (between Q and 1). According to the minimalist assumption, if the status quo is less integrationist than the least integrationist member, the Council would unanimously vote for the position of this state (U or 7), while if it is more integrationist than the position of the most integrationist member (1 in Figure 5.3), the Council would unanimously vote for 1. So the Parliament has to make an offer that makes the majority better off than the status quo or the position that the Council could unanimously adopt (1 or U depending on the position of the status quo) do. Reasoning as in the previous case, we can produce the line (M,U) that shows the outcomes as a function of the position of the status quo when acceptance requires simple majority m and modification requires unanimity. Again, the final outcome will always be inside the segment between the median council member and the member closest to Parliament (between M and 1). A comparison of lines (Q,U) and (M,U) reveals that the more powerful the Parliament is, the easier it is to have its position accepted, which in our case happens when simple as opposed to qualified majority is required for acceptance. The final outcome is in the interval between the pivotal member for acceptance (Q or M) and the most integrationist member (1). Consequently, the Parliament's position will not prevail (unless that position itself lies in this interval). The relationship between the position of the status quo and the position of the final outcome is more complicated. The interval covered by the positions of the members of the Council is called the Pareto interval. If the status quo is in the Pareto interval it cannot be modified by a unanimous vote, because at least one member of the Council will object. This means that when the status quo is inside the Pareto interval, if the Council rejects Parliament's proposal, it will have to accept the status quo. Therefore, when the status quo is in the Pareto interval, Parliament has unconditional agenda setting power. If the status quo is outside this interval, the Council on its own, according to the minimalist assumption (see above), can bring the outcome to position U or 1, requiring Parliament to make a proposal that wins over U (by making the pivotal voter Q or M indifferent) or 1 (there is no Parliamentary proposal that can win 1).

Summary 2

In a conditional agenda setting procedure in one dimension, the final outcome is always between the position of the member of Council (that is closest to the Parliament) and the position of the pivotal voter (Q or M) in the Council (which is closer to the position of the Parliament the smaller the required majority in the Council). If the status quo is in the Pareto interval, then the outcome is identical to the one attainable under unconditional agenda setting; otherwise, the outcome is as if the status quo were on one of the extreme points of the Pareto interval. Comparison of summaries 1 and 2, and inspection of Figures 5.2 and 5.3, indicate the differences between unconditional and conditional agenda setting powers. The differences stem from the fact that an unconditional agenda setter has to take only the position of the status quo into account when it makes a proposal, while a conditional agenda setter has to consider what the Council can do on its own. It is only when the status quo cannot be modified by the Council that the powers of the conditional and unconditional agenda setter coincide. In all other cases, the unconditional agenda setter is able to bring the final outcome closer to his own ideal position than the conditional agenda setter.

Conditional Agenda Setting in Two Dimensions

The one-dimensional representation of the members of the Council was helpful as a heuristic device to understand the logic of Parliamentary calculations. However, it presents two problems. First, from an empirical point of view, reasonable objections can be raised as to how realistic the one-dimensional assumption is. Second, from a theoretical point of view, it is questionable whether the conclusions presented in summary 2 can be generalized to more than one dimension.[16] Moreover, all the results presented in the previous part of this section were derived under the minimalist assumption, which as I said is too strong a requirement. Here I will relax both the one-dimensional and the minimalist assumptions.

Consider that the members of the Council are concerned simultaneously about two different issues, say European integration *and* the environment. Figure 5.4 presents a graphic representation of the position of the members of the Council. Again, for reasons I explained in footnote 16, we will assume that the Council is composed of seven members, that a qualified majority of five is required for acceptance of Parliament's proposal, and that the members of the Council have circular indifference curves (Euclidian preferences), that is, they are indifferent between proposals that are of equal distances from their ideal point.

In the Appendix a series of definitions and elementary geometric properties necessary to analyze the powers of the conditional agenda setter in two dimensions are provided. Here I provide the logic of the argument in a non-technical way.

Figure 5.4
Pareto Surface and Q-Core of Council (Q = 5/7, 6/6)

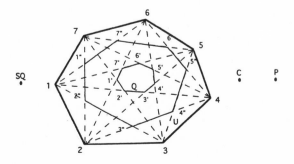

The reasoning is similar to that used in the one-dimensional case. The Parliament has to find out what the Council can do on its own, and present a proposal that makes the Commission and a qualified majority of the Council better off than either the status quo or what the Council can do on its own.

In the one-dimensional case we simplified matters by assuming that the Council would select unanimously the position of the least integrationist member. We called this the minimalist assumption. Here, in two dimensions such an assumption cannot be defended. For example, what is the point that will be selected unanimously by the Council if the status quo is as presented in Figure 5.4? Would point 1 be selected? Why not 2? It all depends on how convincing different governments are in proposing their own ideal points for a vote. For example, the Danish parliament is known to have a permanent committee on European Union legislation, which extracts statements from the government prior to Council meetings, so that the Danish representative in the Council is particularly inflexible (Williams 1991:159).[17] Under such circumstances would other members of the community accept the Danish position as the alternative to the status quo? Since the unanimity position is not unique, I will impose on Parliamentary proposals a severe restriction. I will require that in order to be accepted they must be preferred by the Commission and by a qualified majority of the Council to *any* proposal that can be voted on unanimously by the Council. This way we will have a (very conservative) estimate of the conditional agenda setting power of the Parliament.

In two dimensions, for the qualified majority specified by the Cooperation Procedure (54/76), a central area of the Council, which technically is called Q-core, is guaranteed to exist. Q-core is the set of points that cannot be modified by any Q-majority. It is represented in Figure 5.4 by the heptagon 1'2'3'4'5'6'7'. Figure 5.4 presents also the Q-core if a higher qualified majority of 6/7 is required. It is the heptagon 1"2"3"4"5"6"7". If the status quo is located in this central area of the preferences of the members of the Council, it cannot be modified by either the Parliament's proposal or by the Council on its own.

Figure 5.5 divides the plane into four different areas. If the status quo is inside the Q-core it cannot be changed. If the status quo is outside this central area, but inside the area defined by the preferences of the states—that is, inside the heptagon 1234567 (which is called the Pareto set)—then the Council cannot modify the status quo by unanimity. In this case, Parliament can select a majority in the Commission and a qualified majority Q in the Council as allies and make a proposal that is preferred by its allies to the status quo.

If the status quo is outside the Pareto set, then the set of alternatives unanimously preferred to the status quo may or may not intersect with the Q-core. If there is an intersection, then there is no point that can command a Q qualified majority of the Council, so the Parliament has no agenda setting power. The set of status quo points for which the unanimity set intersects with the Q-core is defined by the curve I(Q-core).

Figure 5.5
Existence of Proposal Commanding a Q-Majority in Council (X) as a Function of Position of Status Quo (SQ)

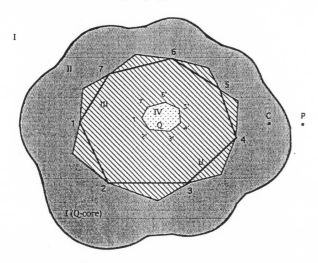

If SQ in:
Area I : no X proposal exists
Area II : X proposal may or may not exist
Area III : X proposal exists
Area IV : no X proposal exists

If the status quo is outside this line, Parliament has no agenda setting power and the Council will select its preferred solution by unanimity. If, however, the status quo is in the area between the I(Q-core) curve and the sides of the heptagon, a winning proposal of the Parliament may exist. In the Appendix, I prove that if the status quo is close to the sides of the heptagon of the states (indicated by the shaded area outside the Pareto set in Figure 5.5), a winning proposal exists (provided the Commission adopts it in its report). This proposal will be the final outcome of the Cooperation Procedure.

Figure 5.6 presents the winning proposal if the status quo is located inside the Pareto set. Figure 5.7 presents a case where there is no winning proposal. Finally, Figure 5.8 presents a case where the status quo is outside the Pareto set but a winning proposal exists. In all these figures, the winning proposal is constructed by finding the set Q(U(SQ)) that is preferred by both the qualified majority of the Council and the Commission to *any* point of the unanimity set of the status quo (U(SQ)). If such a set exists, the Parliament selects from it the point X that is closest to its own ideal point.

In all these figures I have presented the Parliament and the Commission as having ideal points close to each other. This is usually the case because both are supranational actors and because the Commission is politically accountable to the Parliament, as in a parliamentary system.

Figure 5.6
Winning Proposal (X) When Status Quo Is in the Pareto Surface

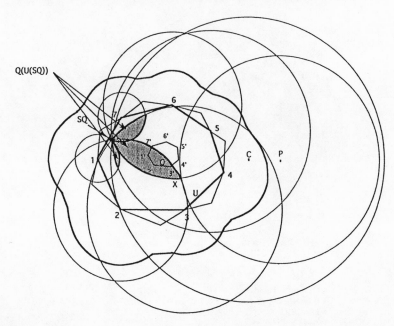

Figure 5.7
Status Quo in Area II; Winning Proposal X Does Not Exist

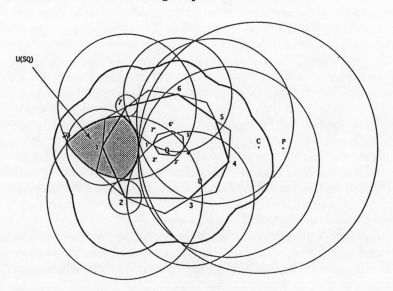

Figure 5.8
Status Quo in Area II; Winning Proposal Exists

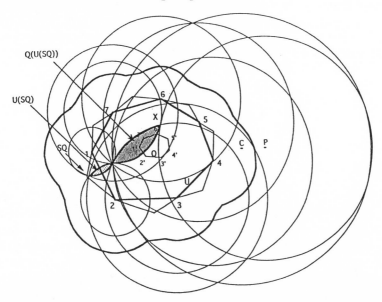

However, if the position of the Commission is far away from the position of the Parliament, it may be that there is no winning parliamentary proposal because a parliamentary amendment would be rejected by the Commission *before* it reaches the Q majority in the Council.

Paradoxes can arise from this institutional setting. For example, it is possible that the final outcome selected by the Cooperation Procedure is not in the Pareto set. Consider a case where the status quo (SQ) is in the Pareto set, Q(SQ) has points outside the heptagon 1234567, and the Parliament's and the Commission's ideal points are located in such a way that they make a proposal outside the Pareto set. Figure 5.6 would present such a case if states 3, 4, and 5 were moved to the left of X (say to the points 3', 4', and 5', respectively). In this case, while all members of the Council would prefer points inside the Pareto set, they would be unable to select them unanimously because at least one of them would prefer the SQ itself. This result is the opposite of Weber and Wiesmeth's (1991:265) conclusion; they claim that the outcomes of the Cooperation Procedure are always efficient.[18]

Another paradoxical property of the Cooperation Procedure is non-monotonicity. Consider that the status quo is at the position presented in Figure 5.7, where there is no winning proposal by Parliament. Consider now that the country called 1 moves to a less integrationist position to the left of the status quo (think for example of Thatcher replacing Major as Prime Minister of the United Kingdom). Since the status quo is now inside the Pareto set, there is always a proposal that the Parliament can make to move the status quo to further integrationist levels. In this hypothetical example the only change is a movement of one government to a less integrationist position, and the resulting change in the outcome was more integration (non-monotonicity). Why did this happen? Because before there was a wide range of unanimity outcomes, and no qualified majority could win all of them, while afterwards the movement of the United Kingdom persuades the other governments that there is no unanimously preferred change of the status quo, so they have to accept the proposal of the Parliament by qualified majority.

Summary 3

A 54/76-core is guaranteed to exist in two dimensions. In this case, the curvilinear property described in Theorem 2 holds: When the status quo is inside the Q-core, or far way from it, there is no winning proposal by the Parliament, and so the conditional agenda setting power of the Parliament is null. But whenever the status quo is in intermediate positions, a winning parliamentary proposal (assuming adoption by the Commission) is either guaranteed or may exist. This is the conditional agenda setting power of the Parliament in two dimensions. One other interesting feature of conditional agenda setting is the importance of information. According to the informational property (Theorem 3 in the Appendix), when the Parliament's information about what the Council will unanimously do increases, its agenda setting power increases. In the limiting case, when the Parliament knows which point inside the Pareto set the Council will select, it will always have agenda setting power (unless there is a Q-core and the Council decides to a select a point in it). This informational property is the reason why I discovered a curvilinear pattern in the agenda setting power of the Parliament in two dimensions but not in one. In the one-dimensional case, I used the minimalist assumption and argued that the Council would select the position of the least common denominator. In two or more dimensions the choice is not so simple, and so I cannot approximate it by assumption. If, however, information about the Council member's positions exists, the power of the Parliament increases. As we saw above in section two, the Parliament and the Council fought bitterly about the informational content of the common position rendered by the Council. Some commentators regarded this struggle and the subsequent shift in the Council's position as "preconditions for rationalizing and coordinating the legislative procedure" (Bieber 1988:720). The informational property helps us to view this struggle in a different light: It is a fight between a national and a supranational institution for control of the agenda. What happens if the actor's calculations are made in a three- or a four-dimensional space? In this case, a Q-core is not guaranteed to exist, and consequently, as long as the status quo is inside or close to the Pareto set, Parliament will have agenda setting powers. On the other hand, if the status quo is far away from the Pareto set, there is no winning proposal from the Parliament.

The conclusions of this analysis are fourfold:

A. *The position of the final outcome.* The final outcome of the Cooperation Procedure will most likely be inside the heptagon defined by the states. However, it is possible that Q(U(SQ)) has points outside the Pareto set, and if one of these points is the closest to the Parliament (and accepted by the Commission), then the Cooperation Procedure leads to an inefficient outcome for the members of the Council.

B. *Curvilinear property.* The agenda setting power of the Parliament is a function of the position of the status quo. If there is a Q-core, this power is a curvilinear function of the position of the status quo. It does not exist if the status quo is inside the Q-core or far away, and it exists or it may exist in intermediate positions.

C. *Existence of a Q-core.* If there is no Q-core, the agenda setting power of the Parliament exists when the status quo is inside the Pareto set, may exist when the status quo is close to it, and does not exist when the status quo is far away.

D. *Informational property.* Accurate information in Parliament about the positions that are likely to be adopted by unanimity in the Council increases the agenda setting power of the Parliament.

EUROPEAN PARLIAMENT AND EUROPEAN INSTITUTIONS

The previous analysis sheds light on the way the three EU institutional actors interact within the context of the Cooperation Procedure. In this section, I contrast the conclusions of my analysis with those of other treatments of the Cooperation Procedure. In the next section, I generalize my findings, proposing that the institution of a supranational conditional agenda setter is a feature that the European Union uses quite frequently.

I began this article with the paradox of the European Parliament, which is generally considered to be weak, nonetheless successfully imposing its will on both the Commission and the Council. As has been shown, the puzzle is resolved by recognizing that the Parliament has conditional agenda setting power, and that consequently it may find proposals that have the property of making both the Commission and a qualified majority in the Council better off than the status quo. The fact that such proposals do not always exist is the reason that cases like the car exhaust emissions are not the rule. This conditional agenda setting power of the Parliament has not always been understood or analyzed correctly. Most analyses base their conclusions overwhelmingly on the observation that the final decision in the Cooperation Procedure is made by the Council; some are incorrect in terms of the strategic calculations of the actors, in others the role of the Parliament has been underestimated because the agenda setting power is attributed to some other actor. Bieber et al. (1986:791) argue that: "With regard to the European Parliament, the Single Act is an inconsistent document: Where it increases the Parliament's powers of participation in decision-making the practical effect is either very limited or diminished because the exercise of the powers is conditional on the *attitude* of the Council and the Commission" (emphasis added). Similarly, Fitzmaurice (1988:391) argues that "despite the appearances of a co-decision model, the Council virtually retains the last word." Both accounts underestimate the role of the Parliament. My analysis demonstrates that the Council has the last word only if the Parliament fails to make a winning proposal; moreover, if the "attitude" of the Council and the Commission are not whimsical and if each actor when confronted with a choice selects the best alternative for himself (thereby adopting maximizing behavior), the Parliament through astute selection of its proposals sometimes has the power to impose its will upon the other actors. Lodge (1987:23) attributes the power of the Parliament to "an alliance with one or more member states prepared to thwart the attainment of the necessary majorities (qualified or unanimous) unless Parliament's views and amendments were accommodated." If Lodge's analysis concerns the power of the Parliament to block the decision in the Council, one or two allies in the Council are not necessary. Both the Parliament and the Council can block legislation by simply sitting forever on a proposal during the first reading of the Cooperation Procedure. However, the Parliament in the second reading has more than blocking power. If the analysis concerns the power of the Parliament to impose its will on the Council, one or two members in the Council are not enough; a qualified majority is required. To make this point clear, consider the configuration in Figure 5.7. Move the Parliament's ideal point to coincide with state 4. There is now an objective alliance between the Parliament and state 4. However, there is no winning proposal that the Parliament can make, and if the Parliament makes a proposal, even if state 4 argues that it supports Parliament and will vote down an otherwise unanimous proposal causing the status quo to prevail, it will not be believed by the other members of the Council. Most analyses of the Cooperation Procedure attribute agenda setting power to the Commission, not the Parliament. For example, Garrett (1991:551) argues that "parliament amendments merely allow the commission again to make its own proposals." Lenaerts (1991:22) argues that the Commission has a "monopoly of legislative initiative." I have already argued that in practice the initiative may come from any one of the three actors. The real question is whether the Commission is constrained in its proposal by the amendments of the Parliament in the second reading. This is not a major difference, because the positions of the Parliament and the Commission are usually close to each other. Figure 5.9 helps the reader to visualize the difference.

Figure 5.9
Winning Proposals by Parliament (X) and Commission (Y) if Their Preferences Diverge

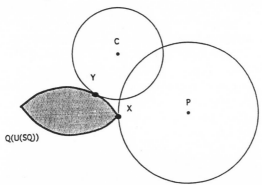

In this figure, I present the set of points that command a qualified majority over anything that can be voted unanimously by the Council, Q(U(SQ)), and the ideal points of the Parliament and the Commission. If the Commission has to accept or reject Parliamentary amendments, the outcome of the procedure will be X (the best the Parliament can do, subject to the constraint that the Commission accepts it). If the Commission can make a proposal of its own, the outcome will be Y (the best the Commission can do regardless of the Parliament's position).

Which approach is the correct one? Texts and practices are ambiguous at this point. Article 149(2) (d) of the EC Treaty specifies:

> The Commission shall, within a period of one month, re-examine the proposal on the basis of which the Council adopted its common position, by taking into account the amendments proposed by the European Parliament. The Commission shall forward to the Council at the same time as its re-examined proposal, the amendments of the European Parliament which it has not accepted, and shall express its opinion on them. The Council may adopt these amendments unanimously.

The wording seems to indicate that the reexamined proposal is not restricted to the adoption or rejection of Parliamentary amendments, but could incorporate a new proposal. However, empirical reports on the Cooperation Procedure, which do not mention the proportion of Commission amendments adopted or rejected by the Council, indicate that the Commission does not make amendments of its own.

According to my account, the Parliament has agenda setting power as long as it can make a winning proposal in the second stage of the Cooperation Procedure. There are essentially four relevant points, and I will discuss each one of them in turn.

A. *Existence of an absolute majority in Parliament.* This is the requirement for successful parliamentary proposals least discussed in the paper. I
went around it by assuming that Parliament is a unified actor and by
studying the internal divisions of the Council. However, as I said earlier,
the 260 vote requirement for a second round proposal is not a trivial
matter. It essentially requires congruence of Socialists and Christian
Democrats of different countries. This is not a frequently observed alliance
at the national level.[19] I think that such a coalition can be formed more
frequently on social or quality of life issues (environment, health, education, and research) than on economic issues. To the extent that the former
prevail on the agenda, the Parliament will see its influence increased.

B. *Acceptance by Commission.* The Parliament and the Commission have
had positions close to each other in the past. The statistics reported earlier
indicate that the Commission accepted 66 percent of Parliamentary
amendments in the first round and, 53 percent in the second round of the
Cooperation Procedure. There are two ways in which the Parliament can
keep this relationship close in the future. The first is through the political
responsibility of the Commission in front of the Parliament. The second is
by the means that it used in the car emissions case: It can threaten to reject
a proposal in its second reading. Such a measure requires unanimity in the
Council, and consequently would probably kill the Commission proposal,
damaging the Commission's reputation. However, if there is sufficient divergence between the positions of Parliament and the Commission, a
winning proposal of Parliament may not exist, since it will not be adopted
by the Commission.

C. *Position of the status quo.* An unconditional agenda setter has more
power when the status quo is far away, because then he has more leeway to
make a take it or leave it offer. In contrast, the European Parliament (a
conditional agenda setter) has less power the further away the status quo,
because there are many positions that the Council can adopt on its own by
unanimity to avoid both the status quo and Parliament's position. It is reasonable to assume that throughout the history of the European Community
the status quo has continued to move towards more integration. If this is a
reasonable assumption, and if integration continues, as the status quo approaches or gets inside the Pareto set of the Council, the role of the Parliament is likely to increase. This is a simple explanation of the second
paradox that motivated this study: In the past the Parliament has been unable to make more than 20 percent of its second-reading amendments
winning proposals. The simple displacement of the status quo towards
more integration will transform winning Parliamentary proposals from the
exception to the rule. Obviously, this is a *ceteris paribus* prediction, and it
assumes the same institutional structure (Cooperation Procedure) and the
same distribution of tastes among the different actors.

D. *Existence of a Q-core.* A 54/76 core is guaranteed to exist in two dimensions, but not in three or more dimensions. Lack of a core increases the likelihood that a Parliamentary winning proposal will exist. Consequently, if issues become more complicated, the role of the Parliament is likely to be enhanced. This conclusion is congruent with the argument in Weber and Wiesmeth (1991) that the likelihood of cooperation increases through issue linkage. The only difference is that issue linkage is a conscious effort (i.e., a strategy) to connect different issues, while my argument is that regardless of the reason of the connection (conscious effort or objective complication), the outcome is not only more cooperation, but a shift of power to the Parliament.

CONDITIONAL AGENDA SETTING AND EUROPEAN INTEGRATION

The European Community has fascinated observers and scholars because it is a unique object of study. Accordingly, a series of neologisms have been invented to describe it. Alberta Sbragia (1992:257) characterizes it as "unique in its institutional structure, neither a state nor an international organization." For William Wallace (1983:403), it is "Less than a Federation, More than a Regime" and is "stuck between sovereignty and integration" (1982:67). For Helen Wallace (1983:205), it is a "part formed political system." David Cameron (1992:66) calls it "institutionalized intergovernmentalism in a supranational organization." Fritz Scharpf (1988:242) argues: "The European Community seems to have become just that 'stable middle ground between the cooperation of existing nations and the breaking of a new one' which Stanley Hoffman [1966:910] thought impossible."

In addition to the uniqueness of the structure, the evolution of the EC has been unpredictable. After a decline in the '60s and '70s, it was revitalized in the mid to late '80s. This "frustration without disintegration and resilience without progress" (Scharpf 1989:265) has spawned a series of theories and innumerable empirical studies aimed at explaining whether and how European integration proceeds.

Theories of European integration have been classified into two broad categories: (Neo)functionalism and intergovernmentalism (Scharpf 1988:266).[20] According to (neo)functionalism, the mechanism driving the integration process is expressed by the concept of "spillover" from one sector to another.

This means that if decisions taken by some interests in some sectors influence other interests and sectors, demands, expectations, and loyalties would be redirected to the European political process. Spillover does not necessarily involve the manifestation of support or enthusiasm for integration. Haas (1958:243), for example, writes, "Lack of agreement among governments can give rise to increased delegated powers on the part of these (supranational) institutions." Later neofunctionalists (Haas 1971, Lindberg 1963, Scheingold 1970) continued to place emphasis upon the expectations, actions, and loyalties of a plurality of political elites, rather than upon the interests of national governments. William Wallace (1982:64-5) argues "the success of the neo-functionalist approach depended upon national governments not noticing—in effect—the gradual draining away of their lifeblood to Brussels." The same non-institutional perspective characterized the "communications" approach developed by Deutsch (Deutsch et al. 1957, Merrit and Russett 1981).

The intergovernmentalist approach stresses the importance of national governments in the development of the European Union. For example, Moravcsik (1991) affirms that the primary source of integration "lies in the interests of the states themselves." As Carole Webb (1983:11) puts it: "The debate between the so-called 'billiard-ball' and 'cobweb' schools in the study of international politics over the relevance of formal state boundaries is one 'marker' dividing intergovernmentalists, on the one hand, from neo-functionalists and advocates of interdependence on the other."

However, while the markers may be clear, a series of empirical studies have found evidence to support and to contradict both theories (Lange 1992, Cameron 1992, Peters 1992, Shapiro 1992, Bieber 1988, Corbett 1989, De Zwaan 1986, Edward 1987, Fitzmaurice 1988, Lodge 1987, 1989). Some scholars have seen advantages in this situation. Sbragia (1992:258) quotes with approval Krislov, Ehlermann, and Weiler claiming: "The absence of a clear model, for one thing, makes ad hoc analogies more appropriate and justifiable. If one may not specify what are clear analogies, less clear ones may be appropriate."

Since European integration progresses through international treaty-making, the process is in the *final analysis* controlled by governments. Indeed, it is inconceivable that governments would continue to sign treaties calling for more and more integration if they did not find it in their interests to do so. The previous sentence sounds like a truism, yet it includes the most important elements of both functionalism and intergovernmentalism: Governments act as specified by intergovernmentalist theories, but they act on their interests, which are determined by a functionalist logic of gains from international cooperation. In other words, the principals in the European Union are the states, and the agents are any transnational institutions that they may create (including the EU itself).

However, these statements specify neither the mechanisms that will be selected by the principals nor the outcomes that these mechanisms are likely to produce. The EU is currently a series of institutions that have promoted, by conflict or by cooperation, a legal system superseding national legal systems. How do they do it? And what is the role of supranational institutions like the Parliament, the Commission, and the Court in the process of integration? In this chapter I analyzed the logic of the interactions among European institutions instead of using "ad hoc analogies." Now I will conclude by arguing that the concept of conditional agenda setting can help us understand the process of integration. The Cooperation Procedure provides a *formal expression of the conditional agenda setting concept*. The idea is simple: There is a delegation of powers *as long as* certain limits are not crossed; and a loss of these powers in the opposite case. One can hardly think of a principal-agent relation where the delegation of powers is unconditional. Simple and universal though the concept of conditional delegation may be, the Cooperation Procedure presents the rare feature of specifying the conditions instead of leaving them to an implicit understanding.[21]

One important feature of the Cooperation Procedure is that the outcome is not necessarily Pareto optimal for the states. In this sense, it is not necessarily an efficient institution (Tsebelis 1990:chapter 4). However, most of the time the outcome will be inside the heptagon defined by the ideal positions of the states. But which Pareto optimal outcome will be selected? Krasner (1991) raises this point with respect to the international regime of communications. Garrett and Weingast (1992) forcefully present the problem of equilibrium selection and argue that ideas as well as the interests of the most powerful states are important in equilibrium selection. The Cooperation Procedure presents an important mechanism for equilibrium selection combined with other desirable features.

European integration proceeds through a series of measures that may have redistributive or investment aspects. In both cases sacrifices are required by some social or national actors. It is obvious that such actors would prefer alternative policies with lower or no cost for them. If such actors represent brakes on European integration, what is the accelerator? Figures 5.6, 5.7, and 5.8 provide a visual representation of the answer.

In all of these cases, a supranational actor (Parliament) is provided with conditional control of the agenda. Anytime the Parliament exercises this power, the outcome is more pro-integrationist than that which the members of the Council would have selected on their own. Moreover, if efficiency gains from the common policy are high (if the status quo is far away), the Council can resolve redistributive issues on its own (remember that in this case the Parliament has no agenda setting power). If efficiency gains are low (i.e., the status quo is close to or in the Pareto set) the Parliament is empowered to solve the problem of equilibrium selection. So, equilibrium selection is one feature of the conditional agenda setting mechanism. But conditional agenda setting by Parliament presents two additional important advantages for countries of the Union. The responsibility for unpopular measures is not taken by national governments, but by some supranational institution that was able to impose its will despite existing objections. Finally, conditional agenda setting will not get out of hand, since most likely (but not necessarily) the outcomes are inside the Pareto set.

Consequently, the mechanism of conditional agenda setting by Parliament has three important advantages: It promotes integration more than the Council on its own can; it keeps the speed of this process under control; and finally, it diffuses responsibility for unpopular measures away from national governments.

Other European institutions offer the same advantages. When the European Court of Justice made the decision concerning *cassis de Dijon*, which created the doctrine of mutual recognition, it was making a decision that was bound to be in serious disagreement with important social interests in all countries at some time or another. Similarly, the Court practically re-wrote the interpretation of the Community value-added tax directive. Such measures were subsequently adopted by the SEA (that is, by the unanimity of governments). In all of these cases, governments in disagreement can opt out of the application of particular legislation or of the system altogether. It is up to the supranational actor to make the decision that will carry the Union further along, as opposed to decisions that will lead to disagreement, dissent, and ultimately to disintegration.

It is widely believed (Shapiro 1992) that the European Court of Justice was instrumental in pushing European integration in the pre-SEA phase. After SEA, issues become more complicated, so legislative supranational institutions (Parliament and Commission) took over the role as the engine of integration. However, the mechanism was the same: Delegation of conditional powers. Conditional agenda setting powers are likely to increase in the future for two reasons: The status quo approaches the positions of the members of the Council; and issues become more complicated, so a 54/76 qualified majority core is not likely to exist. As I demonstrated, both features lead to an increase in the powers of the conditional agenda setter.

In conclusion, European integration does not happen despite the will of national governments, but *because* these national governments have taken measures to build institutions attributing conditional agenda setting power to supranational actors.

APPENDIX

Definition 1: Pareto set: The set of points where the welfare of all members[22] cannot be improved simultaneously.

Lemma 1: The Pareto set of the states in Figure 5.4 is defined by the contour of the heptagon 1234567.

Definition 2: Q-core: The set of points where the welfare of Q out of N states cannot be improved simultaneously.

Lemma 2: The Q-core of the states in Figure 5.4 is defined by the contour of the heptagon 1'2'3'4'5'6'7' for Q=5/7, and 1"2"3"4"5"6"7" for Q=6/7.

Lemma 3: (Greenberg (1979, Theorem 2)). The Q-core exists if $Q > n/(n+1)$ where n is the dimension of the space.

Corollary 1: In the Cooperation Procedure a 54/76-core always exists in two dimensions; a 54/76-core is not guaranteed to exist in more than two dimensions.

Definition 3: Unanimity winset of a point: For any point SQ, define U(SQ) the set of points that are unanimity preferred to it.

Corollary 2: U(SQ) is empty if SQ belongs to the Pareto set.

Definition 4: Qualified majority winset of a point: For any point SQ, define Q(SQ) the set of points that are qualified majority Q preferred to it.

Corollary 3: Q(SQ) is empty if SQ belongs to the Q-core.

Definition 5: Qualified majority winset of a set: For any set of points X, define Q(X) the set of points that are qualified majority Q preferred to any point in X.

Corollary 4: If X intersects with the Q-core, Q(X)=0.

Proof: Follows from definitions 2 and 5. Call x one of the points of intersection. According to definition 2 there is no point preferred to x by a Q-majority. Consequently, Q(X) is empty.

Definition 6: Conditional (Q,U) agenda setting power: For a status quo point SQ, an actor has conditional (Q,U) agenda setting power if when U(SQ) is not empty, Q(U(SQ)) is not empty, or when U(SQ) is empty Q(SQ) is not empty.

Corollary 5: If SQ belongs to the Q-core, there is no conditional (Q,U) agenda setting power.

Proof: Both U(SQ) and Q(SQ) are empty.

Corollary 7: If SQ belongs to U/(Q-core), there is conditional (Q,U) agenda setting power.

Proof: U(SQ) is empty, therefore we have to examine Q(SQ). But Q(SQ) is not empty since SQ does not belong to the Q-core.

Theorem 1: If SQ is in the "neighborhood" of U, there is conditional (Q,U) agenda setting power.

Proof: Select a point SQ close but outside the Pareto set (the sides of the heptagon 1234567), say along the segment 17. In this case U(SQ) will be a small set defined by the indifference curves of 1 and 7. Call SQ' the symmetric of SQ with respect to the segment 17. If SQ is close enough to 17, the other 5 members will prefer SQ' to any point inside U(SQ), and SQ' will not be included in the Q-core. So, Q(U(SQ))=Q(SQ'), and Q(SQ') exists (Corollary 7).

Construction of "neighborhood" of U: In the proof I used the point SQ' which is preferred to any point inside U(SQ) by all other 5 members. All points SQ' inside the 11"7 in Figure 5.4 have this property. The circles from 2 and 7 through SQ' intersect once to the right and once to the left of segment 27. But since SQ' is to the left of 27, the other point is to the right, which means that there is no point of U(SQ) preferred to SQ' by 2. A similar argument can be made with respect to the other 4 points of the heptagon (in particular for point 6). For SQ' to be inside the triangle 171", SQ has to be in the symmetric with respect to 17 triangle. This is how the shaded triangles adjacent to the sides of the heptagon in Figure 5.5 are constructed.

Definition 7: Call Inverse Q-core I(Q-core) the set of points x with the property the intersection of U(x) and Q-core is non-empty.

Corollary 7: If SQ belongs to I(Q-core), there is no conditional (Q,U) agenda setting power.

Proof: By definition 7 there is at least one point of U(SQ) that belongs to the Q-core. Call this point x. By the definition of the Q-core Q(x) is empty, therefore, Q(U(SQ)) is empty.

Construction of boundary of I(Q-core): The boundary of the Inverse Q-core is defined the following way: Construct the symmetric of segment 1'2' of the Q-core with respect to the segment 12 of the Pareto set. Repeat the construction for the other six sides of the heptagon. Connect these segments by circles with centers the vertices of the heptagon. The first circle has center 1 and radius 11', etc.

By construction, if SQ lies on the boundary of I(Q-core), the boundary of U(SQ) (the points that are preferred to SQ by 6 out of the 7 members, while the seventh is indifferent between these points and SQ) will be on the heptagon 1'2'3'4'5'6'7'. Indeed, if SQ lies on a segment of straight line (say the one symmetric to 1'7' in Figure 5.5) the U(SQ) will include the indifference curves of 1 and 7, which intersect in symmetric points along the axis 17; if SQ lies on a segment of a circle (say center 1 and radius 11') the U(SQ) will include the indifference curve of 1, which by definition goes through 1'. Since points SQ along the boundary of I(Q-core) produce U(SQ) which are on the boundary of the Q-core, points further away (area I in Figure 5.1) will produce U(SQ) which intersect with the Q-core.

Theorem 2 (Curvilinear property): For any two-dimensional configuration of the Council, the plane is divided in four subsets according to the position of SQ as in Figure 5.5: AREA I: The Inverse Q-core of the Council for which there is no conditional (Q,U) agenda setting power. AREA II: In this area the Parliament may or may not have agenda setting powers. AREA III: The Pareto set, along with "neighboring" areas, and excluding the Q-core. In this area there is always conditional (Q,U) agenda setting power. AREA IV: The Q-core where there is no conditional (Q,U) agenda setting power.

Theorem 3: Informational property: For any two points x and y, if U(x) is a subset of U(y), then Q(U(y)) is a subset of Q(U(x)).

Proof: From the definition of Q(A) follows that Q(AUB) is a subset of Q(A). The proof follows if one calls U(x)=A and U(x)\U(y)=B.

NOTES

This chapter won the Franklin L. Burdette-Pi Sigma Alpha prize as the best paper presented at the 1992 Annual Meeting of the American Political Science Association. The analysis refers to the pre-Maastricht period of the European integration process. However, the results are still valid since the Treaty on European Union further empowered the European Parliament. I would like to acknowledge financial support by the Hoover Institution and the Center of German and European Studies of the University of California. I thank John Fitzmaurice, Jeffry Frieden, Miriam Golden, Peter Lange, Gary Schwartz, Ken Shepsle, and the participants of the Political Economy group at UCLA, the Political Economy of Europe at UC Berkeley for useful comments. I thank Neal Jesse and Bernadette Kilroy for their research assistance. Finally, I thank Matt Olmsted for his comments as well as for providing me the story on exhaust emission standards.

1. Scharpf (1988) studies the decision making process of the Community, and he argues that it resembles German much more than American federalism and that the fact that decisions are taken by the governments and by the unanimity rule leads to "a joint-decision trap" with suboptimal outcomes. Weber and Wiesmeth (1991) analyze the Single European Act, and find, that the outcome is always "efficient" for the members of the Council and that issue linkage is likely to increase the powers of the Commission. Garrett (1992) studies the interaction among all four institutional actors (Commission, Parliament, Council, and Court) in decision making as well as in the implementation of decisions. Garrett and Weingast (1992) focus more on the Court and the implementation of its decisions. These studies echo a series of papers in congressional studies that have examined the properties of several institutions: electoral strategies of legislators (Fenno 1978, Mayhew 1974); relation of legislatures with government (Hammond and Miller 1987); their internal rules, in particular agenda setting (McKelvey 1976, Schofield 1978, Shepsle and Weingast 1984, Ordeshook and Schwartz 1987, Baron and Ferejohn 1989, Gilligan and Krehbiel 1989), their committee systems (Shepsle and Weingast 1987a, Fenno 1973), and their interaction with bureaucracies (McCubbins and Schwartz 1984).

2. The Treaty on European Union extended the application of the Cooperation procedure to further issues. The newly invented Codecision procedure covers most areas to which the Cooperation procedure was previously applied.

3. For a discussion, see Lodge 1987:14-15.

4. For a detailed description of the navette system in comparative perspective see Money and Tsebelis (1992). For a more detailed institutional analysis of the French case, see Tsebelis and Money (forthcoming).

5. The accounts diverge on this point. Most of the empirical literature speaks about qualified majority (Lodge 1989, Nugent 1989); others (Jacobs and Corbett 1990) speak about qualified majority *or* unanimity, Van Hamme (1989) argues that qualified majority is needed to approve and unanimity to modify (see Table 5.1). Bieber (1988:719) comes to the conclusion that the translation of the Single European Act in different

languages is ambiguous, and, therefore, unanimity is required. However, on several occasions the Council has decided by qualified majority, so in the remainder of my account I will assume that only qualified majority is required for the adoption of a common position.

6. Parliamentary silence at this point is equivalent to acceptance.

7. The Council could give the Parliament legislation or justification of its common position in only one language, in which case Parliament would be forced to rush a reaction given the limited time of parliamentary sessions (Lodge 1987:16).

8. Most institutional accounts attribute the role of the agenda setter to the Commission. Lenaerts (1991:22) argues that the Commission has a "monopoly of legislative initiative." See also Garrett (1992:552), Weber and Wiesmeth (1991:265).

9. The following account is based mainly on Kim (1992); auxiliary sources are Jacobs and Corbett (1990:170), and Stephen (1992).

10. However, a few weeks later (July 1988), France replaced its environmental Minister, Brice Lalonde, and withdrew its support from this common position.

11. The data comes from Jacobs and Corbett (1990:170-71), who analyze the July 1987 to June 1989 period. Bogdanor (1989) and Lodge (1989) cover subsets of this period.

12. Guy Peters (1992:102) argues that the case of occupational health provides another example of the power of Parliament, and Juliet Lodge (1989:75) adds the case of a medical research program to the list.

13. The reader is reminded that an absolute majority of Parliamentary votes is required for a proposal.

14. $5/7 = .714$, and $54/76 = .710$.

15. Similarly, P_q is the symmetric of P with respect to the fifth member of the Council (5 or Q), and P_m is the symmetric of P with respect to the median voter (M or 4). These points are useful for the calculation of the final outcome when qualified majority of simple majority is the decision rule in the Council.

16. It is well known that most results generated by one-dimensional models do not hold in multiple dimensions.

17. What Denmark does in this case is nest the international game of European policy making inside its domestic politics game in order to achieve a credible threat (Tsebelis 1990, Putnam 1988).

18. In a previous draft of this chapter I made the same mistaken argument. I thought that since all members of the Council preferred Pareto optimal outcomes they would unanimously modify the Parliamentary proposal. The mistake in this reasoning is that since the status quo is inside the Pareto set, it cannot be modified unanimously.

19. Exceptions include tripartism in post-World War II France, the Grand Coalition in Germany (1966 to 1969), post-'60s coalitions in Italy, and some coalitions in the Netherlands.

20. Keohane and Nye (1991:18) distinguish three hyptheses, neofunctionalism, international political economy (which they claim is another form of functionalism), and preference convergence.

21. Other cases of such conditional delegation that I can think of are the veto power of the American president (conditional upon not violating the will of two-thirds of either House of Congress), and the power of the German president to nominate the Chancelor (conditional upon selecting a candidate acceptable to the Bundestag in the first round).

22. In all the propositions of this Appendix, I refer to the members of the Council of Ministers.

6

Wider and Deeper: The Links between Expansion and Integration in the European Union

Robert Pahre

INTRODUCTION

The conventional wisdom concerning the expansion of the European Union is that it makes deeper integration more difficult. The argument depends heavily on the experience of the 1970s, when the first expansion seemed to stymie further integration. Expansion meant that the Franco-German core of the Community was no longer dominant, that new members were an increasing drain on Community resources, and that a reluctant Britain was now a member (Taylor 1983:302-304, cf. Michalski and Wallace 1992:1-31, Nugent 1992). Widening the Community also increased the number of conflicts of interest and made agreement over integrating measures more difficult. For instance, the Mediterranean expansion made annual negotiations over agricultural policy more difficult because the southern-tier countries were interested in very different crops than were the northern-tier countries. The dangers of expansion are especially great under unanimity rule, since a single recalcitrant state can hold everyone back.[1]

The tradeoffs between widening and deepening are also evident in the 1990s. Adding new members means a further drain on EU finances (except for Austria and the Scandinavian countries). Expansion weakens public loyalty to the EU, reducing internal coherence and therefore the administrative capacity of central authorities (Cederman, this volume). Finally, the tradeoff between widening and deepening works both ways. The deeper integration of the Single European Act (SEA) and Maastricht treaty lengthen the list of *acquis communautaires* that a new entrant must accept, making accession negotiations more difficult. The problems have led scholars to suggest that a widened Europe will require a multi-tiered, multi-speed, variable geometry, *Europe à la carte* (Keohane and Hoffman, eds. 1991, Martin 1993, Michalski and Wallace 1992:29-31, 45-46).

Plausible as it is, I will argue that the conventional analysis of widening is wrong and that a formal model can help us understand the relationship between widening and deepening. Member states' demand for integration increases with expansion, because adding members worsens the non-integration outcome and raises the optimal level of integration. The supply of integration also increases with expansion. In a world of sovereign states, integration requires a willingness to punish those who cheat on previous bargains. Since a state will fear isolation as the number of isolating states increases, widening strengthens the enforcement of multilateral cooperation.

A series of illustrations and some simple quantitative tests show that the model usefully explains many features of the European Union. In addition, the model formally unifies several things we know from casual observation. For instance, the model suggests that large states—France in the 1960s, Britain in the 1970s—are the most likely opponents of deeper integration, but that widening the Union can break down this resistance. In fact, expansion may be a necessary but not sufficient condition for bringing large states into a pro-integration coalition; to some extent, this has happened to France and may be happening to Britain.

The model highlights what we should have noticed before: In the 1980s and 1990s, the Community grew wider before it could grow deeper, and the Mediterranean Expansion helped lead to the SEA and Maastricht. For that matter, the Nine accomplished numerous deepening measures, such as creation of the European Council, direct election of Parliament, and creation of the European Monetary System (EMS). Moreover, the *narrow* Community of the 1960s was as frustrated by national interest as the wider Community of the 1970s. Not surprisingly, then, I am optimistic about the Union's future even after the third expansion.

COLLECTIVE GOODS AND THE EUROPEAN UNION

European Union members negotiate over issues in which one country's actions have externalities affecting other countries.[2] I model these policies as spending on an economic "good," that is, consumed by the governments (and publics) of the Union. We can decompose these policies into two parts: the purely private good that affects only that country and the public good (or bad) that affects others. Analytically, the public component of such quasi-public goods is the most interesting, so for simplicity, I model *all* matters of Community interest as pure public goods.[3] This does not mean that the Union only supplies pure public goods, but merely that any matter of Union relevance has a public-good component on which we can focus for analytical purposes. Deeper integration is understandable, then, as the increasingly optimal provision of public goods.[4] Additional details of the model are loosely based on an abstraction from the pre-Maastricht Common Agricultural Policy, which made up about two-thirds of the Union budget. Like most other Union programs, the CAP is based on "fiscal solidarity." Members jointly choose a single budget for the program. Directly and indirectly, each state contributes to the CAP through tariffs, VAT (value-added tax), and fiscal support, without negotiation over each state's share.[5] States are aware of the distributional effects of any program; when facing the question of a larger or smaller CAP, clearly France considers that her net benefits depend on her share of contributions and the share of French farmers in total benefits. This conceptualization follows some Union rhetoric that thinks of the EU as providing public goods. The European idea, for instance, sees the nations of Europe as a group seeking to achieve certain common ends. Other Union rhetoric obscures the public good component of EU programs, emphasizing the redistributive effects of programs such as the CAP. However, if the CAP were purely redistributive, the net losers would never contribute. Since apparent net losers voluntarily participate, there must be externalities, economic or political, sufficient to give them a net utility gain.

NONCOOPERATIVE[6] PROVISIONS OF PUBLIC GOODS AND THE DEMAND FOR INTEGRATION

Analysis of the EU requires a counterfactual analysis of what would happen in its absence or, in the words of Schneider and Weitsman (this volume:1), "a theory of integration has ultimately to be a theory of disintegration." To do this, I present a noncooperative model of public goods provision.[7] In this section, I prove several propositions familiar to the public goods literature. Unlike that literature, I use the same model for all the results. In the next section, I use this model to study how and when states will successfully coordinate their contributions to public goods, making everyone better off. The gap between this noncooperative level and a Pareto-efficient provision of public goods represents the demand for international coordination (cf. Keohane 1982, 1984). If the absence of cooperation is particularly unattractive, there will be a greater demand for integration; if the absence of cooperation is not too inefficient, the demand for integration will be less.

States (governments) are the unit of analysis. Within the traditional categories of scholars of European integration, this makes my analysis an "intergovernmental" or "federalist" one (cf. Cohen 1993, Keohane and Hoffman 1991, Moravcsik 1991, Sandholtz 1993, Sandholtz and Zysman 1989, Scharpf 1988, Schneider 1995, Taylor 1983). Intergovernmentalism is often seen as anti-Union (i.e., Taylor 1983:60-92), but I will show here that there is no necessary connection. This intergovernmentalist perspective is a modeling decision, not a theoretical proposition. The assumption makes the world tractable by focusing on only part of the problem of integration, but it does not imply that governments are the only important actors in the EU.

Label the amount of the collective good provided C. I assume that the collective good supplied is the sum of the contributions of each actor, c_i, so that $C = \Sigma c_i$.[8] The choice of c_i is costly, since it consumes resources that might be used for private ends. This implies that each actor i operates under a resource constraint, B_i , which is the sum of its contributions to the public good, c_i, and its spending on private goods, p_i, such that $\forall i$, $B_i = c_i + p_i$. (In what follows, I often use B_i as a proxy for GDP.) Utility is a function of both private and public goods:

$$U_i = U(p_i ; C) \qquad C = \Sigma c_i \qquad B_i = p_i + c_i \qquad \forall i$$

$$\partial U_i / \partial p_i > 0 \qquad \partial U_i / \partial C > 0$$

There are two common arguments about such models of collective goods provision, both stemming from Mancur Olson's *Logic of Collective Action* (1965/1971). Many argue that a small group, or a "privileged" group with one or more large members, can more easily provide public goods. Therefore, a concentration of resources into a few hands may make everyone better off (Olson 1965/1971, cf. Kindleberger 1981, McPherson 1971, Stigler 1971). Applied to the EU, the small-group argument suggests that expansion makes public good provision more difficult by increasing the number of members who must coordinate their policies. The privileged-group argument implies that leadership by one or two large states, such as the Franco-German condominium in the 1950s and 1970s, is essential for success. Today, the privileged-group argument would favor strong German (or Franco-German) leadership of the EU. The model here calls these arguments into question. Holding everything else constant—the number of actors, aggregate GDP—we can think of resource concentration as a redistribution of resources from the small states to the large ones. The privileged-group argument is that the *total* contributions to a public good increase as the disproportionality of resource distribution increases. The model here yields a very different result:

Proposition 1. (The Neutrality Theorem.) The noncooperative level of public good provision is independent of the concentration of resources among the actors.

Proof.[9] Begin with the unique Cournot-Nash equilibrium, and label the equilibrium values of the choice variables p_i', c_i' (Cornes and Sandler 1986 show that this equilibrium is unique if both p_i and C are normal goods). Substituting and then rearranging the equations in (1), we have $U_i = U(p_i ; B_i - p_i + \Sigma B_j - \Sigma p_j)$, $\forall j \neq i$. (Throughout this chapter, ΣB_i is the sum of all budgets, while ΣB_j is the sum of all budgets excluding one, B_i .) Then suppose that the distribution of resources changes without changing the sum $(B_i + \Sigma B_j)$. Any change of $dB_i > 0$ implying $\Sigma dB_j = -dB_i < 0$ indicates resources becoming more concentrated in the hands of i. Now suppose that all $p_j{}'$ remain unchanged. There exists a new Cournot-Nash equilibrium for i, $p_i{}''$, in which $p_i{}' = p_i{}''$, there is no reason to change this choice because the second term of i's utility function—in which all constraints appear—has not changed. A similar analysis will hold for each j, so that there exists a post-redistribution Cournot-Nash equilibrium where all C'', $c_i{}''$, $p_i{}''$ equal the original C', $c_i{}'$, $p_i{}'$. QED. This result may surprise Olsonians, but the intuition is clear. A redistribution of income from state i to state j will induce i to spend less on all goods, including the public good, and state j to spend more. The reduction in i's spending reduces j's utility. To make up the utility loss, j will spend still more on the public good; j's increased spending will increase i's utility, inducing i to spend less than before. If both i and j spend *something* on the collective good, any redistribution of income induces changes in spending that cancel one another out. The aggregate supply of public goods remains unchanged, although the distribution of costs changes (as I will show below). It is just as well that the conventional wisdom is wrong in theory, for it is nonsensical in fact. Imagine an account of European integration that relied on concentration as a key explanatory variable.

As Figure 6.1 shows, using the standard Herfindahl index as a measure of concentration, such a narrative would have to describe a process of generally stagnant integration punctuated by occasional dramatic *decreases* in integration. (These decreases in concentration reflect expansion and only minor redistributions of resources among members.)

Figure 6.1
Resource Concentration in the EU

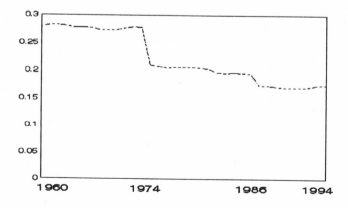

Moreover, the Olsonian concentration argument would suggest that the EU is less well integrated today than it was thirty years ago. Both implications are clearly wrong. Experimental evidence, too, suggests that Proposition 1 is correct and the Olsonian argument wrong. Equally endowed actors supply public goods at a higher level than unequally endowed actors (Marwell and Ames 1979), which is consistent with Proposition 1 if some poorly endowed actors do not contribute to the public good at all.[10]

While contradicting part of the conventional wisdom on collective action, the model is consistent with a different Olsonian argument:

Proposition 2. (The Disproportionality Result.) The share of each actor's contributions to a public good increases more rapidly than each actor's share of group resources.[11]

Proof. By the Neutrality Theorem (Proposition 1), $p_i''=p_i'$ for any resources transferred from j to i as dB_i, $c_i''=(B_i+dB_i)-p_i'=c_i'+dB_i$ and $c_j''=c_j'-dB_i$.

Thus, $dB_i=-dB_j=dc_i=-dc_j$. Since $c_i<B_i$ and $c_j<B_j$, the ratio of contributions, $(c_i + dc_i)/(c_j-dc_i)$, will change at a higher rate than will the ratio of resources, $(B_i + dB_i)/(B_j-dB_j)$. QED

Concentration changes the distribution of costs among the two parties, even though a redistribution of income does not change the total supply of the public good. Large actors pay more than their "fair" share, and small actors less—in the absence of cooperation. As I will show below, cooperation changes the distribution of costs among member states, so the disproportionality result does not describe the actual pattern of contributions by member states.

If both the private good and the collective good are normal, intuition suggests that an increase in resources to i and/or j will increase spending on both goods. So we also have:

Proposition 3. (The Resource Effect.) The noncooperative level of collective goods increases as the resources available to the group increase (that is, C is an increasing function of ΣB_i).

Proof by contradiction. Each i's first-order condition is $\partial U_i/\partial p_i'=\partial U_i/\partial C'$. Suppose that in equilibrium, Σp_i is constant and then increase ΣB_i by dB_i. Since $C=\Sigma(B_i-p_i)$, this lowers the marginal utility of the collective good from $\partial U_i/\partial C'$ to $\partial U_i/\partial C''$, and the first-order condition no longer holds. Therefore, this cannot be an equilibrium. Furthermore, there cannot be any new equilibrium such that $\partial U_i/\partial C'<\partial U_i/\partial C''$ and $C'>C''$, because then $p_i'<p_i''$ and $\partial U_i/\partial p_i''<\partial U_i/\partial p_i'$ for at least some i, because $C=\Sigma(B_i-p_i)$. If this were true, then the new first-order condition $\partial U_i/\partial p_i''=\partial U_i/\partial C''$ cannot hold. Therefore, it must be that $\partial U_i''/\partial C''<\partial U_i/\partial C'$ and $\partial U_i/\partial p_i<\partial U_i/\partial p_i$, such that for any increase dB_i, C and p_i also increase. QED

Together, Propositions 1 and 3 imply that provision of Union benefits depends on Union-wide economic growth and not on growth in individual countries. This rules out any analysis arguing, for instance, that German "leadership" can act as a *substitute* for Union-wide integration: Any increase in resources to Germany has an effect on collective good provision no different from an equivalent increase in Luxembourgeois resources. (Of course, a $1 billion increase in German GDP is far more likely to happen than a $1 billion increase in Luxembourgeois GDP.)

Proposition 3 also implies that noncooperative collective goods provision will rise and fall with the business cycle. Drawing conclusions about the effects of these changes on the demand for integration is more difficult, however, since the optimal level of collective goods provision also changes with aggregate GDP (see Propositions 7 and 10 below).

Since we wish to understand the effects of expansion, we would also like to know the effects of increasing the number of members, holding constant the total resources available to the group:

Proposition 4. (The Membership Hypothesis.)[12] Increasing the number of actors, without changing the aggregate resources, decreases the supply of the public good.

Proof of Proposition 4 will require the following lemma:

$\lambda 1$. Increasing the number of actors, where all have identical resources, reduces the supply of the public good.

Proof. With n equally endowed actors, $B_i = (1/n)\Sigma B_i$; the first order conditions are $\partial U_i / \partial p_i' = \partial U_i / \partial c_i' = \partial U_i / \partial C_i'$. Assume that these actors make identical contributions to the collective good,[13] so that $C'/n = c_i'$. By algebraic manipulation, $p_i' = (\Sigma B_i - C')/n$.

Now add one actor, with equilibrium conditions $\partial U_i / \partial p_i'' = dU_i / dC_i''$. Suppose then that $\lambda 1$ is false, such that in the new equilibrium $C'' = C'$. If so, it must be true that $\partial U_i / \partial C_i'' = \partial U_i / \partial C_i' = \partial U_i / \partial p_i' = \partial U_i / \partial p_i''$.

If $\partial U_i / \partial p_i' = \partial U_i / \partial p_i''$, however, it must be true under normal assumptions that $p_i' = p_i''$. Yet, $p_i' = (\Sigma B_i - C')/n$, and similarly $p_i'' = (\Sigma B_i - C')/(n+1)$. Therefore, it must be that $\partial U_i / \partial p_i' < \partial U_i / \partial p_i''$ by diminishing marginal utility. Thus it cannot be true that $C'' = C'$. By similar reasoning, it cannot be true that $C'' > C'$. Therefore, $C'' < C'$. QED

Proposition 4 now follows directly because $\lambda 1$ will generalize to any distribution of resources:

Proof of Proposition 4. Relax the assumption of identical resource endowments. Now change the resources such that endowments are identical. This will not change equilibrium C', by the Neutrality Theorem (Proposition 1). Add actors, reducing the supply of the public goods to C''. Now redistribute to the new resource endowment, again yielding C'' by the Neutrality Theorem (Proposition 1). QED

The intuition behind this result is that each new member of the group consumes additional p_i, thereby reducing the group resources available for spending on C.

These first four propositions all establish the level of noncooperative public goods provision. We cannot test these results directly, since the EU provides public goods cooperatively. Cooperation is necessary to overcome the free riding found in public goods problems.[14] The optimal level differs from the noncooperative level in several ways:

Proposition 5. (Membership and the Demand for Integration.) If states have identical utility functions, increasing n increases the optimal level of C.[15]

Proof. With two states, consider the set of Pareto-optimal points defined by $\alpha_i U_i(p_i, C) + \alpha_j U_j(p_j, C)$ for $\alpha \in (0,1)$. The first order condition for maximization with respect to $\{p_i, p_j\}$ is $\alpha_i(2\partial U_i/\partial C - \partial U_i/\partial p_i) + \alpha_j(2\partial U_j/\partial C - \partial U_j/\partial p_j) = 0$. We may add states indefinitely, finding analogous first-order conditions; generically, $\Sigma_i^n{}_{=1}\alpha_i(n\partial U_i/\partial C - \partial U_i/\partial p_i) = 0$. By visual inspection, increasing n will be accompanied by decreasing $\partial U_i/\partial C$ and/or increasing $\partial U_i/\partial p_i$. As $\partial U_i/\partial C$ decreases, optimal C increases. A similar analysis holds for $U_i^\alpha U_j^{1-\alpha}$ and other sets of Pareto-efficient points. QED

Recall that the noncooperative level of C decreases with n. Since the Pareto-optimal level of C increases with n, the shortfall between the non-cooperative and cooperative levels of public good provision increases dramatically with n. This means that the demand for cooperation rapidly increases with expansion. Expansion and deeper integration go together.

We should also consider the effect of resources on the optimal supply of public goods:

Proposition 6. Changes in the concentration of resources, and in the disproportionality of contributions, do not affect the optimal level of supply.

Proof. Let the Pareto-efficient level of public goods be defined by the set of maxima for some $\alpha \in (0,1)$ in the equations $\alpha U_i + (1-\alpha)U_j$ or $U_i^\alpha + U_j^{(1-\alpha)}$. For any unique interior solution, redistribution of $dB_j = -dB_i$ will affect $\{p_i, p_j\}$ but not $C = c_i + c_j$, following the proofs of Propositions 1 and 2. QED

A final question is how the demand for cooperation will change over time, and in particular, how it will change in response to secular growth or to changes in the business cycle.

Proposition 7. As aggregate resources (ΣB_i) increase, so does the optimal supply of the public good.

Proof. The first-order condition for optimal supply of C is $\alpha_i(2\partial U_i/\partial C - \partial U_i/\partial p_i) + \alpha_j(2\partial U_j/\partial C - \partial U_j/\partial p_j) = 0$. Suppose that ΣB_i increases by dB_i. By inspection, the first-order condition will not hold if this dB_i is allocated solely to C; neither will it hold if none of it is allocated to C at all. Therefore, optimal C will increase by some dC: $0<dC<dB_i$. QED

Proposition 7 implies that the demand for collective goods will increase during economic booms and decline during recessions (see Proposition 3). The noncooperative supply of collective goods also increases during economic booms and declines during recessions, so it is not clear how the resulting demand changes. Still, once we consider states' willingness to supply public goods cooperatively, we will see that widening the EU makes it easier to reach ever-higher levels of public goods provision in response to economic growth.

DEEPER INTEGRATION: OUTCOMES WHEN NATIONS COOPERATE

The above model characterizes the supply of public goods when states provide these goods noncooperatively. In this section, I will consider a situation much closer to the EU norm: states negotiate over how much public good to provide, above and beyond the noncooperative levels. I present the analysis in a two-actor model (for an *n*-player analysis, see Pahre 1994). It does not matter for the results whether a country is playing a game with one other player or against "the rest of the world."

This approach has its most obvious empirical referent when member states negotiate over the cost of some new program, since this will require incremental contributions from all. It also captures well situations in which the Community relied on member contributions—as was true of the EEC and Euratom in the mid-1970s. It is less apt after 1970, when the creation of the Community's "own resources" (*resource propre*) began. Even so, the EU has continued to require funds beyond its own resources, such as regular Supplementary Budgets agreed by the Council, regularized in the Maastricht treaty under the so-called "fourth resource." All these resemble national "contributions" as modelled here.

In the single-play game of the previous section, we have a Cournot-Nash equilibrium, with equilibrium values p_i', c_i', and so on. If there are sufficiently few iterations, and/or if the future is valued sufficiently little, this will remain the equilibrium.

On the other hand, if it is repeated enough with sufficiently little discounting, this game has an infinite set of equilibria. I assume that the single-play equilibrium will result even in the iterated game unless there is explicit agreement on another point, because with an infinity of possible equilibria, coordination around anything else seems most unlikely without mutual agreement.[16] I ignore how the exact agreement is chosen (but see Bueno de Mesquita and Stokman 1994).

Now suppose that under some proposed agreement, i will increase his spending on C by αh, and j will increase hers by $(1-\alpha)h$, where $h \in R^+$ represents the "size" of the bargain, and $\alpha \in (0, 1)$ captures the states' shares of the additional contributions.[17] In the EU, for instance, members use the share of aggregate GDP to determine their share of fourth resource contributions (α). Mutual acceptance of the bargain yields both states the rewards from mutual cooperation (traditionally labelled R), while mutual rejection of the bargain yields both states the punishment payoffs from mutual defection (P). Cheating on a bargain yields the temptation payoff (T).[18] The states discount future payoffs by a parameter $w_i \in (0, 1)$. Given the utility functions assumed above, the payoffs for i are (dropping superscripts to conserve notation):

$P: U(p', C')$ $\qquad$ $R: U(p' - \alpha h, C' + h)$ $\qquad$ $T: U(p', C' + (1-\alpha)h)$

Notice that this changes our budget constraint to

$B_i = p_i + c_i + \alpha_i h, \forall i$.

I assume that any agreement will be enforced by the meta-strategy of Grim Trigger: If j ever cheats, i defects forevermore, and vice versa. This is the strongest possible enforcement meta-strategy, and best suited for analyzing enforcement problems in cooperation. This leads directly to the following definition:

Definition 1. A bargain is "feasible" if enforceable by GT; that is, it must satisfy the following condition:

$$w^i > \frac{T^i - R^i}{T^i - P^i}$$ which I will relabel $w_i > X_i$

Proof. In GT, a player stops cooperating if anyone cheats, so a cheater is deterred if the rewards for cooperation, $R + (w_i/1-w_i)R$, exceed the one-time gains from defection plus the subsequent punishment, $T + (w_i/1-w_i)P$. Rearranging this inequality gives the condition. QED

In the EU context, GT implies that states sanction cheaters with a partial exclusion from the EU. A state might also sanction others by withdrawing from the EMS or EMU, or refusing to contribute to the CAP or to the Regional Funds. These kinds of threats are not uncommon. When the European Parliament decided in late 1980 that the budget should be increased, some French and Germans suggested not making their contributions. Britain made similar threats during its renegotiation of entry terms in the 1970s, and De

Gaulle's policy of the empty chair in the 1960s was a case of temporary exit from the EEC (Taylor 1983:76, Schneider and Cederman 1994).[19]

Withdrawal from the EU itself appears not to be a real issue only because it has not happened—but *threats* of withdrawal or expulsion have occurred. Prime Minister Harold Wilson refused to rule out the possibility that Britain would leave the EC when he renegotiated the terms of British entry. In January 1980 and May 1982, France threatened to seek an undefined special status for Britain within the EC unless it was more accommodating in the budget negotiations; the French intended this to look like a threat of expulsion (see Taylor 1983:313). Scharpf (1988:259) notes that secession "continues to be a live political option." For that matter, Kalaadtlit-Nunaat (Greenland) has already seceded, although not for enforcement reasons.

Cooperation is more stable, and therefore more likely, as w_i increases and as X_i decreases, since these changes make it more likely that the inequality $w_i > X_i$ will be satisfied. Unfortunately, w_i is unobservable, and we do not have a theory explaining where discount rates come from. Therefore, I limit analysis to changes in X_i as a function of α and h. Where $\partial X_i / \partial \alpha > 0$, cooperation is more likely as a state's share of a bargain (α) decreases, holding constant the size h; where $\partial X_i / \partial h < 0$, cooperation is more likely as the aggregate bargain (contributions by all states) increases, with i's share of contributions constant at α. Our first proposition concerns shares:

Proposition 8. Reducing a state's share in a bargain makes ist cooperation more likely.

Proof. We first determine how changes in α affect the payoffs P, R, and T. Dropping subscripts to conserve notation, and using $\partial U / \partial p |_R$ for $\partial U_i / \partial p_i$ evaluated at R, this yields the following partial derivatives:

$$\partial P / \partial \alpha = 0 \qquad \partial R / \partial \alpha = -h \partial U / \partial p |_R \qquad \partial T / \partial \alpha = -h \partial U / \partial C |_T$$

Substituting these values into $\partial X_i / \partial \alpha$ and rearranging, we find that $\partial X_i / \partial \alpha > 0$ if and only if:

$$\frac{\frac{\partial U}{\partial C}|_T}{\frac{\partial U}{\partial p_i}|_R} < \frac{T-P}{R-P}$$

Because $T>R$, $(T-P)/(R-P)>1$; by the single-play equilibrium conditions and by diminishing marginal utility $\partial U / \partial p |_R > \partial U / \partial p |_P = \partial U / \partial C |_P > \partial U / \partial C |_T$. Thus, $(\partial U / \partial C |_T)/(\partial U / \partial p |_R)<1$, so the condition is always true. QED

The intuition behind Proposition 8 is straightforward: reducing the cost to a state of a given level of benefits (h) reduces the temptation to defect (T) and increases that state's utility when cooperation occurs (*R*). Intuitively, both changes make cooperation easier.

Testing this presents a small problem. Since we cannot observe utility functions, we cannot tell how large a change in α is sufficient to induce cooperation. Even so, we know that *some* change will be necessary. Therefore:

Corollary 8a. If a state refuses to cooperate, then reducing its share is a necessary but not sufficient condition for cooperation.[20]

Proof. Follows from Proposition 8, holding *h* constant. QED

This corollary captures nicely the logic of Britain's renegotiation of its entry conditions. Britain did not object to the EEC in general, nor did it have an objection in principle to any particular EEC policy. The core of Britain's complaint was that it paid too great a share of the costs of the EEC, and it wished to reduce that share. In such cases, the most important constraint on reducing one state's share is that this increases the other state's share. This change may or may not make the second state less likely to cooperate (as the inequality $w_i > X_i$ may or may not still hold.)

While it is impossible to reduce both actors' shares simultaneously in a two-player game, we see a quite different situation if consider the possibility of adding new states to an existing bilateral bargain. In that case, all existing states' shares in a bargain would decrease. This could only make cooperation more likely. Therefore:

Corollary 8b. Adding states to a bargain is a sufficient condition for reducing all states' shares, thereby meeting the necessary condition in Proposition 8.

Proof. If all states use Grim Trigger against *any* defection,[21] the condition in Definition 1 holds, and the corollary follows from Proposition 8, again holding *h* constant. QED

Adding states in a cooperative bargain (Corollary 8b) contrasts sharply with the effect of adding states in a noncooperative situation (Proposition 4). Adding actors reduces the supply of a public good if there is no cooperation, but adding actors makes cooperation easier by reducing everyone's share in the bargain. Applied to the EU, this corollary suggests that expansion makes further integration more likely.

By reducing each state's share, expansion also strengthens the multilateral nature of the EU:

Corollary 8c. As each *i*'s contribution grows smaller compared with that of all other *j*, it is more likely that cooperation will take multilateral form instead of a series of interconnected bilateral bargains.

Proof. See Pahre (1994).

The intuition behind this result is simple: as each i's contributions go down compared with that of all j, the larger sanction available to all states in a multilateral bargain is more likely to be critical. The easiest way to achieve this is by increasing the number of cooperating states.

Because this result is driven by the increased sanction that multi-lateralization provides, it may illuminate the consensual norm for EU decision making. This norm stresses the importance of unanimity even where it is not formally required to make a decision. If more states agree to a given decision, then there are more states that are willing to sanction defectors; making a decision palatable to as many members as possible strengthens enforcement.

By relying on this form of sanction, expansion also makes it more likely that the multilateral structure of the EU is important for cooperation. This has important implications for the common recommendation that future integration take the form of multi-tiered cooperation, with different states integrating in different issue areas, in a "Europe à la carte." The analysis here suggests that such a plan makes the enforcement problems of multilateralism more difficult because fewer states will enforce cooperation in each issue area.

Expansion also affects the ability of states to gain bargaining leverage by threatening to exit the Union. Integration is "robust" if it is feasible even if some state decides to withdraw from it. Again, relative shares of contributions have an important effect.

Corollary 8d. For all j making sufficiently small contributions to a multi-lateral Union, integration will be robust.

Proof. See Pahre (1994).

This result implies that the wider the EU becomes, the more robust it is to secessions. Moreover, the EU is robust to the secession of any sufficiently small state. Certainly this is reasonable. After all, the EU weathered the secession of Kalaadtlit-Nunaat without difficulty (or even without noticing it). Recall, too, the discussions during the Maastricht ratifications. Most observers agreed that continued Danish rejection of Maastricht would not be fatal to the EU; in fact, the Portuguese Presidency issued a statement after an emergency meeting of foreign ministers that there was "strong unanimity that the Eleven should go ahead, without any hesitation, to fulfil the [Maastricht] obligations" (cited in Michalski and Wallace 1992:68). A failed French referendum, on the other hand, would have had serious consequences. This suggests that the threshold for a "sufficiently" small state lies somewhere between France and Denmark. This is perhaps not very precise, but it is at least a start on answering the question of robustness.

Proposition 8 and its corollaries examine the effects of changes in α, holding h constant. Let us now turn to examine the effects of h on X_i, holding α constant. If h increases, the bargain is increasing in size, because i is increasing his contributions to the public good by αh, and j is increasing hers by $(1-\alpha)h$.

Increasing the size of the bargain obviously increases the rewards of cooperation. This makes cooperation more likely. On the other hand, increasing the size of the bargain also increases the temptation to defect, because your partner is contributing more than previously, and so are you. This intuitively makes cooperation *less* likely. Because increasing the size of the bargain affects R and T simultaneously, careful analysts have noticed that it is difficult to reach any conclusions about the likelihood of cooperation (see Jervis 1978, 1986:64, Van Evera 1986).

Here, by assuming the utility function $U_i = (p_i, C)$, and by defining the bargain in terms of αh and $(1-\alpha)h$ as contributions to C, some specific conclusions are possible. We must first examine how the PD payoffs change as h changes:

$$\partial P/\partial h = 0 \quad \partial R/\partial h = -\alpha \partial U/\partial p\,|_R + \partial U/\partial C\,|_R \quad \partial T/\partial h = (1-\alpha)\partial U/\partial C\,|_T$$

Increasing a bargain may make cooperation either more or less difficult:

Proposition 9. If a state's share of a bargain (α) is sufficiently small, it will be more likely to cooperate as the size of the total bargain (h) increases; if a state's share of a bargain is sufficiently large, it will be more likely to cooperate as the total size of the bargain decreases.

Proof. Recall that cooperation is stable when $w_i > X_i$, so that if X_i *decreases*, cooperation is more likely to be stable for i. To see the precise effects, we find the derivative:

$$\frac{\partial X}{\partial h} = \frac{(T-P)(\frac{\partial T}{\partial h} - \frac{\partial R}{\partial h}) - (T-R)(\frac{\partial T}{\partial h} - \frac{\partial P}{\partial h})}{(T-P)^2} = \frac{(R-P)\frac{\partial T}{\partial h} - (T-P)\frac{\partial R}{\partial h}}{(T-P)^2}$$

$$sgn\{\partial X_i/\partial h\} = sgn\{(R-P)\partial T/\partial h - (T-P)\partial R/\partial h\}.$$

Substituting and rearranging terms produces the following condition:

$\partial X_i/\partial h < 0$ if

$$\frac{(R-P)-(T-P)\frac{\partial U}{\partial C}\big|_R}{(R-P)\frac{\partial U}{\partial C}\big|_T-(T-P)\frac{\partial U}{\partial p}\big|_R} > \alpha$$

The denominator of the ratio on the LHS is negative because $\partial U/\partial p\big|_R > \partial U/\partial C\big|_T$. If we normalize $\partial U/\partial C\big|_R = 1$, then the numerator is also negative, making the ratio a positive number. Because $\alpha \in (0, 1)$, the inequality always holds if the LHS is greater than one; *all* states are "sufficiently" small. However, the ratio may easily be less than one. In particular, with $\partial U/\partial C\big|_R$ normalized to 1, the LHS is less than one when

$$R(\partial U/\partial C\big|_T -1)/(\partial U/\partial p\big|_R -1) + P(\partial U/\partial p\big|_R - \partial U/\partial C\big|_T)/(\partial U/\partial p\big|_R -1) < T.$$

This condition is not at all stringent. When it holds, then the condition will hold for a sufficiently small α, and cooperation is more likely as the bargain increases. The inequality will *not* hold for a sufficiently large α, and then cooperation is more likely as the bargain decreases. QED

The intuition here is straightforward. Where a state's share of a bargain is small,[22] it makes relatively small contributions in exchange for large benefits from the contributions of the other party. The incentives for i to defect are small, since the contribution is small and the potential gains large. When a state's share is large, the reverse is true. The result is distinct from Proposition 8. When it comes to shares, all states are alike and prefer paying smaller shares of any bargain (Proposition 8). When states negotiate the optimal *size* of a bargain, however, they may differ: Some types of states prefer larger bargains, others will demand a smaller bargain (Proposition 9).

I will operationalize Proposition 9 through three related corollaries. I assume that cost-sharing is based on some ratio dependent on the relative size of the two countries. (Again, this corresponds to EU rules for fourth resource contributions.) Now $\alpha/(1-\alpha) \sim B_i /B_j$, and α stands for the relative size of the first country. The first corollary retains the logical structure of Proposition 9, in that changing h is a necessary but not sufficient condition for an unacceptable bargain to be made acceptable. The second corollary interprets Proposition 9 probabilistically. Since there are variables affecting cooperation that are not in the model, we may conclude that changing h only affects the probability of a bargain being acceptable, given the existence of these unmodeled variables. The third corollary is a loose rule-of-thumb based on Proposition 9 and its corollaries. These different assumptions give us:

Corollary 9a. If the larger state in a dyad rejects a bargain, then reducing the size of the bargain is necessary but not sufficient to obtain its agreement; if the smaller state rejects a bargain, then increasing the size of the bargain is necessary but not sufficient to obtain its agreement.

Corollary 9b. The larger the state, the more likely it is to demand the reduction of a bargain as a condition of agreement; the smaller the state, the more likely it is to demand an increase in the size of a bargain as a condition for agreement.

Corollary 9c. In any negotiation between states of different sizes, the smaller states are likely to want larger (deeper) agreements than will the larger states.

These various interpretations are consistent with the existing "small state" literature, which argues that small states are natural supporters of extensive international cooperation (East 1973, Heckscher 1966, Hoadley 1980, Keohane 1969).

As was true for Proposition 8, the United Kingdom provides the best examples. The British, who pay a large share of the costs of the EU, regularly oppose increases in the size of EU programs. Britain's reluctance to enter too large a bargain was largely responsible for keeping her out of the development of the European Communities (EC) in the 1950s. Even after deciding to participate in talks over a customs union and payments union in 1948, Britain consistently sought to reduce the size of any bargain by advocating an "empirical" approach to cooperation (see Hogan 1987, Milward 1984, 1992). In the negotiations preceding the Treaty of Rome, Britain sought to reduce the proposed customs union to a free trade area with no common external tariff, no provision for labor or capital mobility, and with agriculture excluded. These demands proved too much for the other states to accept.

Britain's renegotiation of its terms of entry is also interesting because we can analyze with some confidence what a (counterfactual) rejected bargain would look like. Since Britain is a large country, we predict that it will demand either *smaller* bargains or a reduction in the *share* it pays within existing bargains. Foreign Secretary James Callaghan's April 1974 statement on renegotiation (Swann 1990:33-34) provides a good summary of Britain's demands:

1. less ambitious plans for monetary union than the planned EMU;
2. a reduction in the UK share of Community financing;
3. reform of the CAP, to achieve greater financial control and better recognition of consumer concerns;
4. no harmonization of VATs that would entail taxing necessities;
5. the British Parliament should retain its powers of effective regional, industrial, and fiscal politicies, and its ability to control capital movements to protect the British balance of payments and to maintain full employment;

6. better safeguarding of Commonwealth and Lomé Convention interests.

Of these, two are obvious demands for the reduction of existing bargains (1 and 2); three prevent any increase in existing bargains and probably require modest reductions in plans for greater integration (4, 5, 6), and the last seeks to reduce the British share in paying for the EEC (3). All are consistent with the hypotheses of the model.[23]

These demands are also interesting in what they exclude. The United Kingdom might have argued for increases in programs from which it is a major beneficiary. For instance, the United Kingdom might have sought to increase the Regional Fund or Investment Bank in 1978, for it receives substantial net benefits from both. It is striking that this did not happen. This suggests that the size of the bargain and not the distribution of benefits was the issue. Taylor (1983:180) argues that increases in the Regional Fund or Investment Bank "would have involved deciding to pay much more in order to get considerably more out, and it would probably increase the status of the Communities' institutions. Instead they [the United Kingdom] preferred the rather short-term and unimaginative approach of paying less in the first place."

The assumptions of my model very nicely capture the British choice: Should we pay more in and get more out, or do we pay less and get less? The model predicts that a large state is likely to choose the latter, for it prefers smaller total bargains.

Britain is not alone among the larger states in opposing the growth of EU programs. In 1965, Germany was reluctant to approve financing of the CAP, and this helped lead to Charles de Gaulle's policy of the empty chair. Occasionally, two large countries have objected to further integration, as did the Germans and French in 1978, when they proposed a "scaled-down intergovernmental version" of a monetary union, which became the foundation for the less ambitious EMS (Taylor 1983:175).

As relative GDPs have changed, German hesitation has become more evident, even if it does not reach the levels of Britain's almost ritualistic opposition. A good example of the new German role as a "large" state is the position of the Bundesbank on European Monetary Union (EMU) at Maastricht. The Bundesbank clearly favors less integration over deeper integration, smaller bargains over larger ones. At the same time, monetary hardliners are willing to entertain the possibility of deep monetary coordination among only a few countries (such as Germany, the Netherlands, and one or two others). This tradeoff between deep and narrow cooperation versus wide and shallow cooperation hinges upon the technical characteristics of monetary integration (see von Hagen and Fratianni 1993), and poses an interesting line for future research.

Since all this evidence is anecdotal, one might be tempted to find small-state counterexamples, such as the Danish public's initial rejection of Maastricht. Therefore, some systematic test is appropriate. One way to test these corollaries would be to use the crossnational variation in political support for integration as a proxy for the concerns reflected in Corollaries 9a-9c. This logic produces the following two corollaries:

Corollary 9d. Political support for integration decreases as GNP increases.

Corollary 9e. In large states, political support for integrative measures decreases as the measures become more integrative; in small states, political support for integrative measures increases as they become more integrative.

I will present two kinds of evidence in support of this hypothesis. First, there was a systematic pattern to the degree of parliamentary support for the original Treaty of Rome and for the treaty establishing the European Coal and Steel Community (ECSC). As Table 6.1 shows, the support for both the EEC and the ECSC decreased as the size of the country increased. It is also striking that the support for the ECSC, which was a smaller bargain than the EEC, was greater in the large countries than was support for the EEC. In the small countries, on the other hand, support for the larger EEC was greater than support for the ECSC. The pattern reported in Table 6.1 exactly matches Corollaries 9d and 9e. Another source of evidence for testing these corollaries is the public support for integration uncovered by survey research. As we would expect, public evaluation of the EU in Eurobarometer surveys is negatively and significantly related to each country's GDP (see Table 6.2). While I have deliberately ignored other possibly relevant variables since they are not to be found in the model, other work suggests that this result holds even after controlling for them (Gabel 1994, Gabel and Palmer 1994).[24]

Table 6.1
Parliamentary Support for Integration

	EEC	ECSC
France	59%	61%
Germany	*	62%
Italy	68%	73%
Netherlands	92%	91%
Belgium	98%	93%
Luxembourg	94%	92%

Source: Kitzinger (1963:20)
Note:*Large majority by show of hands.

These hypotheses also have implications for cost sharing. If a state rejects a given bargain, its negotiating partners have two choices. Regardless of the state's size, it will wish to pay a smaller share of any bargain.

Alternatively, a small state may accept a larger bargain, a large state a smaller bargain. Any plan for greater integration therefore meets the normal desire of small states for larger bargains, but conflicts with large states' feasibility conditions. Reducing the share of large states may be a necessary part of deeper integration.

This reduction in large states' shares works against the disproportionality result (Proposition 2), which hypothesizes that large states pay a disproportionate share of the costs of public goods in the single-play Nash equilibrium.

Table 6.2
Evaluation of EC Membership (1993)

	GDP	A	B
Belgium	175.4	59	48
Denmark	114.4	58	65
Germany	1609.6	53	41
Greece	63.1	77	79
Spain	407.5	54	40
France	1073.7	55	41
Ireland	38.8	73	80
Italy	849.7	68	52
Luxembourg	8.7	72	69
Netherlands	262.4	80	68
Portugal	64.5	59	69
United Kingdom	798.2	43	33

A:"Do you think your country's EC membership is a good thing?" (%)
B:"Has your nation benefited from EC membership?" (%)

SUPPORT = CONSTANT + β LOGGDP + e
A: - 9.266 (4.302)   standard errors
B: -19.237 (4.564)   in parentheses

A simple test can distinguish between the disproportionality prediction and the logic of the bargaining model. Both predict that there should be a significant relationship between relative size and the share of the contributions to public goods. The disproportionality result predicts a coefficient greater than one;

Proposition 9 can explain a coefficient less than one, showing that the larger states successfully negotiate reductions in their share of any bargain.

Table 6.3 shows that the relationship in 1980, the last year for which I could find data, is inconsistent with Proposition 2 but not Proposition 9.[25] Taken as a whole, all the results in this section have several interesting implications for the pattern of negotiation in the EU. Obviously, a potential bargain cannot be both reduced and increased to gain acceptance. Bargaining must therefore consist of exploiting differences in the states' utility functions, reducing the bargain in areas of most concern to large states and increasing the bargain in areas of most concern to small states.[26]

Case study evidence or data showing the salience of issues across nations should illustrate the usefulness of this claim.

Table 6.3
GDP and EU Contributions, 1980

	Share of EEC GDP (percent)	Share of Contributions (percent)
Belgium-Luxembourg	5.1	6.1
Denmark	2.9	2.4
France	24.1	20.0
Germany	32.7	30.2
Ireland	0.6	0.9
Italy	12.4	11.5
Netherlands	6.7	8.4
United Kingdom	15.5	20.5

CONTRIBUTIONS = CONSTANT + β GDP   + e   standard error

1.43   0.89 (.089)   in parantheses

A final implication of the model is relevant for traditionalist debates over integration:

Proposition 10. It is possible for Pareto-efficient bargains to be unattainable when enforced by Grim Trigger, while some smaller bargain is feasible.[27]

Proof by construction. For some

$$[(R\text{-}P) - (T\text{-}P)(\partial U/\partial C \mid_R)]/[(R\text{-}P)(\partial U/\partial C \mid_T) - (T\text{-}P)(\partial U/\partial p \mid_R)] < 1,$$

set

$$\alpha > [(R\text{-}P) - (T\text{-}P)(\partial U/\partial C \mid_R)]/[(R\text{-}P)(\partial U/\partial C \mid_T) - (T\text{-}P)(\partial U/\partial p \mid_R)]$$

so that the inequality in the proof of Proposition 9 does not hold and $\partial X_i / \partial h > 0$. Because $0 < X_i < 1$, we can now find some $w_i \in (0,1)$ slightly smaller than X_i, so that the bargain is not stable. Now reduce h such that $X_i < w_i$ and the bargain is stable. QED

This result is consistent with Scharpf's (1988) argument that "bargaining" has led to less than optimal outcomes, though a "problem-solving" approach optimal integration. It might produce is also consistent with the neofunctionalist argument for gradual integration, although resting on a completely different theoretical foundation. Desirable integration may not be practical, because it cannot be enforced by GT. In particular, the larger states will face too great an incentive to defect, and the punishment available to smaller states may be insufficient to deter them. For pragmatic reasons, then, small bargains may be necessary to elicit the agreement of the larger member states.

The result might give cause for concern during economic growth. Growth increases the optimal provision of public goods (see Proposition 7), but Proposition 10 suggests that these higher provision levels might be unattainable. Fortunately, expansion makes it easier to reach these optimal levels; by reducing each state's share, expansion makes larger bargains easier to enforce (by Proposition 9). Thus, expansion makes it easier for the EU to take advantage of greater demands for integration stemming from future secular growth.

CONCLUSIONS

In this chapter, I have presented a formal model of collective goods provision to argue that widening the Union facilitates deeper integration. The proposition relies on a model of public goods provision in which adding states increases both the demand for integration and its supply. The same model generates hypotheses consistent with a variety of stylized facts about the Union. For instance, the cooperative model shows that small states are more likely to favor *any* integration than are large states, and small states are more likely to favor large increases in integration. I also show that multilateral cooperation, such as that found in the European Union, is an increasingly attractive alternative to bilateral cooperation as the share of each state's contributions decline. This means that multilateral cooperation grows easier with expansion. Multilateral cooperation is also more resistant to defections by individual states as the number of actors increases.

The model captures the stop-and-go process of European integration largely as a result of expansion. Expansion increases the demand for integration, while also making cooperation easier. A secondary cause of integration is exogenous changes in relative size among EU members, caused by different rates of economic growth, since these might reduce the share of bargains for reluctant large countries such as Britain. Both of these causes are best seen as structural explanations for the stop-and-go process of integration.

The model helps us evaluate a variety of proposals for reforming the EU. Some have suggested that one way to get around some states' opposition to further integration is to proceed with *Europe à la carte* (see Taylor 1983:305-307, Garrett 1993). The model here highlights the enforcement problems created by such a scheme. The states willing to sanction cheaters in one issue area are only the states who have agreed to that particular bargain. This lowers the sanctions and makes cooperation more difficult.

When applying the model, it is obviously important to be sensitive to the limitations of the approach I have used. For instance, I have treated all problems of integration as essentially similar, focusing on the collective goods aspect of integration. Obviously, issue areas vary enormously in the degree to which developments in one country affect others. Trade and international monetary policy are the most "public," while domestic welfare or health and safety policies only affect other countries indirectly.

It is also true that EU negotiations do not always take the inter-state form that I have modelled. In particular, the Commission, the Parliament, the Council, and COREPER all play an important role in EU decision making (Moravcsik 1993, Tsebelis 1994). Moreover, the growing importance of qualified majority rules may make it easier for large states to support a given proposal.

Another limitation stems from the fact that several propositions of the model imply that states always welcome additional contributors–which is simply not true. One reason groups do not always welcome new members is that distributional issues may begin to outweigh joint gains.[28] For instance, side-payments to less-wealthy countries were important for obtaining approval of the EMS (see Taylor 1983); side payments to the Mediterranean countries in the form of Regional Funds were essential for passage of the SEA; giving Britain the option to remain outside the Social Charter and the EMU was important for obtaining approval of the Maastricht treaty. Distribution also will be a critical issue for further expansion into Eastern Europe, Turkey, Malta, or Cyprus.

States might also oppose adding new members because they can anticipate the outcomes of voting mechanisms among groups with variable sets of members (Hösli 1993). As an example, EMU voting is different among a small Germany-France-Denmark-Netherlands group than it would be with Britain, Spain, Portugal, and others as members (Alesina and Grilli 1993). Understanding expansion decisions will therefore also require analysis of voting mechanisms within the EU.

Despite these limits, the model should provide a useful background for the decision making processes studied by others. It explicates the general patterns of the demand for integration and the willingness of member states to supply integrative measures, abstracting away from negotiation, domestic politics, and the like. Analysis of group size, resources, and concentration provides the structural background necessary for understanding the national preferences lying behind models of EU decision making.

NOTES

I would like to thank Lars-Erik Cederman, Matthew Gabel, Madeleine Hösli, and Gerald Schneider for comments on a previous version.

1. For formal models suggesting similar conclusions, see Bueno de Mesquita and Stokman, eds. 1994, Schneider and Cederman 1994, and Fearon 1993. Qualified majority voting reduces some of these problems of expansion.

2. The subsidiarity principle in Article 3b of the Maastricht treaty states that Union-level intervention should be limited to those cases in which cross-border externalities or economies of scale exist (Bureau and Champsaur 1992:89, Michalski and Wallace 1992:40-42, Hösli 1994). Subsidiarity has not been applied to external relations or defence policy, both of which fit the technical criteria.

3. For an excellent summary of the contemporary state of the theory of collective action, see Sandler (1992).

4. This conceptualization is quite different from the spatial model of policy often used to study public choice in American politics and, increasingly, the EU itself (i.e., Bueno de Mesquita and Stokman, eds. 1994, Schneider 1995, Tsebelis 1994). Spatial modelling is more useful for the study of decision making processes than is the model here, but it is less well suited for explaining the interests that actors bring to a given5.

5. It is considered that discussing national shares is *non-communautaire*. The principle of *juste retour*, arising from Britain's successful renegotiation of its Treaty of Accession, is a partial exception. While contributions are very roughly proportional to GDP (see Table 6.1), heavy reliance on tariff revenue means that countries that import relatively more from non members—especially Britain—pay higher shares than we might otherwise expect.

6. I use the term "cooperation" in its nonformal sense, and not in the formal sense of "cooperative games." The formal equivalent of this term is "coordination."

7. Unfortunately, the *empirical* analogue of extra-Union provision of public goods is generally murky. We can, with difficulty, imagine a package of national agricultural policies in France and Germany that would produce the same crossnational redistribution as the CAP does—but the claims based on the model must be weaker in such cases.

8. There are many other possible public goods production functions (see Cornes and Sandler 1986). The summation form is a useful shorthand for a general externalities problem where some externality $E= \sum a_i c_i$, $a_i \in (0, 1)$ $\forall_i$, and $U_i=(p_i, c_i, E)$. The "joint product" model of NATO is such a mixed-goods model; for discussion, see Bernauer (this volume).

9. This approach stems from Cornes and Sandler (1986), see also Warr (1983) and Sandler (1992a). The analysis does not generally hold for solutions in which some actors contribute nothing to collective action—but noncontribution is not an issue for the EU.

10. Unfortunately, Marwell and Ames (1979) do not provide any information about noncontributors, so I cannot verify my assertion.

11. The first statement of this result was Olson and Zeckhauser (1966). Subsequent work has shown that as the number of actors increases, only the richest actors contribute anything at all (Andreoni 1988).

12. Chamberlin (1974) and McGuire (1974) show that with identical actors, increasing n increases the aggregate supply of collective goods because adding actors increases the aggregate resources of the group. Here I hold aggregate resources constant when adding members, and hold the number of members constant when adding resources, separating the effects they analyze. However, they also showed that average contributions decline when the number of members increases, so their analysis does imply the result here—as is clear from my method of proof. For the same result in a simulation, see Hirshleifer (1983); for experimental evidence, see Issac, Walter, and Thomas (1984).

13. Unfortunately, it is possible for an equilibrium to involve identical contributors making different contributions (Cornes and Sandler 1986:77). Despite this possibility, Cornes and Sandler (1986:82-84) also prove Proposition 3 with a representative contributor and a quasi-linear utility function, assuming that identical contributors make identical contributions. The method of proof in Propositions 2-3 should extend to the case of asymetric contributions. For a computer simulation yielding similar results, see Hirshleifer (1983).

14. There is a substantial experimental literature on free riding; see especially Isaac, McCue, and Plott (1985); Issac, Walker, and Thomas (1984), Kim and Walker (1984), Marwell and Ames (1979). Suboptimal supply is common, and Nash levels are the norm in those experiments designed by economists. All these experiments prohibit communication and explicit coordination, so they are not relevant for the results of my model in the following section.

15. Mueller (1989:18-21) shows that if actors have Cobb-Douglas utility functions, the ratio of the Pareto-optimal C to the Nash level increases in n. Cornes and Sandler (1986:83-84) show that with quasi-linear utility functions, the Nash level is unaffected by n, while the optimal level increases. Thus, their analysis of the Nash level is inconsistent with my Proposition 5, with the differences stemming from the lack of diminishing marginal utility in the linear portion of their utility functions. Notice that Proposition 6 suggests that we can relax the assumption of identical actors, following

the proof of Proposition 4.

16. Normatively defensible symetric equilibria might act as focal points for cooperation, making explicit agreement unnecessary. "Fair shares" is one such norm, but with nonidentical actors this has more than one interpretation—equal contributions, contributions proportional to endowments, or contributions proportional to the single-shot contributions. According to Proposition 2, these will differ. This gives us multiple focal points, requiring explicit agreement.

17. The assumption of simultaneous agreement differs from models of sequential reciprocity, in which one actor makes a concession in expectation of future concessions from the others (see Calvert 1989). The share parameter differs from that used in Lindahl equilibria in that it is defined in terms of the relative contributions in addition to the single-play contributions. Where $qi = qj = 0$, however, the two are the same. I reject the Lindahl equilibrium because I am aware of no evidence that actors use the Lindahl mechanism, and experimental evidence suggests that they do not (Isaac, Walker, and Thomas 1984, Issac, McCue, and Plott 1985).

18. The Sucker's payoff (S) is irrelevant to the problem here.

19. The Maastricht treaty allows for additional sanctions. Article 104c allows a qualified majority of the Council of Ministers to fine a member state, or require that state to maintain non-interest-bearing accounts in the European Central Bank, if that member has "excessively" loose fiscal policies (Garrett 1993:111). Moreover, the European Court of Justice (ECJ) can now fine members who do not comply with its judgments. These smaller sanctions may make defection more attractive, but whenever states are uncertain about one another's willingness to punish, smaller sanctions may be more credible than large sanctions.

20. As I will show below, changing either α or h is necessary but not sufficient for cooperation; therefore, changing α alone is not, strictly speaking, necessary. To be precise, then, changing α is an insufficient but necessary part of an unnecessary but sufficient condition (INUS) for cooperation (see Mackie 1965).

21. This is a nontrivial assumption (see Pahre 1994).

22. Notice that the definition of "large" or "small" will depend on the payoffs P, R, and T, and on $\partial U/\partial c\,|R$, $\partial U/\partial c\,|T$, and $\partial U/\partial p\,|R$, all of which are unobservable. For this reason, one, neither, or both states in a bargain may have a "small" share of the bargain.

23. The Community accommodated these demands in a variety of ways, from an insignificant study of CAP reform to important changes in Community financing.

24. Checks for robustness revealed that, surprisingly, per capita income has no significant effect; dummy variables for the First and Second Expansions have intermittently significant effects. Including these has virtually no effect on the estimate or standard error for the GDP variable.

25. Not surprisingly, the Commission does not make public national shares in its annual reports. If we were to use *net benefits* instead of contributions, direct test of the disproportionality hypothesis is impossible because several countries would have "negative shares" of the total benefits. Moreover, the existing measures of net benefits are inappropriate because they consider only the fiscal costs to each state and the direct benefit (subsidies) to a nation's citizens, most of which comes in the form of crop price supports and monetary compensatory amounts. Clearly, the *economic* costs (distortions) are significant, as are the *economic* benefits (higher prices for farmers who sell their crop privately; greater European sales for industry because of the customs union).

For a good discussion of both the accounting problems and the related issues of economic opportunity costs in making such a calculation, see Godfrey (1980).

26. Notice that proper specification of this process requires a more complicated bargain than modelled here, where the utility of bargain x to state i, $A_i^x(\cdot)$ is a function of at least two goods, differently weighted by states i, j, such that for two proposals 1 and 2, $A_i^2 \geq A_i^1$ while $A_j^2 \leq A_j^1$.

27. Contrast Guttman (1978, cf. 1987), where actors can find optimal rates at which to match each others' contributions in a one-period game, guaranteeing a Pareto-efficient Nash solution. My analysis relies on the existence of discount rates such that this matching strategy would not yield an equilibrium, because one actor might have an incentive to cheat. There are also problems of consistent conjectures in the matching approach (Sugden 1985), which do not occur in this game-theoretic formulation

28. Another reason is country-specific political concerns. For instance, Turkey and Cyprus will not be admitted until the problem of northern Cyprus is resolved.

7

Regional Integration and the Enlargement Issue: A Macroanalysis

Walter Mattli

INTRODUCTION

Regional integration schemes have multiplied in the past few years, and the importance of regional groups in trade, money, and politics is ascending. Numerous speculative bits and pieces have been put forward to address the question of why nation-states *voluntarily* merge with their neighbors thereby shifting the locus of decision making towards supranational levels. Theories both in political science and economics have treated separate facets of regional integration (see De la Torre and Kelly 1992, De Melo and Panagariya 1993, Burley and Mattli 1993, Garrett 1992, Mattli and Slaughter 1995, Moravcsik 1991, Sandholtz 1993, Sandholtz and Zysman 1989). Political scientists who study regional integration typically examine the institutional relationships among the subnational, national, supranational levels within a region in which economic transactions take place. These studies, however, typically neglect economic markets, while focusing on political actors and institutions. In contrast, economists who study regional integration look only at market relationships among goods and factors of production within a region and assume away the relevance of political forces.[1]

This chapter addresses the enlargement issue of communities by looking at the interaction between economic markets and political institutions. More precisely, it seeks to answer a question that theorists both in political science and economics have left untouched: *Why does a country seek to join an already existing regional community, and what determines the timing of such a request for membership?*

A simple model, the Integrated Production Frontier (IPF) model, is elaborated to address the enlargement issue. The IPF first elucidates the inter-relationship between two aspects of integration: Merging markets and provision of regional public goods. Second, it examines the effect of exogenous shocks, such as new transportation and communication technologies and new production techniques on integration. Third, it explicitly models the political actors' utility functions.

One strong implication of IPF with regard to the enlargement issue states that *a country seeks to integrate its economy only when there is a significant positive cost of maintaining its present governance structure in terms of foregone growth (as measured by a continuing performance gap between it and a more integrated rival governance structure).* This proposition is tested on data from the enlargement of the European Union. The test provides a striking confirmation of the proposition: Eighteen out of twenty applications for membership by eleven countries were submitted after one or—more typically—several years of mostly substantially below EC-Six average growth rates. Also remarkable is the tendency for growth rate differentials to be, for the most part, above the EC-Six average during the first year of membership.

The finding that a country seeks membership in an economic union only when its growth rate declines *relative* to the countries in a union is robust across time and space.[2] The enlargement of the German Zollverein in the nineteenth century conforms to this logic, as do recent enlargements of regional economic groups on the American continent (see Mattli 1994). The time it takes for countries to react to below average growth varies, however. In the European case, the reaction time appears to be normally distributed around a mean of two and a half years. This study contends itself with this finding and is thus labeled a macroanalysis. Explaining the varying reaction times would require an examination of how differences in domestic politico-institutional structures affect the responsiveness of countries to systemic events. Finally, it is worth noting that the question of why a country seeks to join an already existing regional community begs a corollary inquiry that relates to the *supply side* of integration: Why does a union have an interest in accepting new members? A comprehensive theory of regional integration will eventually have to address both the demand and the supply side of integration.[3] The following section introduces the IPF model. The section after it illustrates some of the implications of IPF using data from the European Union.

THE INTEGRATED PRODUCTION FRONTIER MODEL (IPF)

The X-axis of IPF

The Integrated Production Frontier model (see Figure 7.1) considers the interrelationship between integration in the realm of public goods and market integration in the following way.

Figure 7.1
Integrated Production Frontier Model

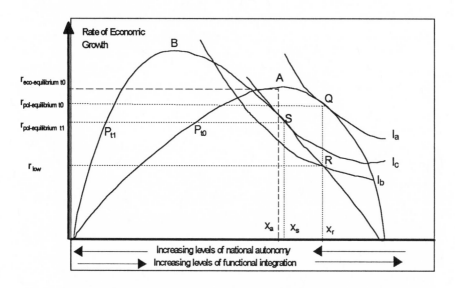

Market integration is referred to as the degree to which international exchange in goods, services, labor, and money takes place. Countries trade with each other, first, to exploit their comparative advantages, second, to achieve economies of scale in production, and third, to minimize risks through diversification. It is a well-known fact that the size elasticity of foreign trade is negative. That is, the smaller the state, the higher its economy's degree of openness.[4] While openness permits a small country to benefit from the same gains of specialization as a large nation, it increases the small state's vulnerability. Nationalizations, confiscations, tariff changes, new non-tariff barriers, differing rates of inflation, devaluations or foreign exchange restrictions to balance payments problems, all render reliance upon foreign markets precarious. This is true not only for small states but also holds more generally. Transactions across politically disjoint surfaces involve uninsured risks and are consequently quite costly. Insurance schemes, in the form of integration in the realm of public goods (also called functional integration), will be obtained when increased frequency of market transactions (due to new technologies) raises the potential for gains high enough to justify the costs of establishing such schemes.[5] Examples of functional integration designed to facilitate economic exchange range from international standards of measurement (such as the metric system or standardized railway gauges) to rules of navigation in the air and on the oceans; from the gold standard or other fixed exchange rate regimes to common rules of fiscal and monetary policies, from tax harmonization treaties to common regional and social policies. Market integration and functional integration thus go hand in hand. The x-axis of IPF captures precisely this idea of jointness. Functional integration may start in the area of exchange rate coordination, then move on—as market integration accelerates —to macroeconomic policy coordination, monetary union, common regional policy, common social policy, and so forth. The x-axis measures, from right to left, increasing levels of functional integration necessitated by expanding markets.

Y-axis and P-curve

The preceding section can be restated as follows: The extension of markets well beyond the political jurisdiction of a state increases the profit opportunities for economic agents in competitive industries. This, in turn, puts pressure on existing governance structures for readjustment to permit the realization of these opportunities. At any moment in time, there exists an optimal level of functional integration that maximizes gross domestic output. A and B on P_{t0} and P_{t1} respectively are such optimality points that assure maximum economic growth.

Points on P_{t0} to the right of A indicate insufficient levels of functional integration. They raise the cost of economic exchange and reduce the rate of growth.[6] Functional integration beyond the optimality points is likewise damaging to economic growth. Functions exhibiting diminishing returns would be costlier to execute at the supranational level. This captures the idea of the European Union's *subsidiarity principle* according to which supranational agencies should act only when measures taken nationally would be ineffectual. There are two forces driving the expansion of markets (which causes the P-curve to shift to the left). The first is an improvement in communication and transportation technologies. But equally important are new production techniques that make products cheaper to produce. Holding the product valuation by the marginal buyer and delivery cost per unit distance constant, cheaper goods will cover larger markets. But here again, an inadequately integrated governance structure, i.e., one that fails to insure against the vagaries of foreign market exposure, will deter firms from expanding production to the full potential of the new production methods. In other words, an inadequately integrated governance structure will permit the new production technology to operate only below capacity. This may even deter the adoption of new techniques and result in the deterioration of economic conditions relative to other countries. The ensuing growth gap may widen for two further reasons. First, firms in competitive industries will exit inhospitable jurisdictions and settle where the institutional environment is most conducive to profitable trade and investment. For such firms, exit is not an option but a question of survival. Exit of capital and entrepreneurship will naturally depress economic growth. Second, foreign investors deciding whether to operate in the large and well integrated market of a community or the functionally insufficiently integrated economy of a non-community country are likely to opt for the former (*ceteris paribus*). These capital inflows strengthen the dynamic effects of market integration (through greater competition) and thus help economic growth. Robust growth, in turn, may attract further capital investment, thereby accelerating growth.

Political Agents' Utility Functions

IPF assumes that national political agents value on the one hand national autonomy or *independence* in their job, i.e., absence of interference by supranational agents, and on the other hand *economic growth* which at relatively high levels assures them reelection (see Erikson 1989, Erikson 1990, Norpoth, Lewis-Beck, and Lafay 1991, Eulau and Lewis-Beck 1985). Their convex monotonic indifference curves are represented by the I's (I_a, I_b, I_c).[7]

The implicit notion of a tradeoff between economic well-being and autonomy is a very old theme. Dahl and Tufte, summarizing the views of influential Greeks from Pericles to Aristotle, note: "If a democratic polity was to be both small and completely autonomous, there was a price to be paid: the citizen body must be self-sufficient and life must be frugal" (Dahl and Tufte 1973). Some 2,500 years after Aristotle, Britain's Prime Minister Callaghan echoed these themes while debating whether the United Kingdom should become a member of the European Monetary System (EMS):

> When we joined NATO we removed some powers from ourselves but it was the general view of the House that in removing these powers we increased our security. That is surely the test that one needs to apply to this sort of proposal. If it means less powers in order to increase prosperity, the House would have to take a decision whether it wished to remain poor and independent or whether it was willing to sacrifice some powers and be more prosperous. (Ludlow 1982:144)

The Mechanics and Implications of IPF

By combining the Integrated Production Frontier and the utility functions, we obtain the Integrated Production Frontier Model. A few implications of Figure 7.1 are immediately apparent. The politically efficient level of integration is reached where the indifference curve I_a is tangent to P_{t0}. This occurs at Q where the level of integration is x_r. This level differs from the economically optimal level of integration, x_a which corresponds to the highest point on the P_{t0} curve. In other words, governments elected to design governance structures most conducive to economic growth choose to do so only imperfectly ($r_{pol\text{-}equilibrium\ t0} < r_{eco\text{-}equilibrium\ t0}$).[8] Assume now that due to some exogenous technological change the combination frontier of growth rates and levels of integration shifts from P_{t0} to P_{t1}. That is, for any given level of growth, the implied level of integration is higher. And, for relatively autonomous governments, for any given level of autonomy, the growth level will be absolutely lower as a result of technological change. If the political agent foregoes any pro-integrative readjustment of the governance structure, growth will fall from $r_{pol\text{-}equilibrium}$ at time t_0 to r_{low} at time t placing him at R. However, even though the political agent values independence, the cost in terms of foregone growth $r_{pol\text{-}equilibrium\ 1}$ minus r_{low} from failing to adjust pushes him to sacrifice the distance $x_s x_r$ of national sovereignty, making him better off at S than at R (since $I_c > I_b$). At S, economic growth always improves over R ($r_{low} < r_{pol\text{-}equilibrium\ 1}$).[9]

In conclusion, one limitation of IPF is worth pondering. The logic of regional integration is triggered only once two states seek closer integration by forming a community. If such novel governance structure corresponds to the new needs of markets, it will attract capital and entrepreneurship. In other words, only an original move towards closer integration renders the latest P-frontier visible and opens a performance gap between the community and other states. The performance gap will motivate other states to imitate or join the community. But what forces motivated the original two states to form closer ties? My model remains silent on this issue. The British historian J. R. Seeley wrote in 1885:

> We often hear abstract panegyrics upon the happiness of small states. But observe that a small state among small states is one thing and a small state among large states quite another. Nothing is more delightful than to read of the bright days of Athens and Florence, but those bright days lasted only so long as the states with which Athens and Florence had to do were states on a similar scale of magnitude. Both states sank at once as soon as large country-states of consolidated strength grew up in their neighbourhood. (Seeley 1885, quoted in Reed 1967:62)[10]

IPF explains why a country merges with a larger area or why states grow together to form a community equal in economic power to a rival common market, but it fails to account for the *original* rise of a community.

A TEST REGARDING THE ENLARGEMENT ISSUE

The Timing of the Enlargement of the EU: Overview of Results

This section offers a test of a proposition that derives from the Integrated Production Frontier Model (IPF), namely, *a country seeks to integrate its economy only when there is a significant positive cost of maintaining its present governance structure in terms of foregone growth (as measured by a continuing performance gap between it and a more integrated rival governance structure).* Data from the enlargement of the European Union are analyzed.[11]

In 1957, Germany, France, Italy, Belgium, the Netherlands, and Luxembourg signed the Treaty of Rome, which committed them to a far-reaching exercise in economic integration. By the end of the transition period in 1969, the basic ingredients of the customs union—elimination of internal tariff and quotas and erection of a common external tariff—were established, and steps were taken to deal with the many non-tariff barriers to the free movement of goods and services. Measures were proposed with respect to the free movement of factors of production. The Common Agricultural Policy was fully operational, as were the European Social Fund and the European Investment Bank. A rudimentary system of macroeconomic policy coordination was established, and plans for speedy monetary integration were being concocted. In short, the European Community represented an ambitious *novel governance structure* with key domains of policy-making delegated to supranational bodies. The EC-Six were joined in 1973 by Ireland and two former members of the European Free Trade Association (EFTA), the United Kingdom, and Denmark. Greece joined in 1981, Portugal and Spain in 1986. Austria submitted an application for membership in 1989, Sweden in 1991, Finland in 1992. Switzerland and Norway expressed their intention to do so in 1992.

A comparison of the timing of submission of applications for membership in the EC with the evolution of the growth rates of countries inside and outside the EC reveals a striking regularity summarized in Table 7.1. *Eighteen out of twenty applications for membership by eleven countries were submitted after one or—more typically—several years of mostly substantially below EC-Six average growth rates.*[12]

Also remarkable is the tendency for growth rate differentials to be mostly above the EC-Six average during the first year of membership. The single exception is Denmark, but it is a weak exception. In this case the year prior to membership showed a reversal from a four-year-long trend of significantly below EC-Six average growth rates. A similar reversal is perhaps most stunning in the British case, where almost all years (the insignificant exception being 1963) since the incipience of the European Community in 1958 produced growth rates well below the Community average. Its growth rate jumped from 2.4 percent in 1972 to 7.7 percent in 1973, the United Kingdom's first year of membership.

Note further that after joining the EC, the more advanced countries' growth rates tend to fluctuate randomly around the EC-Six average. The poorer European countries, however, tend to experience sustained above EC-Six average growth upon becoming members of the Community.[13]

Table 7.1
The Timing of Application for Membership in the European Union

Country	Application	Year of Application	Growth Rate Differential with EC/EU (amount)[a]	# of years of below EC-6 growth rates prior to Application	Growth Rate Differential of Country with EC-6 a year after membership
United Kingdom	1. Appl.	1961	below (6.1%)	3	
	2. Appl.	1967	below (1.5%)	3	above EC-6
	"3." Appl.	1970	below (7.1%)	6	
Ireland	1. Appl.	1961	below (5.5%)	3	
	2. Appl.	1967	below (2.5%)	3	above EC-6
	"3." Appl.	1970	below (2.3%)	1	
Denmark	1. Appl.	1961	below (4.3%)	1	
	2. Appl.	1967	below (1.3%)	1	below EC-6
	"3." Appl.	1970	below (1.9%)	2	
Norway	1. Appl.	1961	below (5.5%)	3	
	2. Appl.	1967	above (0.3%)	0	
	"3." Appl.	1970	below (3.9%)	2	n.a.
	4. Appl.	1992	below (0.2%)	5	
Sweden	1. Appl.	1991	below (2.7%)	3	n.a.
Switzerland	1. Appl.	1992	below (2.5%)	5	n.a.
Finland	1. Appl.	1992	below (8.1%)	2	n.a.
Austria	1. Appl.	1989	below (0.2%)	3	n.a.
Spain	1. Appl.	1977	below (1.9%)	1	above EC-6
Portugal	1. Appl.	1977	above (2.0%)	0	above EC-6
Greece	1. Appl.	1975	below (7.3%)	1	same as EC-6

Sources of the data are at constant prices for years 1957-60: IMF Yearbook 1984, GDP data at constant prices for years 1961-90: IMF Yearbook 1991, GDP data at constant prices for European Community countries, years 1990-91: Commission of the European Communities 1991. For all other 1990-92 data, see OECD 1992.
[a] Year prior to application

Table 7.2 provides an equally revealing trend. It divides each state's history into three phases: Before application to the EC (Phase I starting in 1958); during the application period (Phase II); and finally after admission (Phase III). The application period includes the years of economic downturn until membership. The Growth Gap is the average growth rate differential of a country with the EC-Six during each phase. The Growth Gap numbers are accompanied by a Ratio-index that counts the years of above versus below EC-Six average growth rates during each phase. Several findings are noteworthy. First, the Growth Gaps of Phase I are *in all cases* higher than those of Phase II.

Table 7.2
Summary of Growth Gaps

PHASE I			PHASE II			PHASE III		
	Growth Gap (GG)	Ratio	GG direction change	Growth Gap (GG)	Ratio	GG direction change	Growth Gap (GG)	Ratio
UK	n.a.			-1.6	0/15	<	-0.6	9/11
Ireland	n.a.			-0.6	5/10	<	1.5	15/5
Denmark	1.9	2/0	>	-0.3	5/8	(>)	-0.6	9/11
Norway [1]	n.a.			-0.6	7/9		n.a.	
Norway [2]	2.1	12/1	>	-2.0	0/5		n.a.	
Sweden	-0.4	13/17	>	-2.4	0/5		n.a.	
Switzerl.	-0.7	12/17	>	-0.9	0/6		n.a.	
Finland	0.7	19/13	>	-4.9	0/3		n.a.	
Austria	0.2	15/13	>	-0.5	0/4		n.a.	
Spain	1.6	14/4	>	-0.7	4/6	<	1.0	7/0
Portugal	1.8	14/2	>	(0.2)	7/5	<	1.1	5/2
Greece	2.4	13/3	>	(1.0)	5/2	>?	-0.8	1/11

Sources for GDP data at 1975 prices for years up to 1962: OECD 1984, GDP data at 1985 prices for years 1963-89: OECD 1992, GDP data at constant prices for years 1990-91: OECD 1993. The same calculations were conducted on IMF data and the Penn World Tables by Summers and Heston. (The Penn World Table [Mark 5.5] of 1993 is an updated and revised version of the original Table prepared for Summers and Heston 1991.) The results are consistent with those derived from the OECD data (see Mattli 1994:72).

Second, during Phase I, most Growth Gaps are positive, i.e., countries tend to grow on average faster than the Community Six. The only consistent exceptions are Sweden and Switzerland. The case of these neutral countries is discussed below. Third, during Phase II, all countries grow at below Community rates. There appears no consistent exception to this rule.[14]

Fourth, the discontinuities between Phases I and II are abrupt, averaging 2.8 percent. Finally, the Growth Gaps of Phase III are higher than those of Phase II (the only consistent exception being Greece), i.e., once a country is part of the Community it significantly improves its economic fortune *as measured by the distance to the EC-Six average growth.*

The Enlargement Issue: A Closer Look at the Data

Two questions remain to be answered, one empirical, the other theoretical. First, why did some countries need to apply repeatedly before being accepted; second (and more crucially), why did other countries fail to apply in times persistently below Community growth?

The First Enlargement of the EU

The Treaty of Rome establishing the European Communities came into force on January 1, 1958. As briefly outlined above, it committed the EC-Six (Germany, France, Italy, the Netherlands, Belgium, and Luxembourg) to a far-reaching exercise in economic integration, which envisages free movement of goods, services, capital, and labor aided by common policies in agriculture, transport, regional development, external commerce, research and development, economic cohesion, education, environment, and other domains. On January 4, 1960, the United Kingdom, Sweden, Norway, Denmark, Austria, Switzerland, and Portugal signed the Stockholm Convention establishing the European Free Trade Association (EFTA). Finland signed an association agreement with EFTA in 1961. This rival organization with a minimalist integrative program committed its members to establishing free trade in industrial goods only.

To foreign investors, the European Community was more attractive than EFTA. The percentage of the value of U.S. direct investment in Western Europe apportioned to Community countries rose from 40.5 percent in 1957 to 44.7 percent in 1964. Yannopoulous relates this increase to a diversion of the flow of U.S. investment from the non-EC countries of Western Europe, particularly the United Kingdom to members of the Community (Yannopoulos 1990). This investment diversion undoubtedly contributed to the United Kingdom's worsening economic condition. The United Kingdom grew in the late fifties and early sixties well below the Community average.

Acknowledging defeat, the United Kingdom formally announced in 1961 that it had decided to apply for full membership in the EC. It was followed by Ireland, Denmark, and Norway. Subsequently, Austria, Sweden, and Switzerland made separate applications for association. Negotiations regarding the British application dragged on until January 13, 1963, when General de Gaulle declared at a Paris press conference that Britain was not ripe for membership. Two weeks later, all negotiations were adjourned indefinitely. At that time, talks with Norway and Denmark were advanced. Formal negotiations on the Irish application had hardly begun. In the case of the three applicants for association, Austria, Sweden, and Switzerland, the first round of talks to ascertain the problems to be dealt with had taken place between the EC Commission and a delegation from the countries concerned. But no formal negotiations had been opened (Swann 1988).

Continuing poor economic performance relative to the EC-Six led the British Prime Minister, Harold Wilson, to announce on May 1967 that the United Kingdom had decided to submit its second application. Ireland, Denmark, and Norway followed suit. Negotiations were immediately initiated, but only a few months later, De Gaulle, in one of his famous press conferences, declared that full membership for Britain would lead to the destruction of the Community. This closed the door to entry yet again. The events of May

1968 led to the resignation of De Gaulle and, under President Pompidou, France no longer objected in principle to British membership. In 1970, the United Kingdom along with the three other applicants were invited back to the negotiation table.[15] Since the resumption of talks, the United Kingdom, Ireland, and Denmark registered growth rates substantially below the Community average. This trend narrowed or reverted only as the three acceded to membership three years after the resumption of talks.[16]

In Norway, the proposed accession to the Community was vetoed by a national referendum held in October 1972. This is no surprise in view of our previous conclusion that *countries seek to integrate their economies only when the cost in terms of foregone growth as measured by the performance gap is significantly positive.* Norway was the only country of four applicants where the performance gap of the years 1968 to 1970 had thoroughly disappeared in 1971 to 1972—thus possibly giving the people of Norway the impression that membership was no longer worth the candle.

This is not a farfetched conclusion considering that membership not only implies a relative loss of sovereignty; in addition, an economically successful member of the Community is likely to be a net contributor to the Community's budget. In terms of our model the Norwegian case can be explained by arguing that a second exogenous shock pushed the P-frontier back to its original position. This may, indeed, have happened, for the first commercially important discovery of petroleum on Norway's continental shelf was made at the Ekofisk field in 1969, just as foreign oil companies were about to give up after four years of exploratory drilling. Later, major finds have included the Frigg field, one of the largest offshore natural gas deposits, and the huge Statfjord field. The estimated reserves below the 62nd parallel alone ensured an annual production for twenty years that is several times Norway's domestic consumption of petroleum products. In the mid-eighties, times changed for the worse in Norway. World crude oil prices fell to eight dollars a barrel in 1985 to 1986 delivering to Norway's economy a severe blow from which it took long to recover. Reduction in petroleum revenue slashed Norway's spendable real income by 9 percent. Registered unemployment climbed to nearly 6 percent, the highest suffered in Norway for over sixty years (*The Financial Times* 1992). Consistent with my model, Norway announced in November 1992 its intention to seek membership in the EC.

The Case of Europe's Neutral Countries

The data on Europe's neutral countries seems, *prima facie*, to partially contradict my model. Austria, Sweden, Finland, and Switzerland submitted or announced to submit applications very recently after several years of growth rates continuingly below the Community average. But why did they fail to apply during earlier periods of widening performance gaps? There are two parts to the answer. First, while it is true that these four EFTA countries did not seek application until the late eighties and early nineties, they nevertheless repeatedly sought closer ties with the Community. Membership in a commercial union is only one—though a particularly striking—form of integration. Short of membership, a country can seek more limited variants of integration. Some are sanctioned in bilateral agreements with the Community. For example, when the United Kingdom and Denmark decided to leave EFTA in 1972, the remaining members negotiated free trade agreements (FTAs) in industrial goods with the EC. The FTAs with Austria, Portugal, Sweden, and Switzerland entered into force in January 1973, with Norway in July 1973, and with Iceland in April 1973 (Laursen 1990:311). Further, a joint EC-EFTA ministerial meeting in Luxembourg on April 9, 1984, produced a declaration that sought to continue, deepen, and extend cooperation between the EC and the EFTA with the aim of creating a dynamic *European Economic Area* (EEA) (Ibid.: 312).[17] The dialogue on the EEA intensified and culminated in 1992 with the signing by the two organizations of a treaty establishing a European-wide free trade zone in goods, services, labor, and capital.The EEA came into force on January 1, 1994.[18] Another variant of functional integration is *policy mimicry*. Europe's neutral countries have repeatedly adopted norms and policies forged outside their jurisdiction to avoid economic marginalization. For instance, the Swiss government pledged in 1993 to press ahead with plans to harmonize its laws and regulations with those of the Community despite the Swiss people's rejection of the EEA. In the same year, Switzerland introduced a value added tax as a further step to align its fiscal and economic policies with those of the other European countries. In Norway, steps were taken as early as 1987 to ensure better coordination of European policies by creating a new Secretariat in the Foreign Ministry, together with a Committee of Permanent Secretaries. They scrutinize all new Union directives and seek to involve a wider range of bodies in European affairs. Sweden unilaterally adopted and implemented more than twenty directives by the end of 1989. At the same time, Sweden enlarged its value-added tax base in line with the Community, changed its somewhat restrictive banking and currency laws, and moved to partial deregulation. Finland also followed this rhythm of legislative calibration to Community norms. In the monetary domain, acts of mimicry (i.e., unilateral functional integration) are also quite common. Neither Austria, Switzerland, nor Sweden, for example, are members of the European Monetary System (EMS). Yet, their respective central banks peg their currencies to the Deutsch Mark, the EMS's anchor currency.[19] In short, Europe's neutral countries have gone a long way down the road of unilateral adaptation to EC law and policies to avoid being effectively left out. Their national sovereignty has remained *de jure* intact, but *de facto* it has lost much of its value (Nell 1990:352).

Second, neutrality during the Cold War may well have been a more attractive economic option to some countries than membership in a community.

This is perhaps most apparent in the Finnish case. For Finland, which shares a 780 mile long border with Russia, neutrality was not only a political imperative but above all an economic advantage, permitting it to maintain steady and profitable trade relations with Moscow. The collapse of the Soviet Union has combined with Finland's deepest recession since the 1930s to jettison any moral qualms about betraying its principle of neutrality.[20] Not surprisingly, Finland's application to the EC contains no reference to preserving neutrality as a precondition to membership. The loss of benefits from neutrality due to the end of the Cold War, combined with economic downturns of their economies, have rendered Europe's neutral countries more willing to envisage full membership in the European Union. A recent foreign policy report by the Swiss government contains a revealing chapter devoted to the issue of sovereignty. It argues that neutrality has never been an end in itself, but merely a means of preserving Swiss independence. It then concludes that today, when 70 percent of imports come from EU countries, Swiss independence is threatened more by not having a say in EU policy-making than by any hostile military power. Full membership in the EU must remain, so they report, the goal of Swiss foreign policy (Bundesrat 1993). Similar arguments have convinced the Swedish and Austrian governments to lodge applications for membership in the EU.

CONCLUSION

This study has sought to explain regional integration as the result of the interaction between political and market forces. Exogenous technological shocks disrupt the equilibrium between institutions and markets, thus inducing a redefinition of the optimal distribution of policy tasks between national and supranational levels. The study addressed in particular the *demand side* of integration and found that a country seeks to integrate its economy only when there is a significant positive cost of maintaining its present governance structure in terms of foregone growth (as measured by a continuing performance gap between it and a more integrated rival governance structure). Data from the enlargement of the European Union strongly corroborate this proposition. Eighteen out of twenty applications for membership by eleven countries were submitted after one or—more typically—several years of mostly substantially below EC-Six average growth rates. Future examinations will also need to tackle the *supply side* questions. These are: Why does a community have an interest in accepting new members? Is there an optimal size to integrating communities? What determines this optimal size? However, the findings presented in this chapter constitute a first step towards a fuller dynamic account of regional integration.

NOTES

I am especially indebted to Russell Hardin, Charles Lipson and Duncan Snidal for their extensive comments on previous drafts. I also thank Chris Ansell, Steven Brams, Geoffrey Garrett, Sieglinde Gstoehl, Atsushi Ishida, Andy Kydd, Kate McNamara, Brian Portnoy, Philippe Schmitter, Gerald Schneider, Patricia Weitsman, Yael Wolinsky, the participants in the Program on International Politics, Economics and Security (PIPES) workshop at the University of Chicago and the participants in colloquia at Emory University, Stanford University, and the Institute on Western Europe at Columbia University for valuable comments on earlier drafts. Jim Snyder provided helpful suggestions at the early stage of this research.

1. This unsatisfactory aspect of economic theories of integration has recently been acknowledged by some economists. De Melo and Panagariya, for example, write that "The implications of regional integration go beyond trade in goods, services, and factors. Almost by definition, any regional arrangement worth its name entails the imposition of some common rules of conduct on the countries entering the arrangement and a set of reciprocal commitments and obligations. *The importance of this political dimension of regional integration may well exceed that of the more direct implications having to do with trade flows"* (De Melo and Panagariya 1993:176, emphasis added).

2. A country may improve its economic performance compared with the previous year, but if growth in the union is steeper yet, the country's growth declines relative to the union.

3. These issues are discussed in Mattli 1994.

4. Trade in goods and services as a percentage of GDP (exports and imports combined) amounted, for example, in 1981 to 170.7 percent for Luxembourg, 131.8 percent for Belgium, 118.6 percent for the Netherlands, but only 45.8 percent for France, or 54.9 percent for Germany (Commission of the European Communities 1981).

5. Harold Demsetz expressed a similar idea when referring to the state (as opposed to my interstate) level: "Property rights develop to internalize externalities when the gains of internalization become larger than the cost of internalization. Increased internalization results from changes which stem from the development of new technology and the opening of markets, changes to which old property rights are poorly attuned" (Demsetz 1967:350). Integration in the form of the provision of regional or international public goods is of course similar to defining national property rights. Another recent study that considers the transaction cost economizing motive of integration is Wittman (1991).

6. A similar distinction between optimality and non-optimality points is made in Thrainn Eggertson's discussion of Douglass North's work. He writes: "The stock of knowledge in society and the endowment of resources determine the technical upper limits for productivity and output, the economy's technical production frontier. However, for each structure of property rights there is a *structural production frontier*, which is reached by selecting, from a set of feasible organizations, those structures that minimize costs and maximize output. The set of feasible forms of economic organization is defined by the system of property rights and the system of property rights depends on the community's political structure. *[S]ome political systems create incentives that place the structural production frontier close to the technical production frontier; other political systems do not"* (Eggertson 1990:319; emphasis added).

7. The farther away an indifference curve is from the origin (intersection of x and y axes), the greater the utility.

8. It is worth noticing that this simple model is consistent with insights from the new political economy and the rent-seeking literature. Rather than stipulating that the political agent values independence and high growth, it may instead be relative independence and bribe money from small and effectively organized groups that stand to heavily lose from integration. Whatever the underlying mechanism, the outcome is the same: *The governance structure chosen resists economically optimal levels of integration. The outcome obeys political efficiency* (Magee, Brock, and Young 1989, Krueger 1974, Tullock 1967, Tollison 1982, Stigler 1971, Peltzman 1976, Becker 1983).

9. Note that in the special case of strongly asymmetric trade relations, the same integrative result can be obtained without the occurrence of an exogenous technological shock. A small state heavily dependent on market access to a dominant country may suddenly be faced with prohibitive trade barriers. This will deteriorate its economic health. With no retaliatory power, the small state may have little choice but to trade national autonomy for renewed market access. For a full discussion and illustration of this scenario, see Mattli (1994).

10. Douglass North wrote similarly: "Relatively inefficient property rights threaten the survival of a state *in the context of more efficient neighbors* and the ruler faces the choice of extinction or of modifying the fundamental ownership structure to enable the society to reduce transaction costs and raise the rate of growth. Stagnant states can survive as long as there is no choice in the opportunity cost of the constituents at home or *in the relative strength of competitive states*" (North 1981:29).

11. The logic of IPF suggests that a significant growth differential motivates a country to seek closer functional integration (such as membership in an already existing union) only when there is a preexisting trade relation with a union. A country that has no financial and commercial ties at all with a union does not satisfy the jointness assumption of IPF and may thus react very differently from IPF's prediction.

12. A substitution of the average growth rate of the EC-Six by an updated average that includes the new members of the European Union yields essentially the same results.

13. Countries that are *significantly* poorer than the least wealthy members of the EU have an obvious incentive to join the rich EU club regardless of how their growth rates compare to the Union's economic growth. Their interest lies in reducing the glaring income (per capita) gap with the union. The timing of applications for EU membership by Turkey, Morocco, and formerly communist countries such as Poland, Hungary, Romania, and others will therefore primarily be determined by the willingness of the EU to accept them as new members. A successful incorporation of the economies of these poor countries into the EU would of course require very substantial financial assistance from the Union.

14. In the OECD and IMF data, Portugal and Greece seem to contradict the trend. The Heston and Summers data, however, does not support these exceptions.

15. In Table 7.1 I record these as the "3" application. Formally, however, no new applications were submitted.

16. In the Irish case, the positive impact of membership has been compellingly documented by Farrell 1983. Farrell finds that of the 722 grant-aided overseas enterprises in production in Ireland in December 1980, some 390 (54 percent) had opened in the seven years 1974 to 1980. The main source of direct investment to Ireland was

the U.S., which accounted for 38 percent of employment in foreign firms in 1976. Between 1973 and 1977, U.S. direct investment to Ireland grew at a rate greater than in any other European country and was in fact four times the rate for total U.S. investment abroad. Plants controlled by the United Kingdom and Germany accounted for another 33 percent of the employment generated by foreign firms in Ireland in 1976.

17. For further discussion see Nell 1990. He concludes that EFTA is no longer an adequate framework in which to guarantee the full economic potential of its members. He puts forward an argument that neatly dovetails with the exogenous technological shock hypothesis of my model: "The development of the so-called new technologies opens new opportunities for economic growth and product innovation, and represents a threat to traditional techniques. Outlays or basic and applied research, product development and innovation are such that large integrated markets are needed" (Ibid.: 327, emphasis added).

18. In a referendum held in December 1992, the Swiss people rejected the EEA by a narrow majority.

19. A Swedish diplomat was quoted in the Washington Post as saying: "How long can anyone remain independent vis-a-vis a decision by the *Bundesbank* to change the interest rate or the value of the German Mark? About 20 minutes?" Quoted in Hoagland (1992).

20. Real output declined by 10 percent over 1991 and 1992 and was flat in 1993. Unemployment reached 20 percent. The banking sector lurched into losses, so severe that the state will spend some 60bn markka to bail it out. The budget deficit has balooned to around 10 percent of gross domestic product and foreign debt has doubled to almost 50 percent of GDP. The value of the Finnish markka fell by 50 percent between 1991 and the end of 1992 (*The Financial Times* 1993).

III

POLICY ISSUES FACING THE

EUROPEAN UNION

8

Choosing Central Bankers in Europe

Philippe Martin

INTRODUCTION

One of the most important consequences of the process of European monetary integration is the creation of a new institution, the European Central Bank (ECB) and institutional reform of the national central banks. During the negotiations culminating in the Maastricht treaty, a debate emerged among European countries over the institutional setting of the future ECB; in particular, its independence and stated objectives in terms of price stability. The German government argued in favor of a very independent and conservative central bank, modelled on the Bundesbank. The German government's concern was and continues to be based on the belief that allowing countries that do not have a strong low inflation reputation (e.g., France) and or large budget deficits (e.g., Italy) to share part of the decision power in the ECB might induce a suboptimally high inflation rate in Europe. This concern had already surfaced in the Delors Report (1989) and in Padoa-Schiopa (1990), who explained that "financially weak countries may be inclined to advocate a permissive monetary policy in order to ease the financing of the deficit." Canzoneri and Diba (1991) model explicitly this concern and show that rules constraining the conduct of monetary policy would indeed alleviate the danger of a permissive monetary policy. Further, a very independent ECB with a strong commitment to price stability would help compensate for the absence of a history on which the reputation of such a new institution could be predicted. Hence, the German government has insisted that the future ECB be at least as independent and committed to price stability as the present Bundesbank, and the other Union members have accepted the German view. Indeed, Alesina and Grilli (1992) have examined the proposed statute of the ECB and concluded that the ECB will be as independent and committed to price stability as the Bundesbank, which is the most independent of the twelve member central banks.

The Maastricht treaty also has institutional implications for the national central banks during the transition phase leading to the elimination of national currencies. Article 109C, paragraph 5 states that "during the second stage each Member State shall, as appropriate, start the process leading to the independence of its central bank, in accordance with the provisions of Article 108 paragraph 2." This implies that national legislation on the statutes of the central banks must be compatible with the statute of the ECB. The second stage started on January 1, 1994. Prior to that date, France and Belgium reformed their central banks in accordance with the treaty. In both countries, these institutional changes led to the appointment of new boards of the central banks.

Motivated by these institutional reforms and new appointments, I analyze how monetary unification in Europe should affect the appointment of central bankers. This question is important both for political and economic reasons. As demonstrated by Kydland and Prescott (1977), Barro and Gordon (1983a,b), and Canzoneri (1985), in the presence of output distortions and a perfectly benevolent central bank, discretionary monetary policy can produce an inflation bias that is socially suboptimal. Rogoff (1985) shows that society can partially solve the problem by appointing a "conservative" central banker who dislikes inflation more than society does. However, it is not optimal to appoint an "ultra conservative" central banker, that is, someone who only cares about inflation. A tradeoff exists between the reduction in inflation and the increased variability of output brought by a more conservative central banker.

I analyze the Rogoff argument in a two country model based on Martin (forthcoming). I show that if credibility of monetary policies is an important issue both at the national level (vis-à-vis wage-setters) and at the European level (vis-à-vis central bankers in Europe), monetary unification and conservative central bankers' appointments are imperfect substitutes.[1] After briefly reviewing the main issues related to monetary unification in Europe in the second section, the third section presents the two-country economic model. The fourth section analyzes the economic equilibrium of the model, that is, the equilibrium for a given choice of central bankers. The ECB equilibrium entails a lower average inflation rate and a also a lower variance of the inflation rate than the flexible exchange rate. Hence, for a given choice of central bankers, monetary unification improves welfare. In the fifth section, I investigate the political equilibrium, that is, the equilibrium when the optimal choice of central bankers is made endogenous. The appointment of central bankers is compared in three equilibria: (1) flexible exchange rates without coordination on central bankers' appointments, (2) flexible exchange rates with coordination on the appointments' of central bankers (I interpret this equilibrium as describing the transition period to monetary unification), and (3) monetary union. I find that, if optimally chosen, central bankers will be most conservative during the transition period and least conservative in the final stage of monetary unification. This is because the tradeoff, analyzed by Rogoff (1985), between inflation and output stabilization that determines the optimal appointment of the central bankers differs in the two systems. In the flexible exchange rate regime, when governments which represent the preferences of the country's median voters choose respectively, and noncooperatively, a central banker, they choose a very "conservative" one. A central banker who can fight both the internal inflation bias, and the external inflation bias which comes from an externality between the two countries is selected. In the ECB case, as this external inflation bias disappears, the optimal European central banker need not be as conservative as in the flexible exchange rate regime. It is also proven that the level of ECB welfare is attainable in the flexible exchange rate regime if countries cooperate on the choice of very conservative central bankers.

MONETARY UNIFICATION IN EUROPE: A REVIEW OF THE MAIN ISSUES

The report in 1990 of the Delors Committee, comprising the governors of the national central banks and chaired by Jacques Delors, and the European Commission's own assessment of monetary union (European Commission 1990) consistently linked monetary union to the completion of the Single Market. The economics of this link are not obvious, but one implication of the Single Market, the lifting of most obstacles to intra-European capital flows, makes the present exchange rate arrangement certainly unviable over the long term. The crises of September 1992 and August 1993 have demonstrated that there are only two long-term alternatives: A considerably more flexible exchange rate regime than the EMS in its narrow band version, the current almost flexible exchange rate regime, or a monetary union with a single currency. This should be kept in mind when analyzing the costs and benefits of monetary integration in Europe.

Economists traditionally recognize two main costs of monetary unification: A loss of seigniorage in the high inflation countries and the loss of monetary policy autonomy. Because monetary integration leads to convergence of inflation rates and money supply growth rates, it should also lead to convergence of the "inflation tax," that is, the revenues that the government can expect from money creation, measured as the growth rate of the real monetary base. This has been a significant source of revenues for Southern European countries, which would be largely lost if these countries join a ECB. However, since 1988 the reliance on seigniorage has decreased significatively in these countries, except for Portugal and Greece.[2] This is partially due to the decrease in reserve requirements on the banking sector imposed by the creation of a common financial market. Hence, with or without monetary union reliance on seigniorage revenues will have to fall.

A more important cost comes from the loss of monetary autonomy and is at the base of the optimum currency area literature.[3] If monetary policy can stabilize the economy affected by temporary shocks, the optimal policy will be different in the different countries of the Union, implying changes in the exchange rate that can no longer exist within a monetary union. The more shocks are asymmetric in the monetary union, the more costly the loss of monetary policy autonomy will be. A study by Bayoumi and Eichengreen (1992) suggests that with respect to supply shocks, Europe does not look very different from the United States. In both continents, there is a core (Germany, France, Denmark, and Benelux in the case of the EC) where shocks are highly correlated and a periphery (Portugal, Italy, Spain, Ireland, Greece, and United Kingdom) where shocks are much less correlated with the anchor region (Germany). However, demand shocks are much more asymmetric in Europe than in the United States. On this last account, the loss of monetary policy autonomy may be costly for European countries. However, this will constitute a real cost only to the extent that monetary policy can indeed stabilize output. Certain authors (Bean 1992) argue that because the absence of nominal wage rigidity in Europe raises doubts about the effectiveness of autonomous monetary policy, relatively little is lost by giving up the exchange rate.

The benefits of monetary unification can be analyzed at the micro level and at the macro level. The elimination of transaction costs is the most direct gain of the elimination of multiple currencies. The Commission (1990) optimistically estimates this gain to be 0.5 percent of GDP. This gain is made only once, and is insufficient to compensate unambiguously for the costs that were previously described. Indirect micro gains from the elimination of transaction costs may be more important, but also more difficult to estimate. Like all transaction costs, those derived from the existence of multiple currencies enable firms to discriminate among markets. Their elimination should therefore foster competition in Europe.

Another gain of monetary unification, frequently cited by businessmen, is the reduction of exchange rate volatility and uncertainty. The existence of futures and options markets through which private agents can (partially) insure themselves against exchange rate risk, coupled with the failure to find a strong link between exchange rate volatility and economic activity, suggest that these potential gains may be overstated in the public debate.

At the macroeconomic level, monetary unification can bring monetary credibility and eliminate noncooperative monetary strategies. On the first point, a country that faces a credibility problem at home can "import" monetary discipline by joining a fixed exchange rate zone dominated by a country with a reputation for low inflationary policies. This argument was developed to explain why countries such as France or Italy joined the EMS. The gain in credibility at home depends itself on the credibility of the fixed exchange rate system, which can never be total as long as multiple currencies exist. Hence, this gain can only be fully reaped in the case of the ECB.

The analytical framework of this argument has been developed in the literature on time inconsistency of monetary policies. Because the remainder of this chapter falls within this tradition, I will briefly explain it. The basic model (Barro and Gordon 1983a and b) analyzes an economy in which nominal wages have to be set in advance on the basis of the expected inflation rate. This gives rise to an "expectational" Phillips curve where output is positively related to the difference between the inflation outcome and expected inflation. In the neoclassical tradition, only unexpected inflation can have a positive impact on employment and output because it decreases the real wage in the economy. However, because wage-setters are forward-looking and rational, there cannot be a systematic manipulable tradeoff between output and inflation. If the natural rate of output is too low,[4] the monetary authority will want to exchange a higher inflation rate for a higher output. Wage-setters will understand this and will not believe announcements by monetary authorities to deliver low inflation. If they believed such an announcement and accordingly set a low rate of increase in the nominal wage, the monetary authorities would then deviate and deliver a higher rate of inflation in order to decrease the real wage and increase employment. Hence, the only time consistent equilibrium is one with output at the natural rate and a high enough rate of inflation (expected and actually delivered) so that the monetary authorities will not accept more inflation to get a higher level of output.

The problem of the monetary authorities is therefore to find a commitment technology so that its announcement of low inflation is credible. One possibility is to build a reputation by repeating this game with wage-setters. This takes time and may not be always politically feasible. Another possibility is to appoint an independent and conservative central banker. One of the objectives of this chapter is to show that this strategy may not be enough if chosen at the national level and not at the European level. Fixing the exchange rate to a country with low inflation may then be the best solution.

If the exchange rate is used strategically, to manipulate trade balances or output (as this will be the case in the model presented in this chapter), prisoners'-dilemma types of situations can emerge in flexible exchange rate regimes. The creation of an ECB and the elimination of the exchange rate as a strategic instrument can therefore eliminate the possibility of "competitive devaluations" and increase efficiency. In this case, an ECB can improve welfare because it is closer to the cooperative equilibrium than it is under flexible exchange rates.

The overall picture that emerges from this brief and incomplete review of the main issues related to monetary unification in Europe is that the economic costs and gains that can be estimated may be rather small. Benefits that cannot be easily estimated, discipline and cooperative benefits, depend largely on the institutional structure of the future ECB. This has been laid out in the Maastricht treaty. Monetary policy will be decided by the Governing Council, comprising the six members of the Executive Board appointed by the European Council, and the twelve national central bankers. Hence, the institutional structure of the future ECB closely resembles the Federal Reserve's. Also, the Treaty seems to embody the principle of a conservative and independent central banker as analyzed in this chapter: Article 105 states that the primary objective of the European System of Central Banks (the ECSB, the institution that associates the ECB and the national central banks) is "to maintain price stability." Article 107 prohibits the ECSB or the ECB from "seeking or taking instructions from Community institutions or bodies, from any government of a Member State or from any other body." The succeeding sections of this chapter will attempt to shed some light on just how conservative central bankers should be by analyzing how the optimal appointment of central bankers will differ in the present system from the appointment in a monetary union.

THE ECONOMIC MODEL

In the model, Europe consists of two identical countries 1 and 2 which produce a single identical good for which P.P.P applies. I assume that they do not cooperate on their monetary policy, and that no trigger strategies (à la Friedman, 1971) are possible, reputation building is ruled out as a commitment device for central banks.[5] The two policy makers have the same expected loss function:

$$ L_i = \frac{1}{2} [\pi_i^2 + b (y_i - \overline{y})^2] \quad i = 1,2 \qquad\qquad 1 $$

where L_i is the expected loss function of country i, a function of π_i the inflation rate, and of the deviation of the log of domestic output y_i, from the log of the socially optimal level of output $\overline{y}$, and b is the weight placed on the goal of reaching the optimally social level of output relative to inflation. Time subscripts have been omitted as the game is identical in each period. The supply function is similar to the one in Martin (forthcoming):

$$ y_i = (p_i - w_i) - \theta (p_j - w_j) + \varepsilon \quad i = 1,2 \; j \neq i \qquad\qquad 2 $$

where w is the wage rate, p is the price level, and ε is a random productivity shock distributed normally with zero mean and variance σ_ε common to the two countries.[6] θ is between 0 and 1. If $\theta = 0$, then this equation would be similar to the supply function in a standard Barro-Gordon model with a stochastic shock. If $\theta = 1$, then in equilibrium the Phillips curve is vertical at the European level. I will assume in the rest of the chapter that θ is between 0 and 1. I have assumed, without loss of generality, that the log of the full employment level of output is zero. As in the Barro-Gordon model, the socially optimal level of output is higher than the natural level.

The second part of equation (2) can be explained this way. Imagine a European firm that has production units in these two European countries and has to decide where to increase or decrease its labor demand and its production. What the second part of equation (2) says is that, given that P.P.P holds, i.e., the firm can sell the good at the same price everywhere, the firm will choose to increase labor demand and production relatively more in the country that has a lower real wage. This will create an incentive for each government to inflate away the domestic real wage to import jobs from the foreign country at a given foreign real wage and will be at the origin of a prisoners' dilemma type of situation. Hence, in equilibrium this external-ity will induce an inflationary bias.[7] The case of positive monetary spill-overs has been recently analyzed by Dolado et al. (1994).

Wage-setters want to achieve the equilibrium output y. Their utility can be represented by:

$$U_{wi} = -[p_i - w_i]^2 \quad i = 1,2$$

3

The expected utility-maximizing strategy for wage-setters is thus:

$$w_i = \pi_i^e \quad i = 1,2$$

4

So output can be rewritten as:

$$y_i = \pi_i - \pi_i^e - \theta(\pi_j - \pi_j^e) + \varepsilon \quad i = 1,2 \ j \neq i$$

5

This equation states that output in country i is affected positively by unexpected national inflation and negatively by unexpected foreign inflation.

The next two sections analyze the economic and the political equilibrium in the ECB case and the flexible exchange rate case. I define the economic equilibrium as the equilibrium for which the choice of central bankers is given. The political equilibrium is the equilibrium for which the appointment of central bankers is made endogenous.

THE ECONOMIC EQUILIBRIUM

In this section I compare the inflation rates and output levels in the flexible exchange rate regime and in the monetary union regime for a given choice of central bankers. Because countries are identical, the monetary union regime solves the prisoner's dilemma problem that arises in the flexible exchange rate regime and results in the cooperative equilibrium.

Flexible Exchange Rates

I assume that each central bank controls perfectly the home inflation rate. Alternatively, I could more realistically have assumed that the central banks control the growth rates of money supplies and close the model with a quantity equation.

The results would be qualitatively similar. So the expected loss function of country i can be rewritten as:

$$L_{iFER} = \frac{1}{2} \pi_i^2 + \frac{1}{2} b \left[\pi_i - \pi_i^e - \bar{y} - \theta(\pi_j - \pi_j^e) + \varepsilon \right]^2 \quad i = 1,2 \; j \neq i \qquad 6$$

where the subscript FER stands for flexible exchange rates. At the beginning of each period, inflation expectations are formed and nominal wage contracts are set.

Then, the shock ε is realized and observed by the two central banks, which choose the domestic inflation rate based upon this information.[8]

The problem of the central bank of country is to minimize its loss function with respect to the domestic inflation rate π_i taking as given the domestic expected inflation rate π_i^e and the expected and actual inflation rates π_j^e and π_j of the other country.

In equilibrium, the inflation rates in the two countries are equal as the two countries are identical. The time consistent inflation policy is given by:

$$\pi_i = b \bar{y} - \frac{b}{1+b-b\theta} \varepsilon \quad i = 1,2$$

$$7$$

Each central bank has an incentive to set a higher (lower) inflation rate than the other European countries when a negative (positive) shock is observed. The output levels are:

$$y_i = \frac{1}{1+b-b\theta} \varepsilon \quad i = 1,2$$

$$8$$

Equation (7) shows that the reaction to shocks increases with θ, which can be thought of as the measure of the externality. An employment transfer takes place between the two countries if a difference in the inflation rates and therefore the real wages exists. In equilibrium there is no such net employment transfer because each country tries similarly to counter the shock by transferring it to its partner, and the equilibrium inflation rates and real wages are identical in the two countries as shown in equation (7). Hence, the output levels are identical in both countries as shown in equation (8). Finally, the expected inflation rate is in the two countries:

$$\pi_i^e = b \, \overline{y} \quad i = 1,2$$

9

In addition to the incentive to overreact to shocks, remember that central banks want a higher level of employment than the wage-setters. Hence, as wage-setters understand the incentive to reach the higher level of employment by choosing a higher level of inflation than the foreign country, they will purposely set the nominal wage at a high level.

The Equilibrium with the ECB

It is assumed that members of the ECB are irrevocably committed to the Union once they have joined it. In this case, both the wage-setters and the policymakers know that the inflation rate must be identical in the two countries for the P.P.P to apply. So, equation (2) becomes a standard expectational Phillips curve with the slope $(1-\theta)$:

$$y_i = (1-\theta)(\pi_i - \pi_i^e) + \varepsilon \quad i = 1,2$$

10

and the expected loss function of the ECB is:

$$L_{ECB} = \frac{1}{2} \, \pi_i^2 + \frac{1}{2} b \left[(1-\theta)(\pi_i - \pi_i^e) - \overline{y} + \varepsilon \right] \quad i = 1,2$$

11

The time consistent inflation rate in this case is:

$$\pi_i = b(1-\theta)\overline{y} - \frac{b(1-\theta)}{1 + b(1-\theta)^2}\varepsilon \quad i = 1,2$$

12

And the output is given by:

$$y_i = \frac{1}{1 + b(1-\theta)^2} \, \varepsilon \quad i = 1,2$$

13

The expected inflation rate is:

$$\pi_i^e = b(1-\theta)\bar{y} \quad i = 1,2$$

14

Comparing the equilibria with and without the ECB brings me to the following conclusions:

- First, the inflation bias is reduced in the ECB case, because wage expectations are reduced. Wage-setters understand that national policymakers do not have any systematic incentive to inflate the real wage more than the foreign one to achieve the output target. They therefore reduce their inflation expectations. The extent to which inflation expectations are reduced depends on θ, because it represents the extent of the externality between the two countries, which in turn is fully understood by wage-setters.

- Second, the reaction to shocks is smaller in the ECB case, as governments do not try to accommodate the shocks by importing jobs from the foreign country. In the non-ECB case the reaction to shocks is too large and is not optimal given the tradeoff between inflation and employment stability. So the variance of output is larger in the ECB regime than in the non-ECB regime. Again, the extent to which the variance of inflation is suboptimally high depends on θ, the extent of the externality. This can be shown by calculating the difference in variance between the flexible exchange rate regime and the ECB equilibrium.[9]

- Third, it is shown in the Appendix that welfare is higher in the ECB regime than in the non-ECB regime. This is because the average inflation and the variance of inflation are reduced. The reaction to shocks is optimal in the ECB regime as the slope of the Phillips curve is correctly perceived. Also, in this example, because shocks are perfectly correlated, the outcome with the ECB is the same as the one under flexible exchange rates if governments were to cooperate on monetary policies. Hence, in this sense Europe is an Optimum Currency Area in the model.

So in the non-ECB regime, there is a two-level game in the sense of Putnam (1988): A reciprocal influence of domestic and international affairs exists. At the domestic level, the central bank in each country plays a game with the wage-setters. At the international level, there is a game between the two national central banks. In the ECB regime, this second game is eliminated. In this domestic game, the wage-setters' strategy (i.e., their expectation concerning inflation or nominal wage increases) is based on the expectation of wage-setters of the outcome of the interaction unfolding between the central banks. In the international game between the two central banks, strategies (the inflation rates) depend on the information advantage each central bank has over the wage-setters in the domestic game.

THE POLITICAL EQUILIBRIUM

In this section, an additional political dimension is examined. Until now, the central banker, the government, or the median voter's loss function were assumed implicitly to be identical. However, if monetary policy is delegated to an independent central banker with its own output-inflation preferences, the choice of the central banker will affect the economic equilibrium. Delegation will then be used as a commitment technology.[10] I examine how the choice of the central bankers is affected by the exchange rate regime in Europe. I distinguish three different possibilities. The first one is the one that I interpret as describing the situation in Europe during the 1980s, that is, a flexible exchange rate regime without coordination of central bankers' appointments.[11] In this equilibrium, the choice of central bankers takes the form of a game between countries. The second one is the transitional period instituted by the Maastricht treaty, where preparation for the final stage of monetary unification implies changes of the statutes of European central banks to a common level of independence and common objectives in terms of price stability and output stabilization. Finally, the third equilibrium is one where the two countries form the ECB. I will start by this one because it is the most simple.

Choosing a Central Banker in the ECB

In the ECB regime, choosing the "conservative" banker is done in the same way as in a closed economy. Suppose the governments in each country represent the preferences of the median voter[12] characterized by b_m so that the loss function of the governments is:

$$L_i^m = \frac{1}{2}\,\pi_i^2 + \frac{1}{2}b_m\,\left[(1-\theta)(\pi_i - \pi_i^e) - \overline{y} + \varepsilon\right]^2 \quad i = 1,2 \qquad\qquad 15$$

When choosing the central banker, the government recognizes the credibility problem that the central bank will face when implementing monetary policy. To choose the central banker, the government minimizes the loss function given by equation (15) with respect to b_{ECB}. Hence, we assume, following Rogoff (1985), that the government can appoint a central banker among candidates who differ by their relative preference between inflation and output, that is, choose among different levels of b's. Using equations (12) and (13), the minimization problem implies a first order condition implicitly defining the optimal choice of b_{ECB}:

$$b_{ECB} \; \overline{y}^2 + \frac{b_{ECB} - b_m}{\left[1 + b_{ECB}(1 - \theta)^2\right]^3}\sigma_\varepsilon^2 = 0 \qquad\qquad\qquad 16$$

This condition implies that b_{ECB} must be less than b_m but positive. Therefore, the appointed European central banker will be more "conservative" than the median voter, but not a totally conservative one (Rogoff 1985, Alesina and Grilli 1992). The intuition is the same as in a closed economy model. At the point where $b_{ECB} = b_m$, inflation is suboptimally high because of the time inconsistency problem described in the preceding section. On the other hand, the reaction to shocks is optimal at that point. Because the loss function is quadratic in the output deviation and inflation, this implies that the tradeoff between the two is not optimal at the point where $b_{ECB} = b_m$. It is better to accept more output instability and less inflation. To change the equilibrium tradeoff in this direction, the government can appoint a more conservative banker, that is, an agent who cares more about inflation and less about output stability than the median voter. b_{ECB} should be less than b_m. From equation (13) and (14) one can indeed check that as b decreases average inflation decreases and output instability increases.

Because the shocks are identical in the two countries, a fixed exchange rate regime in our model is equivalent to cooperation on monetary policies, as it delivers the same inflation rate and welfare. However, in this model cooperation on monetary policies or a fixed exchange rate regime are not the only manners to attain the efficient equilibrium.

The Transition Phase: Coordination of Central Bankers' Appointments

Without the ECB, the two countries can attain the same level of inflation and welfare implied by this European "conservative" central banker by choosing an even more conservative banker than when the ECB is formed. If each government appoints a central banker, that is chooses b such that:

$$b_1 \; = \; b_2 \; = \; b_c \; = \; (1 - \theta) \; b_{ECB} \qquad\qquad\qquad 17$$

where b_{ECB} is implicitly defined by equation (16), and b_c stands for the preferences of the central bankers chosen under cooperation, then the two exchange rate regimes are identical. This can be checked by replacing b in equation (7) by the value in equation (17). Hence, if governments cooperate on their choice of national central bankers, the flexible exchange rate regime results in the same equilibrium as in the ECB equilibrium. This is so even though central bankers do not cooperate on monetary policies. There is an equivalence in results between cooperation on monetary policies and cooperation on the appointments of central bankers. The difference between the two types of cooperation might be important in practice. Cooperation on monetary policies must be continuous because policy decisions in reaction to shocks in each period are decided jointly among participatory states. On the contrary, cooperation on the choice of central bankers is required infrequently. Once cooperation has been achieved on the choice of two individuals to run the two central banks, no more cooperation on the reaction to shocks is required. However, cooperation on the appointment of central bankers may be difficult if each government has private information on the preferences of the candidates for the position.

The Maastricht treaty does not represent as high a level of government cooperation as required by the appointment of central bankers in my model. However, it can be interpreted as giving governments common standards in terms of price objectives and output stabilization, as well as in terms of central bank independence. Article 109C, paragraph 5, of the Maastricht treaty reads: "During the second stage each Member State shall, as appropriate, start the process leading to the independence of its central bank, in accordance with the provisions of Article 108 paragraph 2." This implies that national legislation on the statutes of the central banks must be compatible with the statute of the ECB.

Hence, I infer that during the second stage, which started January 1, 1994, central banks in Europe adopt similar legislations in the objectives in terms of price and output stabilization and independence. In the context of my model, I translate this in the constraint that the preferences of the central bankers over the tradeoff between inflation and output stabilization be identical. In our model, this constraint on central bankers' appointments is sufficient to lead to the cooperative equilibrium.

When choosing central bankers in each country, each government takes into account the restriction that $b_1 = b_2 = b_t$ where the subscript t stands for transition. The two governments choose b_t so as to minimize equation (6) where the inflation rates have been replaced by their equilibrium values given in (7). Solving for the first order conditions, I find that b_t is implicitly defined by the equation:

$$b_t \; \overline{y}^2 + \frac{b_t - b_m (1 - \theta)}{\left[1 + b_t (1 - \theta)\right]^3} \sigma_\varepsilon^2 = 0$$

18

Hence, using equations (16) to (18), it can be seen that $b_t = b_c$.

Central Banker's Appointments without Coordination

If governments do not cooperate on the choice of national central bankers, then a new strategic relationship is introduced. Again, in the sense of Putnam (1988), a two-level game unfolds. At the domestic level, the appointment of a central banker will be influenced by the game played by central bankers at the international level.

At the international level, the outcome of the game played by central banks will depend on who was appointed to manage monetary policy. Without cooperation on the appointment of central bankers, the inflation rates will be different in the flexible exchange rate regime and in the ECB regime. I will show that in the flexible exchange rate regime when governments do not cooperate on their choice of national central bankers, the central bankers they appoint are more conservative than in the ECB regime. This means that the central bankers appointed noncooperatively in the flexible exchange rate regime dislike more inflation than in the ECB regime. However, they are less conservative than during the transition period under the Maastricht treaty.

When governments in the two countries (whom I assume to have identical preferences characterized by b_m) appoint their national central bankers, they take the preference of the foreign central banker as given. The preferences of the appointed national central bankers are b_1 and b_2 in countries 1 and 2. Hence, b_1 and b_2 are the choice variables of the governments in countries 1 and 2. First, I determine the first order conditions for inflation rates of each central bank in terms of b_1 and b_2. I get the reaction functions:

$$\pi_1 = b_1 \bar{y} - \frac{b_1 b_2 \theta}{1+b_1}\bar{y} + \frac{b_1 \theta}{1+b_1}\pi_2 - \frac{b_1}{1+b_1}\varepsilon$$

$$\pi_2 = b_2 \bar{y} - \frac{b_1 b_2 \theta}{1+b_2}\bar{y} + \frac{b_2 \theta}{1+b_2}\pi_1 - \frac{b_2}{1+b_2}\varepsilon$$

19

After simplification, the two inflation rates are:

$$\pi_1 = b_1 \bar{y} - \frac{b_1 b_2 \theta + b_1(1+b_2)}{(1+b_1)(1+b_2) - b_1 b_2 \theta^2}\varepsilon$$

$$\pi_2 = b_2 \bar{y} - \frac{b_1 b_2 \theta + b_2(1+b_1)}{(1+b_1)(1+b_2) - b_1 b_2 \theta^2}\varepsilon$$

20

The two governments know equations (19). Hence, the government loss function in country one is represented by:

$$L_1^m = \frac{1}{2} \pi_1^2 + \frac{1}{2} b_m \left[\pi_1 - \pi_1^e - \theta(\pi_2 - \pi_2^e) - \overline{y} + \varepsilon \right]^2$$

21

The government in country 1 minimizes equation (20) (using equation [19] to replace the home and foreign inflation rates) with respect to b_1 and taking b_2 as given. As the two countries are identical and as the two median voters of the two countries have the same preferences, in equilibrium I can simplify by imposing: $b_1 = b_2 = b'$. The equation implicitly defining b', after simplification is:

$$b' \overline{y}^2 + \frac{b'(1+b') - b_m(1+b'-b'\theta^2)}{(1+b'+b'\theta)(1+b'-b'\theta)^3} \sigma_\varepsilon^2 = 0$$

22

It is shown in the Appendix that the central banker chosen noncooperatively in the flexible exchange rate is more conservative than the central banker in the ECB: b' is less than b_{ECB}. However, the central banker chosen noncooperatively in the flexible exchange rate regime is less conservative than if chosen cooperatively or during the transition period under the Maastricht treaty: b' is more than b_t.

The Appointment of Central Bankers in the Three Regimes

Hence, comparing the appointment of central bankers in the three possible institutional equilibria, the result is as follows:

Figure 8.1
The Appointment of Central Bankers in Three Regimes

More conservative central banker

b_{ECB}	>	b'	>	$b_c = b_t$
ECB		Flexible exchange rates, no cooperation		Transition

The intuition is the following. Under the ECB regime, the external inflation bias is eliminated because the expectational Philipps curve at the national level becomes more vertical and is the same as it is at the European level. Under the ECB regime, the exchange rate can no longer, by definition, be used to attract output by lowering the real wage. This eliminates a source of inflation. Hence, the conservative central banker need not be as conservative as in the flexible exchange rate regime. In the flexible exchange rate regime, choosing cooperatively very conservative central bankers constitutes a partial commitment to the foreign central banks. The inflation bias is reduced because wage-setters understand that choosing a very conservative national central banker implies that the incentive to have a lower real wage than abroad is reduced. Choosing, non-cooperatively, very "conservative" central bankers is a substitute to international cooperation or equivalently, in this example, to the commitment mechanism provided by the fixed exchange rate regime.

However, this is only an imperfect substitute, as governments do not cooperate on the choice of central bankers. In this case, if one country was to choose a central banker with the same preferences as in the cooperative equilibrium, the other country would have an incentive to deviate and appoint a slightly less conservative central banker so as to take advantage of more output stabilization at that point. This is why the equilibrium is still a prisoner's-dilemma type of situation.

Walsh (1992) has recently shown that a very simple contract that imposes a linear penalty for inflation on the central bank can eliminate the inflation bias induced by discretionary monetary policy without distorting the optimal response to supply shocks that affect the economy. In my framework, however, inflation is not only too high on average, it is also too volatile because central banks attempt to react to shocks by affecting their real exchange rate. Hence, a contract such as described by Walsh (1992) or Persson and Tabellini (1993) would indeed eliminate the inflation bias but would not make inflation more stable. On the contrary, the suboptimal high volatility of inflation is reduced by the appointment of a conservative central banker, with or without cooperation on their appointment. To see this, it is sufficient to note that the variance of inflation in the flexible exchange rate regime is increasing in b:

$$ var(\pi) = E(\pi)^2 = \frac{b^2(1-\theta)^2}{[1+b(1-\theta)^2]^2}\sigma_\epsilon^2 \ ; \ \frac{\partial var(\pi)}{\partial b} > 0 $$

The Maastricht treaty, by coordinating some common standards for price objectives and central bank independence, has indeed resulted in the appointment of central bankers who are considered as more "conservative" than under the previous regime. Note that this was done in certain countries (France and Belgium) even before the beginning of stage 2. Also, one of the clearly stated objectives of these governments when the reforms of the central banks were implemented was to strengthen the credibility of monetary policy not only towards national agents (wage-setters) but also towards international financial markets in relation to the exchange rate policy. These institutional changes conform exactly with the intuition of our results given above.

CONCLUSION

The insight that the end result of the monetary integration process—the creation of the ECB and the disappearance of national currencies—should trigger the appointment of less conservative central bankers may seem surprising. On political-economy grounds I have shown that it should not. The elimination of a source of an inflationary bias results optimally in the appointment of less conservative central bankers. However, in a model where countries differ in their preferences concerning the tradeoff between output and inflation stabilization, this result would not necessarily hold for all countries. Also, I have not taken into account fiscal issues and the absence of a history of the ECB on which to base reputation. These elements would drive our results in the opposite way; i.e., monetary unification will bring more conservative central bankers. The net effect of these different elements and of the mechanism that I have uncovered here is therefore ambiguous.

Another important implication of the results is that, without any international cooperation on appointments, delegation to an independent and "conservative" central banker can be an (imperfect) substitute for cooperation on policies. However, the appointment of central bankers itself becomes a strategic game between countries. A different type of prisoner's-dilemma situation emerges in which strategies are not based on inflation rates but on the choice of central bankers. If cooperation on appointments of central bankers is possible, it then becomes, in my model, a perfect substitute to cooperation on policies themselves. I suspect that this result applies to areas other than monetary policy. Delegating policies to independent agencies with preferences different from the median voter's ones may be a way to partially solve prisoners' dilemma problems that arise at the level of policies, when formal cooperation is difficult because of credibility problems. There are other areas, such as fiscal policy, environmental policy, and foreign policy, for which externalities are important, especially in the European context, and for which cooperation is difficult.

APPENDIX

Proof that $L_{ECB} < L_{FER}$:

Using equation (7), L_{FER} and L_{ECB} can be transformed into:

$$L_{FER} = \frac{1}{2} b(b+1) \bar{y}^2 + \frac{1}{2} \frac{b(b+1)}{\left[1+b(1-\theta)\right]^2} \sigma_\varepsilon^2$$

(A1)

$$L_{ECB} = \frac{1}{2}b[b(1-\theta)^2 + 1]\,\overline{y}^2 + \frac{1}{2}\frac{b}{\left[1 + b(1-\theta)^2\right]}\,\sigma_\varepsilon^2$$

(A2)

It can easily be checked that both the terms in $\overline{y}$ and σ_ε^2 are less in the second than in the first equation.

Proof that $b' < b_{ECB}$:
Combining equations (16) and (21), I get:

$$b_m = b_{ECB}\left[1 + b_{ECB}(1-\theta)^2\right]^3 \frac{\overline{y}^2}{\sigma^2} + b_{ECB}$$

$$= \frac{b'(1+b'-b'\theta)^3(1+b'+b'\theta)}{1+b'-b'\theta^2}\frac{\overline{y}^2}{\sigma^2} + \frac{b'(1+b')}{1+b'-b'\theta^2}$$

(A3)

After rearranging terms, I get:

(A4)

$$(b'-b_{ECB})(1+b'-b'\theta^2) = -b'^2\theta^2$$

$$1 + \left\{b_{ECB}\left[1 + b_{ECB}(1-\theta)^2\right]^3(1+b'-b'\theta^2) - b'(1+b'-b'\theta)^3(1+b'+b'\theta)\right\}\frac{\overline{y}^2}{\sigma^2}$$

The first term of the right side of equation (A4) is negative. Suppose that $b \geq b_{ECB}$, then:

$$\left[1 + b_{ECB}\left(1-\theta^2\right)\right]^3 < \left(1+b'-b'\theta\right)^3$$
$$1 + b'\left(1-\theta^2\right) < 1 + b'\left(1+\theta\right)$$

(A5)

as θ is less than 1 and positive. Hence, in the right side of equation (A4), the first and second terms are negative; $b \geq b_{ECB}$ cannot be true.

Proof that $b' > b_t$:
Combining equations (18) and (22), I get:

(A6)

$$b_m = \frac{b_t}{1-\theta}[1+b_t(1-\theta)]^3 \frac{\overline{y}^2}{\sigma^2} + \frac{b_t}{1-\theta}$$

$$= \frac{b'(1+b'-b'\theta)^3(1+b'+b'\theta)}{1+b'-b'\theta^2}\frac{\overline{y}^2}{\sigma^2} + \frac{b'(1+b')}{1+b'-b'\theta^2}$$

After rearranging terms, I get: (A7)

$$b_t - b' = b'[b'(1-\theta) - b_t(1-\theta^2) - \theta]$$

$$+\left\{b'(1+b'-b'\theta)^3(1+b'+b'\theta)(1-\theta) - b_t(1+b_t-b_t\theta)^3(1+b'-b'\theta^2)\right\}\frac{\overline{y}^2}{\sigma^2}$$

Suppose that $b' \leq b_t$, then the first term of equation (A7) is negative and it can be checked that:

$$(1+b'-b'\theta)^3 < (1+b_t+b_t\theta)^3$$
$$(1+b'+b'\theta)(1-\theta) < 1+b'-b'\theta^2$$

(A8)

as θ is less than 1 and positive. Hence, in the right side of equation (A7), the first and second terms are negative; $b' \leq b_t$ cannot be true.

NOTES

1. Laskar (1990) and Dolado et al. (1994) look at delegation of monetary policy in an international context. In Laskar, delegation arises because of the existence of a time-inconsistency problem. In Dolado et al., on the contrary, there is no time consistency issue.

2. In 1988, seigniorage in percentage of GDP in Italy, Spain, Portugal, and Greece was respectively 1.1 percent, 1.4 percent, 2.2 percent and 2.8 percent. In 1993, these numbers were 0.4 percent, 0.7 percent, 1.6 percent and 4.8 percent. In the case of Italy and Spain, the numbers are now close to Northern European ones.

3. The classic reference for the optimum currency area theory is Mundell (1961). An extensive review of the issues of monetary unions is provided by Masson and Taylor (1992) and Bean (1992).

4. The difference between the full employment level of output and the socially optimal one can be rationalized by the presence of distortions on the labor market. For example, income taxation, the presence of a minimum wage or unions, can distort the labor-leisure choice decision. This distortion of the labor market equilibrium can then cause the market-determined level of employment and output to be too low. For a discussion of this see Barro and Gordon (1983a), Canzoneri (1985), and Rogoff (1985).

5. See Canzoneri and Henderson (1991) for trigger mechanisms and reputation in repeated games and why such strategies do not always lead to efficient outcomes.

6. The choice of perfect correlation was made for simplification purposes. The main results still hold as long as the correlation between shocks is positive.

7. Empirically, the results of Martin (1994) suggest that externalities present in monetary policies contribute to an inflationary bias in industrial countries.

8. Hence, for simplicity, in the case of the current EMS, I assume that a realignment takes place after each shock and the outcome is similar to the one under flexible exchange rates.

9. The ECB is not the Pareto efficient equilibrium, because even though the inefficiency from the game between the central bankers is removed, the inefficiency from the game between the central bank and the wage-setters is not entirely eliminated.

10. On the microeconomic theory of delegation see in particular Vickers (1984).

11. Again, this implies an extreme interpretation of the EMS which, because of the realignments, produces the same equilibrium as does a flexible exchange rate regime. This assumption, although simplistic, enables us to focus on the main difference between the EMS and the ECB; that is, exchange rates are irrevocably fixed only in the second system. Also, since August 1993 and the enlargement of the bands to 15 percent, the EMS resembles more a flexible exchange rate regime than a fixed one.

12. I assume that the two median voters have the same preferences concerning this tradeoff. I therefore ignore potential conflicts among European median voters. See Alesina and Grilli (1992) for such an analysis.

Full Membership or Full Club? Expansion of NATO and the Future Security Organization of Europe

Thomas Bernauer

INTRODUCTION

The end of East-West confrontation has led to developments in the North Atlantic Treaty Organization (NATO) that pose new puzzles and allow for new tests of theories of international relations. How will NATO—the most institutionalized and enduring form of regional security integration in this century, constituting the principal forum for Europe's further integration in this field—evolve in the future? How will NATO's decisions concerning the new security environment shape the future security arrangements of Europe?

Balance of power and balance of threat theory predict the rapid collapse of NATO, concurrent with the demise of the Warsaw Pact and the disintegration of the former Soviet Union (Mearsheimer 1990, Waltz 1993, Walt 1987). Institutionalists, on the other hand, argue that NATO is likely to persist but that the alliance's mission, strategy, and composition will probably change (Keohane, Nye, and Hoffmann 1993). They hold that international institutions, such as NATO, tend to adapt rather than die. Five years after the collapse of the Berlin Wall, institutionalist predictions seem to have fared better than realist ones. NATO has encountered significant problems in coping with unfamiliar tasks, such as the war in the former Yugoslavia. Nonetheless, it is adapting reasonably well to the new security environment; no one should expect that adapting a complex multilateral institution to fundamentally changing circumstances is possible without some difficulties.

Critical tests for these predictions about the future of NATO are difficult to design and carry out (Hellmann and Wolf 1993). The arguments of balance of power or threat theory and institutionalism overlap to the degree that most observable implications can be claimed by both theories to support their propositions. In addition, the implications *per se* of the propositions are not yet sufficiently observable.

This chapter argues, however, that analyzing the question of whether NATO will expand into Central and Eastern Europe can contribute to theorizing about the evolution of alliances and regional integration in general. This issue has observable outcomes against which propositions can be assessed. Expanding NATO's membership is a question deemed of extreme importance to policymakers and may indeed determine the future of NATO (Asmus et al. 1993, Harries 1993). Moreover, such an examination can provide insights into the form that NATO will assume: Whether the alliance will continue to operate in its traditional way, with sixteen members and full security guarantees, or, at the other extreme, whether and how NATO might be fundamentally transformed so that it would become the core of a pan-European security institution.

Several former member states of the Warsaw Treaty Organization have requested full membership in NATO (Hungary, Poland, and the Czech Republic, henceforth mentioned as HPC) and others may well follow (Hoppe 1994). I will argue that this development is consistent with the predictions of balance of threat theory. But neither balance of threat nor institutionalist theory provides a satisfactory explanation of NATO's response to the applicants. NATO has sought to keep the former allies of the Soviet Union in Central and Eastern Europe at arm's length and has offered them the Partnership for Peace Program. This program includes joint military exercises and exchanges of information. It does not, however, involve any security guarantees and, therefore, is not a military alliance in the traditional sense (Rühl 1994).

I will explore the implications of these events for alliance theories by outlining an alternative model. This model conceptualizes NATO as a club with limited membership that has to make decisions on whether or not to accept new members, subject to a variety of constraints. This constrained optimization model takes variation in the external threat seriously. But it offers a more systematic explanation than balance of threat theory does of the relationships between external threat, defense burdens, the nature of NATO's services, alliance cohesion, and membership decisions.

The question of expanding NATO is similar to the question of widening or deepening integration in the context of the European Union and the Western European Union (WEU), and the relationship between expansion and cohesion. Hence the model outlined in this chapter may also illuminate the dynamics of European political and economic integration, as well as security integration in the framework of the WEU.

The first part of the chapter discusses the principal propositions of balance of threat theory and institutionalist theory with regard to the dynamics of NATO, as well as the shortcomings of these approaches. The second part reviews two types of theories that have been used to explain alliance size and choices of allies: Theories about minimum winning coalitions, and portfolio diversification models. The third part argues that the collective goods aspect of alliances, which is underdeveloped in the two aforementioned theories, is crucial for understanding alliance size and choices of alliance partners. It contends that the services of NATO to its member states are, to a large extent, impure public goods. This argument constitutes the basis for applying the theory of clubs to explain the conditions under which NATO will expand into Central and Eastern Europe. Drawing on work by Buchanan (1965), Sandler and Tschirhart (1980), and Cornes and Sandler (1986), the fourth part outlines a formal model that explains membership decisions in homogeneous and heterogeneous clubs. The final part applies the arguments of the formal model more closely to NATO and advances some predictions.

BALANCE OF THREAT THEORY AND INSTITUTIONALIST THEORY

Balance of power theory argues that states balance against the most power-ful state in the international system. Power, in this context, is usually concep-tualized in terms of military capabilities. States ally with weaker states, or a group of states, to keep the most powerful actor at bay (Waltz 1979). Balance of threat theory holds that states balance against the most threatening state rather than the most powerful state. Threats are primarily a function of capabilities, offensive armaments, geographic proximity, and intentions (Walt 1987:21-26). States balance against threats by increasing their individual defense effort, or by allying with other states. I will henceforth concentrate on balance of threat theory. This theory generates more sophisticated explanations of alliance dynamics than balance of power theory because it does not merely focus on capabilities, but also on geography, behavior, intentions, and other explanatory variables.

Balance of threat theory explains the formation and evolution of alliances exclusively as a function of external threats. Western European countries, the United States, and Canada formed NATO to balance against the threat posed by the former Soviet Union.[1] The Soviet Union was perceived as the most threatening actor because of its vast military capabilities, its declared aim of exporting revolution, its offensive military posture, its geographic proximity, and its history of expansionism. The United States (the state with the largest capabilities in the international system) appeared less threatening to Western Europe because it was not located on the Eurasian landmass, had a similar socioeconomic system, and was willing to provide massive economic assis-tance. This explains why Western Europe allied with the United States rather than with the Soviet Union.

The Warsaw Pact was characterized by bandwagoning rather than balancing behavior. Bandwagoning refers to the dynamics of allying with the enemy; Central and Eastern European countries allied with the most threatening state. Balancing against the Soviet Union was almost impossible for these countries because of the geographic proximity of the threatening state, the presence of the Soviet Army on their territory since the end of the Second World War, and the unwillingness of Western countries to challenge the Soviet sphere of influence.

The level of external threat affects the dynamics of existing alliances by influencing their cohesion.[2] When the threat increases, so does the incentive of the members of an alliance to coordinate their goals and strategies to attain those goals. When the threat declines, policy coordination becomes more difficult. The alliance loses cohesion and is less likely to endure. Bandwagoning cases, such as Central and Eastern Europe until 1989, are more sensitive to variation in the external threat than are cases of balancing. When the most threatening state declines, the bandwagoning allies are likely to defect. Furthermore, both balancing and bandwagoning alliances are more difficult to organize and maintain in multipolar systems because threats are more diffuse and there are more choices with regard to possible allies than in bipolar systems (Waltz 1993).

The propositions of balance of threat theory, as applied to NATO and the Warsaw Pact, are partly inaccurate. Predictions that the Warsaw Pact would disintegrate quickly, which have been derived from the bandwagoning argument, turned out to be correct. But forecasts that the fading external threat would decrease the cohesion of NATO and lead to its disintegration (Waltz 1993, Walt 1987, Mearsheimer 1990) are less convincing. NATO is currently the strongest international security organization in Europe, and there are no signs that it will break down anytime soon.

Institutionalist theory contends that NATO may persist by adapting to its new environment. But it is indeterminate as to how precisely NATO will adapt and what form it could assume in the future. The principal reason why NATO may endure in a modified form is that it is highly institutionalized and performs a variety of functions that the alliance's member regard as useful (Hoffmann, Keohane, and Nye 1993, Hellmann and Wolf 1993). In particular, NATO provides low-cost information, prevents Germany from becoming too powerful, and constitutes the only permanent transatlantic bargaining forum. The value of these functions is only to a small degree affected by variation in the threat posed by Russia. Moreover, NATO members have invested large amounts of time and resources in NATO; that is, the sunk costs are high. States are unlikely to abandon this non-retrievable investment (even though the returns appear to be limited, at least temporarily), because establishing new institutions could be much costlier than adapting old ones.

Critical tests for these competing propositions are very difficult to design.[3] The most important deficiency of the two theories, however, is that they focus exclusively on whether and why NATO will or will not persist. They do not offer a theory of how NATO might adapt or what form it may assume in the future.[4] In particular, they do not explain the conditions under which NATO is more or less likely to expand or how far it will expand into Central and Eastern Europe. Thus they are unable to generate clear predictions as to the future of Europe's security arrangements.

ALLIANCE SIZE AND CHOICE OF ALLIES

Theories of political coalitions and portfolio diversification models can provide some answers as to the size of alliances, the constraints on alliance size, and the choice of allies. I will argue, however, that they are based on ambiguous concepts that are difficult to apply empirically. Moreover, they are underdeveloped in regard to the collective goods aspect of alliances, which is crucial to membership decisions.

Some authors have drawn on Riker's (1962) theory of political coalitions to predict the size of alliances in terms of minimum winning coalitions (Holsti et al. 1973, Zinnes 1970).[5] Applied to the question of NATO's possible eastward expansion, one could argue that the alliance will accept new members only if this expansion is necessary to win anticipated future wars or reach favorable settlements in anticipated political conflicts.

The transformation of Riker's theory into a theory of alliance size has proved to be difficult. Alliances and international security relations are often not zero-sum games. The notions of winning and power are difficult to conceptualize. The costs of forming and maintaining an alliance, including transaction costs, are hard to operationalize and measure. And the translation of Riker's notion of coalition size into a meaningful concept of size in alliance theory (number of states or something else) has remained controversial. Not surprisingly, propositions about alliance size based on the winning coalition argument have generally not stood up well to empirical testing (Holsti, Hopmann, and Sullivan 1973, Ward 1982:23-25).

Another approach to explaining alliance size and choices of alliance partners has been proposed by Conybeare (1992). Applying the theory of finance to alliances before the First World War, he identifies particular states in terms of their risks (standard error in manpower) and returns (manpower). Like diversified investment portfolios, diversified alliances produce a superior combination of risk and return and are thus more likely to form and endure. The idea of ally-risk as a choice variable is intuitive. It can be argued that NATO's choice in regard to new alliance members will be shaped by its desire to obtain a superior combination of risk and return. Riskier candidates for NATO membership will have to offer a greater return to make themselves attractive on the "alliance market."

There are, however, several problems with using the portfolio diversification model to explain NATO's choices of new allies. Risk and return, as well as risk aversion, are difficult to operationalize (Morrow 1987, Bueno de

Mesquita 1985, Conybeare 1992). Portfolio models are much better at assessing the pricing of allies in the alliance market and explaining alliance efficiency *ex post* than at predicting which alliances will form and which allies will be chosen. Such predictions would require the modeling of states' utility functions concerning alliance portfolios attributes in order to arrive at a general equilibrium model. Such utility functions would have to include the state's attitude towards risk as well as other variables, such as income and taste (Conybeare and Sandler 1990). The resulting model is bound to be extremely complex and has, not surprisingly, been suggested rather than developed.[6] Finally, and perhaps most important, the portfolio model ignores the impact of collective goods aspects on the choice of allies. It simply assumes that alliances produce pure public goods.[7]

The theory of clubs offers an explanation of alliance size and ally choices that is more parsimonious than the (as yet underdeveloped) portfolio model. It takes into account the collective goods aspect of alliances. And it avoids the conceptual problems of coalition theories.[8]

WHETHER SIZE MATTERS DEPENDS ON NATO'S SERVICES

This section explains why the nature of NATO's services, in terms of the private or public benefits they yield to their consumers, is among the principal explanatory variables for NATO's choice of allies. It reviews pure public goods models of NATO, explains why they are inaccurate, and outlines the consequences of impure public goods for alliance dynamics. This step in the argument is important because the theory of clubs is applicable to NATO only to the extent that NATO's services to its member states are impure public goods.

Olson and Zeckhauser (1966) argued that NATO's principal function was to deter an invasion by the Warsaw Pact countries. The most important instruments of deterrence were nuclear weapons. The U.S. nuclear umbrella over Western Europe and North America was a pure public good. Each NATO member enjoyed its protective effect without diminishing the benefits of other states, and no NATO member could be excluded from this security benefit.

Based on the assumption that NATO's services were a single and pure public good, Olson and Zeckhauser derived the following propositions. First, larger members contribute proportionally more to the collective good than smaller members.[9] Second, the overall defense provision level in NATO is pareto sub-optimal. Third, and most important for the argument here, the alliance can accept new member states without significant problems. New members increase the overall provision level of the public good (unless they are extremely poor and have no armed forces at all) and do not reduce the benefit of other members (deterrence is indivisible) (Olson and Zeckhauser 1966, Sandler 1993).

The historical record from 1949 until the end of the Cold War appears compatible with this argument. NATO accepted virtually every country that wanted to become a member; or inversely, every state that was asked by NATO to join did join. Greece and Turkey became members in 1952, West Germany in 1954, and Spain in 1982.

Since the end of the Cold War, the situation has changed. Hungary, Poland, and the Czech Republic asked for membership and were rejected. This evidence eliminates the proposition that similarity of political systems determines the choice of allies (Holsti et al. 1973:263). Turkey, an authoritarian state, was accepted, whereas the Czech Republic, a democracy, was not. The argument of balance of threat theory that NATO has not expanded because the threat has declined is equally unconvincing. The commonly expressed reason for not expanding NATO into Central and Eastern Europe is that this step would antagonize Russia and bring extreme nationalists to power. Governments in NATO countries seek to appease Russia by forgoing eastward expansion because an increased Russian threat could force them to increase their defense expenditure, which is politically unpopular. However, new NATO members have been accepted in the past irrespective of fierce Soviet opposition and threats. Acceptance of new members has, therefore, not necessarily been a response to an increased Soviet threat. It is unclear, in any event, whether increases in the Soviet threat have been causes or consequences of increased membership in NATO. The appeasement proposition is also weak because the economic decline of Russia inhibits it from engaging in another arms race with the West, should NATO expand eastward. To the contrary, risk averse military planners in the West might wish to be on the safe side and add to the capabilities of NATO by enlarging the alliance.[10]

The changing character of NATO's services, in terms of public or private goods, provides a better explanation of why NATO's ally choices have become more contentious in recent years. The pure public goods assumption, which implies that adding new members to the alliance is unproblematic, was questioned when, in the early 1970s, it was observed that the share of smaller allies in NATO's total military expenditure had increased (Russett 1970). This observation was inconsistent with the proposition that larger NATO allies shoulder a larger share of the burden. The principal explanation for this inconsistency has been that, since the late 1960s, NATO's services have increasingly become an impure public good. The contribution of each NATO member to the collective effort yields (private) benefits to the provider as well as (public) benefits to all members of the alliance.

If the argument that NATO's services have become an increasingly impure public good is correct, we should expect that requests for NATO membership become, *ceteris paribus*, more contentious. Adding a new member to the alliance produces benefits by increasing overall defense provision of the alliance unless the applicant has no military capability at all and is extremely poor.[11] On the cost side, adding a state under conditions of impure public goods produces a "thinning effect" (spatial rivalry). The extent of these costs depends on geography (longer borders to defend), technology, resource endowments of a prospective new member, negative spillover effects (reaction of the state or alliance that is balanced against), the internal stability of the applicant, and its relation with third states (e.g., the risk of NATO entanglement in disputes not related to Russia), and other factors.

Distinguishing private from public benefits in NATO is difficult (Beer 1972). The available data suggests, however, that NATO's services have indeed become more private over time. The increasing ratio of non-U.S. military expenditure in NATO (SIPRI 1993:367-70) indicates indirectly that relative expenditures for nuclear weapons, which are predominantly provided by the United States, are declining. The ratio of expenditure for conventional armaments over nuclear weapons is thus increasing.[12] This assessment is underlined by the fact that United States, British, and French expenditures for nuclear weapons have not increased significantly in the meantime.[13]

Assuming that expenditures for conventional armaments are associated with more private benefits than expenditures for nuclear weapons, we can argue that the private benefits of military expenditure in NATO have increased relative to public benefits. Conventional arms produce more private benefits because they allow individual states to limit damage on their own territory if NATO's deterrence fails; they yield economic benefits by supporting the provider's defense industry; they allow the provider to create or maintain jobs in the armed forces and arms industry, thus reducing unemployment; they support the provider in disaster relief, drug interdiction, protection against unconventional threats (e.g., terrorism or massive migration), or maintenance of domestic order; and they are instrumental in regional rivalries (e.g., between Turkey and Greece).

The benefits of conventional weapons are largely private because, if one country consumes these weapons through troop and weapon deployments, they are not available to other alliance members (rivalry). In the same vein, individual alliance partners can be excluded from benefits through troop and weapon deployment decisions. With nuclear forces, rivalry and the possibility of exclusion are very small. The share of commonly funded non-nuclear NATO services (headquarters, staff, integrated military command, pipelines, communication infrastructure, airfields, etc.), which are public goods, has remained small throughout NATO's existence (NATO 1989:245-51).

CLUB SIZE AND DEFENSE PROVISION LEVEL

Drawing on the economic theory of clubs (Buchanan 1965, Cornes and Sandler 1986, Fratianni and Pattison 1982, Sterbenz and Sandler 1992, Sandler and Tschirhart 1980), this section outlines a model according to which NATO members seek to optimize alliance size and defense provision level. The model assumes unitary rational actors who seek to maximize their net private benefit and examines the membership condition in homogeneous clubs. NATO can be regarded as a voluntary and self-organized club without third party enforcement. It involves a group of actors (states) that share the production costs of an impure public good. Because clubs allocate the production and consumption of public goods through market-like mechanisms, such as tolls or membership fees, they are hypothesized to be more efficient from the viewpoint of policymakers who control defense expenditure. This argument, which contradicts Olson's suboptimality theorem, has dominated the application of club theory to alliances. It is largely supported by macro-quantitative testing of joint product models (Conybeare and Sandler 1990, Sandler, Cauley, and Forbes 1980). I will concentrate on the membership condition, which has thus far not been systematically applied to alliances. In clubs that produce impure public goods there is a crowding (rivalry) problem. Adding new members diminishes the benefit or quality of services available to other members. This problem is equivalent to the thinning effect referred to above. NATO's member states face two critical issues. First, they have to devise a mechanism that prevents non-members from freeriding on NATO's services. NATO has dealt with this problem by extending full security guarantees and the nuclear umbrella only to member states. Moreover, only attacks against a member state can evoke automatic assistance by the alliance.[14]

NATO's second problem is to regulate membership under conditions where each member seeks to maximize its net benefit. This problem is crucial with regard to the question of expanding NATO. Figure 9.1, a modified geometric representation of Buchanan's (1965) model, shows a stylized version of the decision making problem.[15] The costs and benefits of each NATO member are shown on the vertical axis. The level of provision of the collective good (military expenditure may serve as a proxy) is shown on the horizontal axis. I assume that each member contributes an equal amount to the collective good and consumes NATO's services to an equal extent. Like most other club models, I also assume that NATO is a decentralized club with no transaction costs. Particularly the assumption of homogeneity of membership is unrealistic, but serves as a simple starting point. The next section extends the model to heterogeneous clubs. $Bn1$ indicates the benefit that the representative NATO member obtains through the alliance's services when NATO has $n1$ members. $Cn1$ indicates the cost to each member of providing NATO's services when NATO has $n1$ members.[16] The optimal provision level, assuming these cost and benefit functions, is $Q1$. At this point, the marginal benefit equals the marginal cost of NATO's services (the slope of $Bn1$ equals the slope of $Cn1$). Adding a new member to NATO would push the benefit curve down to $Bn2$ because of the crowding effect. In other words, due to the fact that NATO's services are an impure public good, adding a new member diminishes the benefits available to the other members.

Figure 9.1
The Provision of Collective Security in NATO

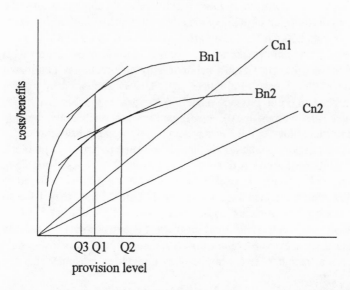

The cost curve Cn1 moves down to Cn2. This indicates that adding a country to NATO decreases the cost to each member, because each NATO member will have to spend less money if and only if the total provision level remains constant.[17]

This model shows that the overall provision level of the collective good and the size of NATO are interdependent. Attempts to expand the membership of the alliance while maintaining an optimal level of NATO's services to its member states must be associated with an increase in total contributions to the collective good.[18] The increase in the provision level is necessary to internalize the crowding effect.[19] If it is not feasible, adding a new member would make everyone in the alliance worse off.

In terms of Figure 9.1, the prospective new member, if accepted to the alliance, would produce a crowding effect. Hence the benefit curve for each member of the alliance would move to Bn2. If the applicant were a poor state that had no armed forces, for example, and if the old NATO members maintained the status quo in defense provision, the cost function would remain at Cn1. In this case, the optimal provision level would drop to Q3 and NATO's services would be pareto-inferior. Maintaining the provision level at Qn1 would require that each alliance member increase its contribution to the collective good.

If adding a new member would make NATO countries worse off, they are likely to reject the applicant, unless there are important costs or benefits exogenous to this model, such as ideological solidarity, issue-linkage, or high exclusion costs. Suboptimality means a higher probability that NATO assistance in case of attack or threat of attack will fail to materialize or will be delayed, or that NATO members will receive insufficient support from their allies if a crisis occurs.

HETEROGENEOUS ALLIANCES

In this section, I make the above model more realistic by extending it to heterogeneous alliances. To simplify the argument, heterogeneity is defined as differential demand for the services of the alliance (taste). Drawing on work by Cornes and Sandler (1986), Buchanan (1965), Sandler and Tschirhart (1980), and Oakland (1972), I outline a decision-theoretic model that examines pareto-optimal conditions for a single club (NATO) and takes into account members and non-members. The model assumes that exclusion and transaction costs are zero, decisions about membership are taken jointly, and existing NATO members and states applying for membership will not join another alliance if rejected or dissatisfied.[20]

NATO member i's utility (Ui) function has the following form.

$$U_i = U_i(y_i, x_i, c(k))$$
where $c_k = \partial c / \partial k > 0$ and $\partial U_i / \partial c \leq 0$ for $i = 1....s$ (1)

For reasons of simplicity, Ui is defined as the function of a private numéraire good (y), an impure public good (x), and a crowding function (c) that is based on average utilization of NATO's services (k), x_i and y_i increase utility, c decreases utility. x_i, the utilization rate of club member i, is a function of the probability and extent of use of NATO's services. s is NATO's size (number of members). Average utilization of NATO's services (k) is constrained by the fact that NATO members cannot allocate more than their total services to one alliance member; that is, $k = \Sigma_{i=1}^{s} x_i / X$, where $x_i \leq X$. In the case of NATO, it is safe to assume that x_i will be substantially smaller than X at any moment, particularly because crises or conflicts are almost never entirely confined to one member state. The equation $c_k = \partial c / \partial k > 0$ expresses the fact that average utilization of NATO's services (k) increases crowding costs. $\partial U_i / \partial c \leq 0$ for $i = 1....s$ indicates that crowding costs reduce utility. The crowding function is shaped by two opposing trends. Increased provision of the impure public good (X), that is, NATO's overall defense provision level, decreases crowding costs ($c_X = \partial c / \partial X < 0$). Increased utilization of NATO's services increases crowding costs ($\partial c / \partial x_i > 0$).

This argument can be easily extended to non-members (identified by *). Equation (2) indicates that non-member i's utility is independent of NATO's services; that is, i's utility is unaffected by the NATO's services and crowding costs.

$$U^*_i = U^*_i(y^*_i, 0, 0) \text{ for } i = s_{i+1}.....s^* \tag{2}$$

The pareto optimal membership condition can be derived by maximizing the marginal entrants utility function (see Sandler and Tschirhart 1980:1487-89). The first order membership condition is expressed by equation (3). It shows the net total effect on NATO of accepting an additional member.

$$\frac{U_s(.)}{\partial U_s/\partial y_s} - \frac{U^*_s(.)}{\partial U^*_s/\partial y^*_s} - (y_s - y^*_s) \geq -x_s (c_k/X)\sum_{i=1}^{s} MRS^i_{cy} \tag{3}$$

$0 < s < s^*$ (s^* is the number of actual and possible member states).

The net benefits of adding a new member ($i = s$) to the alliance must be equal or greater than the crowding costs produced by this state's entire consumption of NATO's services. Crowding costs produced by the new member are shown on the right side of the equation. The total utilization of NATO's services by the new member, x_s, is multiplied with the crowding costs produced by the consumption of one unit of NATO's services ($\sum_{i=1}^{s}(-c_k/X)$ MRS^i_{cy}). The two elements of net benefits of membership are shown on the left side. First, the gain in utility from having the applicant join the alliance is expressed as the difference in utility in terms of the private good between membership and non-membership. The second element concerns the change in private good consumption as a result of membership (similar to a membership fee for the new member).[21]

EXPANSION VERSUS COHESION: EMPIRICAL EVIDENCE AND PREDICTIONS

This part of the chapter applies the above arguments more closely to the question of expanding NATO. It examines how heterogeneity affects the supply and demand of NATO's services, how NATO's services and individual provision of the collective good are allocated in NATO, and how allocation mechanisms influence membership decisions.

The club model implies that, in order to arrive at efficient outcomes, NATO must be able to determine both the price of a unit of the alliance's services (toll)[22] and the membership condition. This task is easier in clubs with homogeneous membership than in heterogeneous clubs, such as NATO. In homogeneous clubs, membership and toll conditions are both part of the same discrete decision, because all members use the club's services to an equal extent. All members contribute the same amount to the collective good.

Heterogeneous clubs, on the other hand, are efficient only if tolls can be levied according to consumption. The crowding effect must be internalized by making heavy users, or users of more costly services, pay more than light users, irrespective of income. Burden-sharing in the war between the United Nations sponsored alliance and Iraq is a recent example. Particularly the United States received significant payments from Kuwait and Saudi Arabia for its military campaign to drive the Iraqi army out of Kuwait and protect Saudi Arabia (Bennett et al. 1994).

What effect would the expansion of NATO into Central and Eastern Europe have on the utility functions of NATO's members?[23] This effect depends primarily on the defense provision level of the prospective members, their demand for NATO's services, and the ability of NATO's allocation mechanisms to internalize crowding effects.

Troop and weapon deployment decisions are largely in the hands of individual NATO countries, both in times of peace and war (see below). Consequently, exclusion is possible not only with regard to non-members, but also members. NATO's services are also subject to a crowding effect (rivalry). As a result, the contributions of most NATO members to the collective good (e.g., military expenditure) have, at least since the 1980s, been a function of three variables: income (e.g., GNP); threat (e.g., the most threatening state's or alliance's military expenditures); and the other allies' contributions (e.g., their military expenditures, also called spill-in).

Threat and income drive individual contributions up. Spill-ins from other allies' defense efforts drive contributions down. The effect of spill-ins is hypothesized to be smaller than the effect of income and threat because of the impure public good character of NATO's services and the possibility of exclusion. However, large-n testing of the spill-in hypothesis has so far produced ambiguous results (Oneal and Whatley 1994, Sandler 1993, Conybeare and Sandler 1990).

Defense efforts of Hungary, Poland, and the Czech Republic (HPC), the most immediate candidates for full NATO membership, are likely to vary with the threat posed by Russia and regional and subnational conflict in Central and Eastern Europe. The dynamics of these threats are very difficult to predict. More predictable is that continuing economic hardship will probably have a negative impact on their defense provision for some time to come. The spill-in effect that NATO membership would have on HPC defense provision is a function of the probability and extent of NATO assistance in the event of crisis or war. The probability and extent of NATO assistance, in turn, are determined by NATO's club arrangements.

NATO members' consumption of the collective good is virtually impossible to measure in absolute units (e.g., number of troops). Moreover, the consumption rate of individual members is not independent.[24] However, those who decide on whether or not to expand NATO are likely to use at least informed guesses of the expected consumption of NATO's services by candidates for membership. The expected consumption is a product of the probability that NATO's services will be required and the extent of services that will be required. At present, the probability that NATO's services will be consumed by HPC is considerably greater than zero because there are contested borders and ethnic conflicts in the area, and there is considerable uncertainty about Russia's future behavior in its "near abroad." The extent of NATO services required could range anywhere from very small to enormous, depending on the type of conflict. In other words, the crowding costs produced by the new members, which are captured by the right side of equation (3), could be substantial. At the same time, the utility of NATO members, shown on the left side of equation (3), will probably not grow significantly if HPC join the alliance.

Both sides of equation (3) can be influenced by NATO's allocation mechanisms. NATO's services and individual members' contributions have been allocated through decentralized, market-like mechanisms rather than a rigid burden-sharing formula.[25] In peacetime, troop and weapon deployment decisions, for example, are coordinated by NATO bodies, but are ultimately taken by individual host and recipient governments. In the event of an attack against a NATO member, all other members are committed to automatic assistance to the victim. But individual governments have considerable freedom as to how much to contribute in this case. Exclusion and rivalry problems are presumably more pronounced in times of crisis or war than in peacetime.

The costs of excluding NATO members from the alliance's services, however, are presumably higher than the costs of excluding non-members. Outright reneging on alliance commitments could lead to the disintegration of the entire alliance, because retaliatory reneging of the victim state on its alliance commitments in the future could lead to a negative tit-for-tat spiral. Delayed or insufficient assistance may not destroy NATO but will decrease the cohesion and deterrence effect of the alliance, thus detracting from the future benefits of the alliance's members.

This analysis suggests that from the viewpoint of present-day NATO members, full security guarantees to HPC, and possibly other Central and Eastern European states, are undesirable. Such guarantees could have a negative impact on defense provision in these countries because they might increase spill-ins (in terms of expected supply of NATO services) at a time when decreasing income already has a depressing effect on defense provision. This argument is based on the assumption that a strong defensive capability of Central and Eastern European states is in the interest of NATO countries because it provides a buffer between NATO and Russia, whose future intentions and capability are uncertain but potentially threatening.

The Partnership for Peace Program (PFP) seems to be an efficient institutional solution from NATO's perspective. It potentially enhances cooperation with Russia, thus keeping the threat low.

A low threat allows NATO countries to adjust their defense provision downward, which is politically popular particularly under present conditions of budget deficits and slow economic growth. The PFP signals a somewhat increased probability and extent of NATO assistance to certain Central and Eastern European countries should they be threatened or attacked. Hence, it contributes to deterring Russia from interfering in these countries and reduces the incentive of these countries to again bandwagon with Russia.

On the other hand, NATO maintains the flexibility to increase (or decrease) the probability and extent of security assistance gradually. This flexibility decreases exclusion costs[26] and lowers incentives of free-riding and moral hazard on the part of HPC in peacetime. In times of crisis or war, NATO maintains the flexibility to reduce crowding costs by lowering the probability and extent of assistance to Central and Eastern Europe. NATO's decision to offer the PFP instead of full membership will leave certain Central and Eastern European countries, particularly HPC, dissatisfied. However, NATO's superior bargaining power in terms of its non-agreement costs[27] has turned the PFP into a take it or leave it proposition, and most countries have accepted the program.[28] Will HPC and perhaps other Central and Eastern European states ever receive full membership in NATO?

This analysis suggests that NATO's decision will hinge on the level of threat, particularly the threat posed by Russia, and the level of income of the applicants. If the threat to HPC increased substantially, and if there was a high risk that this development could have negative repercussions for NATO countries, it will be in NATO's interest to increase the probability and extent of security assistance towards full membership.

Full membership would send the strongest deterrence signal to the threatening power(s) because it involves the highest probability and extent of assistance to the victim. Income is likely to play a secondary role. If income increased substantially in HPC, NATO would have a greater incentive to extend membership to these countries because higher income could compensate for negative effects of spill-ins on defense provision. The likelihood that NATO will be transformed into an all-European security structure is very low.

CONCLUSION

The club model of NATO and the empirical evidence presented in this chapter suggest that the decline of the threat posed by Russia decreases the likelihood that NATO will expand into Central and Eastern Europe for the time being. This conclusion is consistent with the prediction of balance of threat theory, which is the dominant theory of alliance dynamics.

However, the theory of clubs offers a more systematic picture of the causal relationships between external threat, alliance cohesion, and membership decisions. Moreover, contrary to balance of threat theory, the club model and the empirical evidence suggest that NATO's institutional design can be modified to the extent of ensuring efficiency and cohesion of the alliance in a changing environment. It also indicates that NATO will probably not be transformed into an all-European security structure.

The club model outlined in this chapter is also applicable to other forms of regional integration, such as the European Union. The latter excludes non-members by imposing tariffs or other forms of protectionist measures, determines financial and other contributions from member states, and allocates monetary and non-monetary benefits to individual members. The question of alliance cohesion and expansion, and the tradeoffs involved, is analytically similar to the question of widening or deepening integration in the context of the European Union. The club model may thus serve as a starting point for further research on the dynamics of European political and economic integration.

NOTES

The research for this paper was supported by a grant from the Swiss National Fund for Scientific Research (Grant 8220-30628). Earlier versions of the paper were written during a stay at Harvard University's Center for International Affairs, whose support is gratefully acknowledged. I would like to thank Gunther Hellmann, Dieter Ruloff, Gerald Schneider, Markus Spillmann, and Patricia Weitsman for their comments on various versions of this paper.

1. Another important function of NATO has been to tie Germany into a security arrangement that would prevent it from reverting to the threatening posture it took until 1945.

2. Cohesion refers to the ability of member states of an alliance to agree on goals and policy to attain those goals (Holsti et al. 1973:16).

3. Balance of threat theorists can claim that NATO's current difficulties are indicators for its decline. Institutionalists can claim that these problems are merely an indicator of the usual problems that accompany the adaptation of international institutions to a changing environment. The only critical test of the two competing claims is the persistence of NATO over time; the longer it persists, the more the balance of threat proposition is in trouble. Such a test cannot be very attractive to those doing empirical research now.

4. Balance of threat theory is vague on the issue of adaptation partly because it has no arguments on internal versus external adaptation, or on the alignment behavior of third parties. Hellmann and Wolf (1993) touch briefly on this issue but do not discuss it in detail.

5. Riker (1962) argues that in n-person zero-sum games with complete information and the possibility of side-payments, rational actors will form minimum winning coalitions; that is, the coalition would fail to win if any of its members withdrew or did not join.

6. Conybeare (1992) offers a highly simplified version of such a model by hypothesizing that very risk-averse countries will choose low risk/low return allies and that highly risk-acceptant countries choose high risk/high return partners.

7. Conybeare (1992:83) argues that "each ally expects an equal share in the total alliance manpower."

8. Like Morrow (1991:908), I assume that there are no winning coalitions because wars and international politics are quite unpredictable. Adding to an alliance's capabilities increases the chances of winning in war and obtaining favorable outcomes without armed conflict. In principle, therefore, an alliance can grow in size until it possesses all capabilities in the international system. Morrow (1991:908) goes even further and argues that, since all nations shape the status quo, the only winning coalition is one that incorporates all capabilities in the international system. He defines a winning coalition as "a coalition that can determine the status quo regardless of the actions of other actors" (Morrow 1991:908). The club model outlined below shows, however, that Morrow's statement holds only to the extent that alliances can internalize the crowding costs that result from expansion.

9. The United States was, at that time, the only country with an important nuclear arsenal and it discouraged its European allies to acquire such weapons. European NATO members, for their part, were able to free-ride under the U.S. nuclear umbrella in terms of spending less on their (conventional) defense. This argument is reminiscent of the hegemonic stability argument (Keohane 1984).

10. Riker's (1962) argument that under high uncertainty (Russia's internal turmoil) alliances will be larger than just winning coalitions supports this argument.

11. If a state without an army is very poor, it cannot pay its allies to increase their defense provision level. However, such a state may be able to offer other types of benefits, such as providing a buffer zone between the other alliance members and a threatening state that does not belong to the alliance. Buffer zones can lower the costs of maintaining early warning systems or rapid reaction forces.

12. The reasons for the increased weight of conventional armaments in NATO include changes of strategic doctrine (e.g., "mutualy assured destruction" changed to "flexible response" from 1962 to 1967), technology (e.g., precision guided conventional munitions), and the nature of threats. In the 1990s, for example, the nuclear threat posed by Russia has decreased remarkably. U.S. and Russian nuclear warheads are being de-activated and dismantled by the thousands. Unconventional threats, such as terrorism, organized crime, and massive migration, have increased relative to traditional threats (at least in the perception of many NATO decision makers). Finally, it looks as if NATO could become increasingly involved in peacekeeping and peacemaking missions. Most of these tasks cannot be addressed with nuclear weapons.

13. These indicators were originally proposed by Sandler, Cauley, and Forbes 1980.

14. NATO thus avoids becoming entangled in defense commitments that individual NATO members have with non-members (e.g., France and its former colonies in Africa).

15. Adapted from Sandler 1992a:69.

16. The benefit curve reflects declining marginal returns from investment in NATO. To simplify the argument I assume that the cost curve is linear; that is, the cost of each extra unit of NATO services is constant.

17. Figure 9.1 derives from the following argument. The degree to which actor i is

willing to trade consumption of the impure public good X for the consumption of the private good y (the marginal rate of substitution, MRS^i_{xy}) is equivalent to the slope of Bni. The degree to which actor i is willing to trade production of the impure public against the private good (the marginal rate of transformation, MRT^i_{xy}), is equivalent to the slope of Cni for any group size. $MRS^i_{xy} = (\partial Vi/\partial X)/(\partial Vi/\partial yi)$; $MRT^i_{xy} = (\partial Ci/\partial X)/(\partial Ci/\partial yi)$. Vi is the benefit of NATO member i. Ci is the cost to member i of providing NATO's services. X is the total provision of the collective good. And yi is NATO member i's consumption of the impure public good. The optimal club size is reached when NATO member i equates its marginal rate of substitution (MRS) between group size and private good to its marginal rate of transformation (MRT) between the two. That is $MRS^i_{ny} = MRT^i_{ny}$. This equation results from differentiating net benefits [Vi - Ci; Vi = Vi(yi, X, n); Ci = Ci(yi, X, n)] with regard to yi, X, and n. $MRS^i_{ny} = (\partial Vi/\partial n)/(\partial Vi/\partial yi)$; $MRT^i_{ny} = (\partial Ci/\partial n)/(\partial Ci/\partial yi)$. See Buchanan 1965, Sandler and Tschirhart 1980, and Sandler 1992.

18. This argument derives from the fact that $MRS^i_{Qy} = MRT^i_{Qy}$, which expresses the provision level aspect of the decision making issue, and $MRS^i_{ny} = MRT^i_{ny}$, which expresses the membership decision making problem, include identical variables.

19. Clubs will only be inclusive (open) if crowding costs are zero or exclusion costs are extremely high. This is clearly not the case for NATO.

20. The latter assumption seems reasonable at the present time, when there is no alliance in Central and Eastern Europe and security integration in the framework of the Community of Independent States has largely failed.

21. The second component is required because the private good must have the same benefit at the margin before and after the new member joins the alliance. If this is not the case, reallocation is required. See Sandler and Tschirhart 1980:1490.

22. For the above model, the toll condition is $ck/X)\Sigma^s_{i=1} MRS^i_{cy} = MRS^j_{xy}$; j = 1....s. See Sandler and Tschirhart 1980:1489. In this model, each member pays the same price for a unit of service, but the total contribution differs depending on individual use of the club's services.

23. These utility functions were, in the above model, defined as $Ui = Ui(yi, xi, c(k))$, where $ck = \partial c/\partial k > 0$ and $\partial Ui/\partial c \leq 0$ for i = 1....s.

24. In most club models, the crowding effect is defined in an extremely simplified way. It is often assumed that crowding is a function of visitation rates in homogenous clubs, and that visitation rates follow a poisson distribution where the representative member's probability of n visits is $p(n) = e^{-\lambda}\lambda^n/n!$, n = 0, 1, 2,.... and where λ is the expected number of visits by each individual (Sterbenz and Sandler 1992). Such an assumption cannot be made with regard to NATO's crowding function.

25. Expenditures for common items such as the integrated military command, communications infrastructure, pipelines, or airfields are exceptions. But these expenditures amount only to around one percent of total military expenditures by NATO countries and are thus ignored here.

26. This argument implies that excluding members is costlier to NATO than excluding non-members (see above).

27. NATO's non-agreement costs have decreased considerably since the end of the Cold War because threats by a candidate for NATO membership that it could ally with the adversary if rejected are less credible than during the Cold War.

28. An explicit fee-for-service approach in NATO, one of the possible alternatives to internalize crowding effects produced by eastward expansion of NATO, is very

unlikely. First, it would be very difficult to define and measure units of utilization, on which contributions would have to be based. Something like insurance premiums would have to be devised, based on the probability of certain events occurring (such as war). Second, it would be extremely difficult to devise a generally accepted scheme that measures and compares the units of NATO's service and their prices. Opening up this question for debate could result in acrimonious distributional bargaining.

10

Towards a United States of Europe: Future Challenges and Potential Solutions

Thomas Bernauer, Gerald Schneider, and Patricia A. Weitsman

Cooperation among states is rarely simple. The high level of collaboration required for integration to progress brings an additional dimension of complexity. It is no wonder that the path towards European Union has been characterized by both stops and starts. Looking ahead, it would appear that additional challenges have yet to be met. This chapter assesses the issues on the European agenda that will present future challenges. After identifying some of the potential hindrances to future integration, we will then discuss the extent to which the theoretical framework presented in this volume facilitates our understanding of these problems and offers possible solutions to them. We think that applied formal modeling reveals potential trouble spots and also offers at least partial solutions.

We distinguish between the formal and the "informal" agenda of the organization. Many issues on the formal agenda, including the negotiations among member states to develop a European constitution, are controversial. The process of continuing enlargement in the number of states joining the Union will intensify the discussion of whether widening or deepening should be the organization's priority. Any attempt by the Commission or other supranationalist actors to expand the integration agenda will amplify the resistance of some member states. One issue on the "informal" agenda that we see as central to determining the level of dissent or cooperation among Union states is the increasing importance of direct legislation. Some member states of the European Union require referendums; in others, the practice is growing.

THE FORMAL AGENDA OF THE EUROPEAN UNION

There are a number of issues that will dominate the agenda of the European Union for some time to come. These topics range from decision making reforms over the implementation of aspects of the Maastricht treaty to the widening of European integration into Central and Eastern Europe. Some of the chapters of this volume addressed directly or by implication these issues on the formal agenda of the EU.

Institutional innovations require careful analysis. Spatial modeling, with its implicit focus on decision making procedures, is particularly helpful in this respect. Studies have already facilitated our understanding of how the innovations of the Single European Act and the Maastricht treaty have altered the internal balance of power within the European Union. We have seen how the cooperation procedure transformed the European Parliament into an actor with positive, but conditional, agenda setting power. Schneider's (1995) analysis of the codecision procedure of the Treaty on European Union shows that the logic of integration has been completely transformed with this new legislative rule, creating new hindrances for deepening integration. Hence, by employing spatial models to aspects of the integration process, we realize that if future reforms do not address the tension between qualified majority voting and consensus-oriented policy making, member states will continue to be able to resort to a hidden veto right.

In the reform debate, the EU will also have to reconsider the size of the Commission and the European Parliament as well as the distribution of voting power among the member states. Resistance will arise primarily from small and less wealthy member states because the current system is particularly beneficial to them. In the past, northern member states often favored an expansion of the cohesion fund, the structural fund, or the farming subsidies to gain southern members' support for a deepening of integration. In the future, such generosity might be impossible. The competition over the organization's redistributive measures is already fierce and could potentially increase after further enlargements. Most newcomers would be net-recipients of these funds.

Because such crucial decision making rules have distributional effects, the reform debate will inevitably address the threshold for qualified majority voting in the Council of Ministers. This discussion should involve a reassessment of weighted voting. The results of formal theory demonstrate that the distribution of voting weights does not reflect the *a priori* voting power of an actor (for a recent application to the European Union, see Herne and Nurmi 1993). This paradoxical result dictates a need for political theorists to develop new decision rules to prevent non-monotonicity effects (discrepancies between formal and actual voting power). In an interesting paper, Holler (1987) proposes a randomized decision rule to avoid incongruence between the voting weight and the actual voting power of an actor. Unfortunately, implementing such alternatives is difficult.

The EU reform discussion in the domain of the Common Foreign and Security Policy will focus on the question of how consensus solutions can be obtained despite diverging state interests. The formal analysis of regimes (Morrow 1994) offers a promising avenue of research to analyze the current failures of collaboration. It is especially urgent to understand the difficulties in coordinating security policy, given that the end of the Cold War has dramatically altered the nature of the international system and with it the requirements of European defense. The theory of clubs offers a starting point for probing the limits of security integration in Europe. It examines the tradeoffs between expanding membership on the one hand and stability and depth of integration on the other hand.

The instability in some parts of Central and Eastern Europe leads to a need for new instruments in dealing with emerging security risks. Specific institutional mechanisms and strategies of international organizations may facilitate cooperation among states. For example, rules that guide the admittance of new members to an organization may be used in a way that elicits cooperation. Conditions for admitting states to an organization might include positive incentives coupled with certain penalties for noncompliance. An example of this are the conditions imposed on states seeking to become members of the Council of Europe. One such condition is that member states respect minority rights domestically. All of these strategies to elicit cooperative behavior may be evaluated by developing models to assess their effectiveness.

Formal work may be a vehicle for understanding the conditions under which European Union member states will unify their foreign and security policies. In the fluid setting of EU policy making, trust among the member states is the crucial category to explain the achievements and failures of the organization's main foreign policy instrument the so-called European Political Cooperation. Under conditions of uncertainty, member states might fail to adopt a forceful measure despite their wish of acting together and to speak with one voice in foreign affairs (Schneider and Seybold 1995).

A further source of internal disagreement are some of the pending membership applications to the organization.The larger question that lies behind such controversies is over the "right" size of an integration area. Most economic models which are used to analyse such problems are based on narrowly defined efficiency criteria. They do not take into account the wider political benefits of inegration such as conflict prevention. Some contributions in this volume show that is is possible to move beyond the traditional frameworks and to explain large-scale integration and disintegration processes over extended time-frames.

THE INFORMAL AGENDA OF THE EUROPEAN UNION

Presenting additional potential problems to continued future integration is the fact that the domestic populations in Union member states are far from unequivocal in their support for the integration process. This is becoming increasingly salient with the growing practice of holding referendums for the ratification of integration agreements. Bringing the public back in to questions of foreign policy has a number of implications, both theoretically and in predicting the future course of Europe. While in the past the fate of integration was in the hands of mavericks like President De Gaulle or Prime Minister Thatcher, increasingly it is the public that decides the future of the continent.

Formal models (Lupia 1992, Schneider and Weitsman 1996) show us the perils of direct democracy. This work, however, also allows us to point out how a regression back to the days of indivisible sovereignty may be prevented. Contrary to the conventional wisdom (Tocqueville (1986[1835], Friedrich 1968), voters do care about foreign policy. Referendums are not merely opportunities to signal their satisfaction with the government. The two-level aspect of referendums consequently requires decisionmakers to encourage a vote for integration in a number of ways. First, to prevail in these plebiscites it is essential to couple the integration treaty with a domestic reform program. Second, referendum campaigns have a better chance of success when the government is unified in its support for the treaty. In cases where parties are divided over the treaty up for review, the confidence of voters aligned with those parties will go down. Third, proponents of EU membership must try to divide the unholy coalition of the extreme left and right who tend to come together to campaign against integration agreements. And finally, campaigners in support of an integration referendum must avoid complicated messages and the use of intimidation tactics. Decisionmakers cannot frighten their constituencies into compliance; they must illuminate the benefits in a simple way.

In essence, the linkage between the domestic and international level makes ratification of integration agreements via referendum a very complex issue indeed. The fragility of cooperation is exacerbated by the very real conflicts within states over relinquishing sovereignty in the economic and political realm. As yet, there is no common European voice on foreign or security policy. The harmonization of defense and foreign policies is, perhaps, the most symbolic manifestation of supranationalism in the Maastricht treaty. Denmark's response was unambivalent and unequivocal: No opt-out, no ratification. States historically pursuing a policy of non-alignment and neutrality will have a hard time selling an integrated strategy for defense to its constituents. Since the last enlargement, four EU member states are neutral.

RATIONAL CHOICE AND ITS ALTERNATIVES

We have sought, in this volume, to demonstrate how rational choice approaches to the study of integration elucidate and explain the stops and starts in European integration. The different contributions have demonstrated the explanatory power of rational choice approaches in the realm of studies on regional integration. We have proposed a new research program that takes the classical questions seriously, but tries to explain them in a rigorous fashion. Such a reorientation allows us to overcome some of the major drawbacks of traditional studies in the field, namely their ad hoc nature and the lack of cumulation in our knowledge about regional integration.

On a superficial level, there is nothing new in our proposed research program. However, the contributions to this volume clearly point out the advantages of formal modeling over traditional research on regional integration. A first innovative feature of the research program is that it explicitly links individual attitudes towards European integration to collective decisions. Second, the approach views the creation of new institutions as a purposeful endeavor. A third central accomplishment of the research program is that it allows us to synthesize liberal and neorealist explanations of regional cooperation. Micro-level approaches can inform us of the conditions under which cooperation occurs and the conditions under which integration fails. Rationalist integration theory thus allows to analyse the dynamics of integration.

In sum, rational choice approaches are useful for the study of regional cooperation. In our view, they make it possible to question commonly held assumptions about the process of integration. By laying the microfoundations of foreign policy making, formal reasoning provides a parsimonious approach that eliminates the need to explain everything at once; yet it equips us with the necessary tools to understand the stops and starts in regional integration, both from a historical perspective and also for the future.

REFERENCES

Achen, Christopher H. 1992. "Social Psychology, Demographic Variables, and Linear Regression: Breaking the Iron Triangle in Voting Research." *Political Behavior* 14:195-211.

Akerlof, George A. 1991. "Procrastination and Obedience." *American Economic Review* 81:1-19.

Alesina, Alberto, and Vittorio Grilli. 1992. "The European Central Bank: Reshaping Monetary Politics in Europe." In *Establishing a Central Bank: Issues in Europe and Lessons from the U.S.,* eds. M. Canzoneri, V. Grilli, and P. Masson. Cambridge, MA: Cambridge University Press.

——. 1993. "On the Feasibility of a One-Speed or Multispeed European Monetary Union." *Economics and Politics* 5(2):145-165.

Anderson, Benedict. 1983. *Imagined Communities: Reflections on the Origin and Spread of Nationalism.* London: Verso.

Andreoni, James. 1988. "Privately Provided Public Goods in a Large Economy: The Limits of Altruism." *Journal of Public Economics* 35:57-73.

App, Rolf. 1987. "Initiativen und ihre Wirkungen auf Bundesebene seit 1974." *Annuaire Suisse de Science Politique* 27:189-206.

Arrow, Kenneth J. 1951 (rev.1963). *Social Choice and Individual Values.* New York: John Wiley and Sons.

Arthur, W. Brian. 1994. *Increasing Returns and Path Dependence in the Economy.* Ann Arbor, MI: University of Michigan Press.

Asmus, Ronald D., Richard L. Kugler, and F. Stephen Larrabee. 1993."Building a New NATO." *Foreign Affairs* 72:28-40.

Attina, Fulvio. 1990. "The Voting Behaviour of the European Parliament Members and the Problem of Europarties." *European Journal of Political Research* 18:557-79.

Axelrod, Robert. 1984. *The Evolution of Cooperation.* New York: Basic Books.

Baldwin, David A. 1985. *Economic Statecraft.* Princeton: Princeton University Press.

Baron, David, and John Ferejohn. 1989. "Bargaining in Legislatures." *American Political Science Review* 89:1181-1206.

Barro, Robert, and David Gordon. 1983a. "Rules, Discretion and Reputation in a Model of Monetary Policy." *Journal of Monetary Economics* 12:101-22.

———. 1983b. "A Positive Theory of Monetary Policy in a Natural Rate Model." *Journal of Political Economy* 91:589-610.

Bayoumi, Tamin, and Barry Eichengreen. 1992. "Shocking Aspects of European Monetary Unification." CEPR Discussion Paper No. 643.

Bean, Charles R. 1992. "Economic and Monetary Union in Europe." *Journal of Economic Perspectives* 6:31-52.

Bean, Richard. 1973. "War and the Birth of the Nation State." *Journal of Economic History* 33:203-221.

Becker, Gary. 1983. "A Theory of Competition among Pressure Groups for Political Influence." *Quarterly Journal of Economics* 98:371-400.

Beer, Francis A. 1972. *The Political Economy of Alliances: Benefits, Costs, and Institutions in NATO.* Beverly Hills: Sage. Sage Professional Papers in International Studies Series, Vol.1.

Bennett, Andrew, Joseph Lepgold, and Danny Unger. 1994. "Burden-sharing in the Persian Gulf War." *International Organization* 48:39-75.

Bieber, Roland, J. Pantalis, and J. Schoo. 1986. "Implications of the Single Act for the European Parliament." *Common Market Law Review* 23:767-92.

Bieber, Roland. 1988. "Legislative Procedure for the Establishment of the Single Market." *Common Market Review* 25:711-724.

Binmore, Ken. 1990. *Essays on the Foundation of Game Theory.* Cambridge, MA: Basil Blackwell.

Binmore, Ken, and Larry Samuelson. 1994. "Muddling Through Noisy Equilibrium Selection." Mimeo, University College of London and University of Wisconsin.

Bogdanor, Vernon. 1989. "The June 1989 European Elections and the Institutions of the Community." *Government and Opposition* 24:199-214.

Borner, Silvio, Aymo Brunetti, and Thomas Straubhaar. 1990. *Schweiz AG. Vom Sonderfall zum Sanierungsfall.* Zürich: Verlag NZZ.

———. 1994. *Die Schweiz im Alleingang.* Zürich: Verlag NZZ.

Bowler, Shaun, and David M. Farrell. 1993. "Legislator Shirking and Voter Monitoring Impacts of European Parliament Electoral Systems Upon Legislator/Voter Relationships." *Journal of Common Market Studies* 31:45-69.

Brenner, Michael J. 1991. "EC: Confidence Lost." *Foreign Policy* 91:24-43.

Brunetti, Aymo. 1992. *Politisches System und Wirtschaftswachstum.* Chur: Rüegger.

Buchanan, James M. 1965. "An Economic Theory of Clubs." *Economica* 32:1-14.

Buchanan, James M., and Gordon Tullock. 1962. *The Calculus of Consent.* Ann Arbor, MI: University of Michigan Press.

Buchanan, James M., and Y. J. Yoon, eds. 1993. *The Return to Increasing Returns.* Ann Arbor, MI: University of Michigan Press.

Bueno de Mesquita, Bruce, and Frans N. Stokman, eds. 1994. *Twelve Into One:*

Models of Decision-Making in the European Community. New Haven: Yale University Press.

Bueno de Mesquita, Bruce. 1985. "The War Trap Revisited: A Revised Expected Utility Model." *American Political Science Review* 79:56-77.

Bundesrat. 1993. *Bericht über die Aussenpolitik der Schweiz in den 1990er Jahren.* Bern: Bundeshaus.

Bureau, Dominique, and Paul Champsaur. 1992. "Fiscal Federalism and European Economic Integration." *American Economic Review, Papers and Proceedings* 82:88-92.

Burley, Anne-Marie, and Walter Mattli. 1993. "Europe Before the Court: A Political Theory of Legal Integration." *International Organization* 47:41-76.

Calhoun, Craig. 1991. "Indirect Relationships and Imagined Communities: Large-Scale Social Integration and the Transformation of Everyday Life." In *Social Theory for a Changing Society*, eds. Pierre Bourdieu and James S. Coleman. Boulder, CO: Westview.

Calvert, Randall L. 1989. "Reciprocity Among Self-Interested Actors: Uncertainty, Asymmetry, and Distribution." In *Models of Strategic Choice in Politics*, ed. Peter C. Ordeshook. Ann Arbor, MI: University of Michigan Press: 269-293.

Cameron, David R. 1992. "The 1992 Initiative: Causes and Consequences." In *Euro-Politics*, ed. A. Sbragia. Washington, D.C.: Brookings.

Canzoneri, Matthew. 1985. "Monetary Policy Games and the Role of Private Information." *American Economic Review* 75:1056-70.

Canzoneri, Matthew, and Behzad Diba. 1991. "Fiscal Deficits, Financial Integration and a Central Bank for Europe." Presented at the NBER-TCER-CEPR conference on Fiscal Policy in Open Macro Economies.

Canzoneri, Matthew, and Dale Henderson. 1991. *Monetary Policy in Interdependent Economies: A Game Theoretic Approach.* Cambridge, MA: MIT Press.

Caporaso, James A. 1993. "Toward a Sociology of International Institutions: Comments on the Articles by Smouts, de Senarclens and Jonsson." *International Social Science Journal* 45:479-489.

Caporaso, James A., and D. P. Levine. 1992. *Theories of Political Economy.* New York: Cambridge University Press.

Carr, Edward H. 1939. *The Twenty Years' Crisis, 1919-1939.* London: Macmillan.

Cederman, Lars-Erik. 1994a. "Emergent Polarity: Analyzing State-Formation and Power Politics." *International Studies Quarterly* 38:501-534.

———. 1994b. "Emergent Actors: How States and Nations Develop and Dissolve." Ph.D. dissertation, Department of Political Science: University of Michigan.

Chamberlin, John. 1974. "Provision of Collective Goods as a Function of Group Size." *American Political Science Review* 68:707-716.

Coase, Ronald H. 1960. "The Problem of Social Cost." *Journal of Law and Economics* 3:1-44.

Cohen, Benjamin J. 1993. "Beyond EMU: The Problem of Sustainability." *Economics and Politics* 5:187-201.

Cole, John, and Francis Cole. 1993. *The Geography of the European Community.*

London: Routledge.

Coleman, James S., and Thomas J. Fararo. 1992. *Rational Choice Theory: Advocacy and Critique*. Newbury Park, CA: Sage Publications, Inc.

Commission of the European Communities. 1981. *European Economy*. Brussels: EC.

Commission of the European Communities (Directorate General for Economic and Financial Affairs). 1991. *European Economy: Annual Economic Report 1991-92*. Brussels: EC.

Congressional Quarterly Almanac. 1991. *101st Congress 2nd Session*. Washington, D.C.

Connor, Walker. 1972. "Nation-Building or Nation-Destroying." *World Politics* 24:319-355.

———. 1994. "Self Determination: The New Phase." In *Ethnonationalism: The Quest for Understanding*, ed. Walker Connor. Princeton: Princeton University Press.

Conybeare, John A. 1992. "A Portfolio Diversification Model of Alliances: The Triple Alliance and Triple Entente, 1879-1914." *Journal of Conflict Resolution* 36:53-85.

Conybeare, John A., and Todd Sandler. 1990. "The Triple Entente and the Triple Alliance 1880-1914: A Collective Goods Approach." *American Political Science Review* 84:1197-1206.

Cook, Karen Schweers, and Margaret Levi. 1990. *The Limits of Rationality*. Chicago: The University of Chicago Press.

Corbett, Richard. 1989. "Testing the New Procedures: The European Parliament's First Experiences with its New 'Single Act' Powers." *Journal of Common Market Studies* 4: 359-72.

Cornes, Richard, and Todd Sandler. 1986. *The Theory of Externalities, Public Goods, and Club Goods*. Cambridge, MA: Cambridge University Press.

Dahl, Robert, and Edward Tufte. 1973. *Size and Democracy*. Stanford: Stanford University Press.

De la Torre, Augusto, and Margaret Kelly. 1992. *Regional Trade Arrangements* (Occasional Paper 93). Washington, DC: International Monetary Fund.

De Melo, Jaime, and Arvind Panagariya, eds. 1993. *New Dimensions in Regional Integration*. Cambridge, MA: Cambridge University Press.

De Zwaan, J. W. 1986. "The Single European Act: Conclusion of a Unique Document." *Common Market Law Review* 23:747-65.

Delley, Jean-Daniel. 1978. *L'initiative populaire en Suisse. Mythe et réalité de la démocratie directe*. Lausanne: L'âge d'homme.

———. 1987. "La démocratie directe." *Pouvoirs* 43:102-115.

Delors, Jacques et al., 1989. "Report on Economic and Monetary Union in the European Community." Committee for the Study of Economic and Monetary Union. Brussels: EC.

Demsetz, Harold. 1967. "Toward a Theory of Property Rights." *American Economic Review* 59:347-359.

Deutsch, Karl W. 1966a. *Nationalism and Social Communication; an Inquiry into the Foundations of Rationality*. Cambridge, MA: MIT Press.

————. 1966b. *Nerves of Government*. New York: The Free Press.

————. 1976. *Die Schweiz als ein paradigmatischer Fall politischer Integration*. Bern: Haupt.

Deutsch, Karl.W., S. A. Burell, R. A. Kann, M. Lee, M. Lichtermann, and R.W. von Wagenen. 1957. *Political Community and the North Atlantic Area*. Princeton: Princeton University Press.

Deutsch, Karl W., L. J. Edinger, Richard C. Macridis, and R. L. Merritt. 1967. *France, Germany, and the Western Alliance; a Study of Elite Attitudes on European Integration and World Politics*. New York: Scribner.

Dinan, Desmond. 1994. *Ever Closer Union: An Introduction to the European Community*. Boulder: Lynne Rienner.

Dolado, Juan J., Mark Griffiths, and Jorge Padilla. 1994. "Delegation in International Monetary Policy Games." *European Economic Review* 38:1057-1069.

Downing, Brian M. 1992. *The Military Revolution and Political Change: Origins of Democracy and Autocracy in Early Modern Europe*. Princeton: Princeton University Press.

East, Maurice. 1973. "Size and Foreign Policy Behavior: A Test of Two Models." *World Politics* 25:556-576.

Edward, David. 1987. "The Impact of the Single Act on the Institutions." *Common Market Law Review* 24:19-30.

Eggertson, Thrainn. 1990. *Economic Behavior and Institutions*. Cambridge, MA: Cambridge University Press.

Eichenberg, Richard C., and Russell Dalton. 1993. "Public Support for European Integration." *International Organization* 47:507-534.

Eldredge, Niles, and Stephen J. Gould. 1972. "Punctuated Equilibria: an Alternative to Phyletic Gradualism." In *Models in Paleobiology*, ed. T. Schopf. San Francisco: Freeman, Cooper & Co.: 82-115.

Elster, Jon. 1983. *Explaining Technical Change*. Cambridge, MA: Cambridge University Press/Oslo: Universitetsforlaget.

Erikson, Robert. 1989. "Economic Conditions and the Presidential Vote." *American Political Science Review* 83:567-576.

————. 1990. "Economic Conditions and the Congressional Vote: A Review of the Macrolevel Evidence." *American Journal of Political Science* 34:373-399.

Eulau, Heinz, and Michael Lewis-Beck. 1985. *Economic Conditions and Electoral Outcomes: The United States and Western Europe*. New York: Agathon Press.

European Commission. 1990. "One Market, One Money." *European Economy* 44.

Farrell, P.O. 1983. "Ireland." In *Industrial Mobility and Migration in the European Community*, eds. Leo Klaassen and Willem Molle. Aldershot: Gower.

Fearon, James D. 1993. "Cooperation and Bargaining Under Anarchy." University of Chicago: Manuscript.

Fenno, Richard F. Jr. 1973. *Congressmen in Committees*. Boston: Little Brown and Co.

————. 1978. *Home Style*. Boston: Little Brown and Co.

Financial Times. 1992. *Special Survey on Norway*. June 2.

————. 1993. *Special Survey on Finland*. October 11.

Fitzmaurice, John. 1988. "An Analysis of the European Community's Co-operation Procedure." *Journal of Common Market Studies* 4:389-400.

Forrester, Jay W. 1961. *Industrial Dynamics*. Cambridge, MA: MIT Press.

———. 1971a. *World Dynamics*. Cambridge, MA: MIT Press.

———. 1971b. "Counterintuitive Behavior of Social Systems." *Technology Review* 74:52-68.

Fratianni, Michele, and John Pattison. 1982. "The Economics of International Organizations." *Kyklos* 35:244-61.

Frey, Bruno S., and Reiner Eichenberger. 1989. "Should Social Scientists Care About Choice Anomalies?" *Rationality and Society* 1:101-122.

Friedman, David. 1977. "A Theory of the Size and Shape of Nations." *Journal of Political Economy* 87:59-77.

Friedman, James. 1971. "A Noncooperative Equilibrium for Supergames." *Review of Economic Studies* 38:1-12.

Friedrich, Carl Joachim. 1968. *Constitutional Government and Democracy: Theory and Practice in Europe and America*. Waltham, MA: Blaisdoll.

Fudenberg, Drew, and Eric Maskin. 1986. "The Folk Theorem in Repeated Games with Discounting or with Incomplete Information." *Econometrica* 54:533-554.

Gabel, Matthew. 1994. "Understanding the Public Constraint on European Integration: Affective Sentiments, Utilitarian Evaluations, and Public Support." University of Rochester: PhD. Dissertation.

Gabel, Matthew, and Harvey Palmer. 1994. "National Interest, Public Opinion, and European Integration: A Political-Economy Model of National-Level Public Support." University of Rochester: Manuscript.

Garrett, Geoffrey. 1991. "International Cooperation and Institutional Choice." *International Organization* 45:539-564.

———. 1992. "International Cooperation and Institutional Choice: The European Community's Internal Market." *International Organization* 46:533-60.

———. 1993. "The Politics of Maastricht." *Economics and Politics* 5:105-123.

Garret, Geoffrey, and Barry Weingast. 1992. "Ideas, Interests and Institutions: Constructing the EC's Internal Market." In *Ideas and Foreign Policy*, eds. Judith Goldstein and Robert Keohane. Ithaca, NY: Cornell University Press: 173-206.

Geddes, Barbara. 1990. "How the Cases You Choose Affect the Answers You Get: Selection Bias in Comparative Politics." *Political Analysis* 2:131-150.

Gellner, Ernest. 1964. *Thought and Change*. London: Weidenfeld & Nicolson.

———. 1983. *Nations and Nationalism*. Ithaca, NY: Cornell University Press.

George, Stephen. 1985. *Politics and Policy in the European Community*. London: Oxford University Press.

Germann, Raimund E. 1994. *Staatsreform. Der Uebergang zur Konkurenzdemokratie*. Bern: Haupt.

Gersick, Connie J. 1991. "Revolutionary Change Theories: a Multilevel Exploration of the Punctuated Equilibrium Paradigm." *Academy of Management Review* 16:10-36.

Giddens, Anthony. 1985. *The Nation-State and Violence: Volume Two of A Contemporary Critique of Historical Materialism*. Berkeley: University of California Press.

Gilligan, Thomas W., and Keith Krehbiel. 1987. "Collective Decision-Making and Standing Committees: An Informational Rationale for Restrictive Amendment Procedures." *Journal of Law, Economics and Organization* 3:287-335.

Gilpin, Robert. 1981. *War and Change in World Politics*. Cambridge: Cambridge University Press.

Godfrey, Wynne. 1980. "The United Kingdom and the Community Budget." In *Britain in Europe*, ed. William Wallace: Heinemann.

Greenberg, Joseph. 1979. "Consistent Majority Rule over Compact Sets of Alternatives." *Econometrica* 47:627-36.

Grieco, Joseph M. 1990. *Cooperation among Nations*. Ithaca and London: Cornell University Press.

Guttman, Joel M. 1978. "Understanding Collective Action: Matching Behavior." *American Economic Association Papers and Proceedings* 68:251-255.

——. 1987. "A Non-Cournot Model of Voluntary Collective Action." *Economica* 54:1-19.

Haas, Ernst B. 1958a. *The Uniting of Europe: Political, Social, and Economic Forces 1950-57*. London: Stevens and Sons.

——. 1958b. *Beyond the Nation-State*. Stanford: Stanford University Press.

——. 1964. *Beyond the Nation-State. Functionalism and International Organization*. Stanford: Stanford University Press.

——. 1971. "The Study of Regional Integration: Reflections on the Joy and Anguish of Pretheorizing." In *Regional Integration, Theory and Research*, eds. Leon N. Linberg and Stuart A. Scheingold. Cambridge, MA: Harvard University Press.

——. 1975. *The Obsolescence of Regional Integration Theory*. Berkeley: University of California: Institute of International Studies.

Hammond, Thomas H., and Gary J. Miller. 1987. "The Core of the Constitution." *American Political Science Review* 81:1155-74.

Harries, Owen. 1993. "The Collapse of The West." *Foreign Affairs* 72:41-53.

Heckscher, Gunnar. 1966. *The Role of Small Nations—Today and Tomorrow*. London: University of London Athlone Press.

Hellmann, Gunther, and Reinhard Wolf. 1993. "Neorealism, Neoliberal Institutionalism, and the Future of NATO." *Security Studies* 3:3-43.

Herne, Kaisa, and Hannu Nurmi. 1993. "The Distribution of A Priori Voting Power in the EC Council of Ministers and the European Parliament." *Scandinavian Political Studies* 16:269-285.

Hirshleifer, Jack. 1983. "From Weakest-link to Best-shot. The Voluntary Provision of Public Goods." *Public Choice* 41:371-386.

Hoadley, J. Stephen. 1980. "Small States as Aid Donors." *International Organization* 34:121-137.

Hoagland, Jim. 1992. "A Bogeyman Theory of Government." *Washington Post*. June 2.

Hoffman, Stanley. 1966. "Obstinate or Obsolete? The Fate of the Nation-State and the

Case of Western Europe." *Daedalus* 95:862-915.

Hogan, Michael J. 1987. *The Marshall Plan. America, Britain, and the Reconstruction of Western Europe, 1947-1952*. Cambridge, MA: Cambridge University Press.

Hogarth, Robin M., and Melvin W. Reder. 1987. *Rational Choice: The Contrast between Economics and Psychology*. Chicago: The University of Chicago Press.

Holler, Manfred J. 1987. "Paradox Proof Decision Rules in Weighted Voting." In *The Logic of Multiparty Systems*, ed. M. J. Holler. Dordrecht: Martinus Nijhoff: 425-436.

Holsti, Ole R., P. Terrence Hopmann, and John D. Sullivan. 1973. *Unity and Disintegration in International Alliances: Comparative Studies*. New York: Wiley.

Hoppe, Hans-Joachim. 1994. "Die Lage der mittel- und südosteuropäischen Länder." *Aussenpolitik* 45:134-45.

Hösli, Madeleine O. 1993. "Admission of European Free Trade Association States to the European Community: Effects on Voting Power in the European Community Council of Ministers." *International Organization* 47:629-643.

———. 1994 (forthcoming). "The Political Economy of Subsidiarity." In *The Political Economy of European Integration*, ed. Finn Laursen. Maastricht: European Institute of Public Administration.

Huelshoff, Michael G. 1994. "Domestic Politics and Dynamic Issue Linkage: a Reformulation of Integration Theory." *International Studies Quarterly* 38:255-279.

Hug, Simon. 1994. "Mobilisation et loyauté au sein de l'électorat." In *Elites politiques et peuple. Analyse des votations fédérales 1970-1987*, ed. Yannis Papadopoulos. Lausanne: Réalités sociales: 161-201.

IMF (International Monetary Fund). 1984. *Yearbook*. Washington, D.C.: IMF.

———. 1991 *Yearbook*. Washington, D.C.: IMF

Inglehart, Ronald. 1970a. "Cognitive Mobilization and European Identity." *Comparative Politics* 3:45-70.

———. 1970b. "Public Opinion and Regional Integration." *International Organization* 24:746-795.

———. 1977. *The Silent Revolution. Changing Values and Political Styles among Western Publics*. Princeton, NJ: Princeton University Press.

———. 1990. *Culture Shifts in Advanced Industrial Society*. Princeton, NJ: Princeton University Press.

Isaac, R. Mark, James M. Walker, and Susan H. Thomas. 1984. "Divergent Evidence on Free Riding: An Experimental Examination of Possible Explanations." *Public Choice* 43:113-149.

Isaac, R. Mark, Kenneth F. McCue, and Charles R. Plott. 1985. "Public Goods Provision in an Experimental Environment." *Journal of Public Economics* 26:51-74.

Jacobs, Francis, and Richard Corbett. 1990. *The European Parliament* Harlow, Essex: Longman.

Jacobson, Harold K., William Reisinger, and Todd Mathers. 1986. "National

Entanglements in International Govermental Organizations." *American Political Science Review* 80:141-159.

Jacoby, W. 1994a. "Industrial Relations in Eastern Germany: the Politics of Imitation." Presented at the Harvard University Center for European Studies: Workshop on European Political Economy and Institutional Analysis.

———. 1994b. "Two Postwar Reconstructions: Institutional Transfer in Germany, 1945-94." Presented at the Annual Meeting of the Western Political Science Association.

Janssen, Joseph I. H. 1991. "Postmaterialism, Cognitive Mobilization and Public Support for European Integration." *British Journal of Political Science* 21:443-468.

Jervis, Robert. 1978. "Cooperation Under the Security Dilemma." *World Politics* 30:167-214.

———. 1986. "From Balance to Concert: A Study of International Security Cooperation." In *Cooperation Under Anarchy*, ed. Kenneth A. Oye. Princeton: Princeton University Press.

Kahneman, David, and Amos Tversky. 1979. "Prospect Theory: An Analysis of Decision under Risk." *Econometrica* 47:263-291.

Kaysen, Carl. 1990. "Is War Obsolete? A Review Essay." *International Security* 14:42-64.

Kelstrup, Morten. 1992. "European Integration and Political Theory." In *European Integration and Denmark's Participation,* ed. Morten Kelstrup. Copenhagen: Copenhagen Political Studies Press.

Keohane, Robert O. 1969. "Lilliputians' Dilemmas: Small States in International Politics." *International Organization* 23:291-310.

———. 1982. "The Demand for International Regimes." *International Organization* 36:325-355.

———. 1984. *After Hegemony: Discord in the World Political Economy*. Princeton: Princeton University Press.

———. 1988. "International Institutions: Two Approaches." *International Studies Quarterly* 32:379-396.

Keohane, Robert O., and Stanley Hoffmann. 1990. "Conclusions: Community Politics and Institutional Change." In *The Dynamics of European Integration*, ed. William Wallace. London: Pinter Publishers for the RIIA.

———. 1991. "Institutional Change in Europe in the 1980s." In *The New European Community: Decisionmaking and Institutional Change,* eds. Robert O. Keohane and Stanley Hoffmann. Boulder, CO: Westview Press: 1-39.

———. 1991. *The New European Community. Decisionmaking and Institutional Change*. Boulder, CO: Westview Press.

Keohane, Robert O., and Joseph S. Nye. 1977. *Power and Interdependence*. Cambridge, MA: Harvard University Press.

———. 1977. *Power and Interdependence. World Politics in Transition*. Boston, MA: Little, Brown, and Company.

Keohane, Robert O., Joseph S. Nye, and Stanley Hoffmann. 1993. *After the Cold War:*

International Institutions and State Strategies in Europe: 1989-1991.
Cambridge, MA: Harvard University Press.

Kim, Charlotte. 1992. "Cats and Mice: The Politics of Setting EC Car Emission Standards." CEPS Standards Programme: Paper # 2. Harvard University.

Kim, Oliver, and Mark Walker. 1984. "The Free Rider Problem: Experimental Evidence." *Public Choice* 43:3-24.

Kindleberger, Charles P. 1981. "Dominance and Leadership in the International Economy." *International Studies Quarterly* 25:242-254.

Kitzinger, Uwe Webster. 1963. *The Politics and Economics of European Integration: Britain, Europe, and the United States.* New York: Harper and Row.

Knight, Jack. 1992. *Institutions and Social Conflict.* New York: Columbia University Press.

Krasner, Stephen. 1991. "Global Communications and National Power: Life on the Pareto Frontier." *World Politics* 43:336-66.

Kratochwil, Friedrich. 1989. *Rules, Norms and Decisions.* Cambridge, MA: Cambridge University Press.

Kratochwil, Friedrich, and John G. Ruggie. 1986. "International Organization: A State of the Art or the Art of the State." *International Organization* 40:753-775.

Krehbiel, Keith. 1987. "Why Are Congressional Committees Powerful?" *American Political Science Review* 81:929-35.

——. 1991. *Information and Legislative Organization.* Ann Arbor, MI: Michigan University Press.

Kreps, David M. 1990. *Game Theory and Economic Modeling.* Oxford: Clarendon Press.

Kriesi, Hanspeter. 1980. *Entscheidungsstrukturen und Entscheidungsprozesse in der Schweizer Politik.* Frankfurt: Campus Verlag.

——. 1990. "Federalism and Pillarization: The Netherlands and Switzerland Compared." *Acta Politica.* 25:433-450.

——. 1991. "Direkte Demokratie in der Schweiz." *Aus Politik und Zeitgeschichte.* 23:44-54.

——. 1993. *Citoyenneté et démocratie. Compétence, participation et décision des citoyens et citoyennes suisses.* Zürich: Seismo

Kriesi, Hanspeter, Claude Longchamp, Florence Passy, and Pascal Sciarini. 1993. *Analyses des votations fédérales du 6 décembre 1992.* Adliswil, Genève: GfS Institut de recherche et Département de science politique: Université de Genève.

Krueger, Anne. 1974. "The Political Economy of the Rent-Seeking Society." *American Economic Review* 64:291-303.

Krugman, Paul R. 1991. *Geography and Trade.* Cambridge, MA: MIT Press.

Kundera, Milan. 1981. *The Book of Laughter and Forgetting.* New York: Penguin.

Kydland, Finn, and Edward Prescott. 1977. "Rules Rather than Discretion: The Inconsistency of Optimal Plans." *Journal of Political Economy* 85:473-490.

Lange, Peter. 1992. "The Politics of the Social Dimension." In *Euro-Politics,* ed. A. Sbragia. Washington, D.C.: Brookings.

Laskar, Daniel. 1990. "The Role of a Fixed Exchange Rate System When Central Bankers are Independent." Mimeo. CEPREMAP: Paris.

Lattimore, Owen. 1962. *Studies in Frontier History*. London: Oxford University Press.

Laursen, Finn. 1990. "The Community's Policy Towards EFTA: Regime Formation in the European Economic Space (EES)." *Journal of Common Market Studies* 28:303-325.

Lehmbruch, Gerhard. 1967. *Proporzdemokratie. Politisches System und politische Kultur in der Schweiz und in Österreich*. Tübingen: Mohr.

Lenaerts, Koen. 1991. "Some Reflections on the Separation of Powers in the European Community." *Common Market Law Review* 28:11-35.

Levi, Margaret. 1988. *Of Rule and Revenue*. Berkeley: University of California Press.

Lijphart, Arend. 1974. *Democracy in Plural Societies*. New Haven: Yale University Press.

Lindberg, Leon N. 1963. *The Political Dynamics of European Integration*. Stanford: Stanford University Press.

Lindberg, Leon N., and Stuart A. Scheingold. 1970. *Europe's Would-Be Polity*. Englewood Cliffs, NJ: Prentice-Hall, Inc.

Linder, Wolf. 1987. *La décision politique en Suisse*. Lausanne: Réalités sociales.

——. 1994. *Swiss Democracy : Possible Solutions to Conflict in Multicultural Societies*. New York: St. Martin's Press.

Lodge, Juliet, ed. 1986. *European Union: The European Community in Search of a Future*. London: MacMillan.

——. 1987. "The Single European Act: Towards a New Euro-Dynamism?" *Journal of Common Market Studies* 24: 203-23.

——. 1989. "The European Parliament—From 'Assembly' to Co-legislature: Changing the Institutional Dynamics." In *The European Community and the Challenge of the Future*, ed. J. Lodge. London: Pinter:59-79.

——. 1993. "EC Policymaking: Institutional Dynamics." In *The European Community and the Challenge of the Future*, ed. Juliet Lodge. New York: St. Martin's Press.

Lofdahl, Corey. L. 1994. "Global Politics and the Time Arrow." Paper presented at the Annual Meeting of the Western Political Science Association.

Longchamp, Claude, and Peter Kraut. 1994. *Hindernisse für eine klare Zielsetzung in der bundesrätlichen Europa-Strategie*. Zürich/Bern: GfS-Forschungsinstitut.

Ludlow, Peter. 1982. *The Making of the European Monetary System: A Case Study of the Politics of the European Community*. London: Butterworth Scientific.

Lupia, Arthur. 1992. "Busy Voters, Agenda Control, and the Power of Information." *American Political Science Review* 86:390-403.

Lüthi, Ruth, Luzius Meyer, and Hans Hirter. 1991. "Fraktionsdisziplin und die Vertretung von Partikulärinteressen im Nationalrat." In *Das Parlament: Oberste Gewalt des Bundes?*, ed. Parlamentsdienste. Bern: Haupt: 53-72.

Mackie, John L. 1965. "Causes and Conditions." *American Philosophical Quarterly* 2:245-264.

Maggee, Stephen, William Brock, and Leslie Young. 1989. *Black Hole Tariffs and*

Endogenous Policy Theory. Cambridge, MA: Cambridge University Press.

Mann, Michael. 1986. *The Sources of Social Power. Vol I.* Cambridge, MA: Cambridge University Press.

———. 1992. "The Emergence of Modern European Nationalism." In *Transition to Modernity: Essays on Power, Wealth and Belief*, eds. John A. Hall and Ian Jarvie. Cambridge, MA: Cambridge University Press.

March, James G., and Johan P. Olsen. 1989. *Rediscovering Institutions*. New York: Free Press.

Martin, Lisa L. 1993. ""International and Domestic Institutions in the EMU Process." *Economics and Politics* 5:125-143.

Martin, Philippe. 1994. "Monetary Policy and Country Size." *Journal of International Money and Finance* 13:573-586.

———. Forthcoming. "Free-Riding, Convergence and Two-Speed Monetary Unification in Europe." *European Economic Review.*

Marwell, Gerald, and Ruth E. Ames. 1979. "Experiments on the Provision of Public Goods: Resources, Interest, Group Size, and the Free-Rider Problem." *American Journal of Sociology* 84:1335-1360.

Masson, Paul, and Mark Taylor. 1992. "Common Currency Areas and Currency Unions: An Analysis of the Issues." CEPR Working Paper n° 617.

Mattli, Walter. 1994. "The Logic of Regional Integration." Ph.D. dissertation, Department of Political Science, University of Chicago.

Mattli, Walter, and Anne-Marie Slaughter. 1995 (forthcoming). "Judicial Politics in the European Union." *International Organization.*

Mayhew, David. 1974. *Congress: The Electoral Connection.* New Haven, CT: Yale UP.

McCubbins, Matthew D., and Thomas Schwartz. 1984. "Congressional Oversight Overlooked: Police Patrols and Fire Alarms." *American Journal of Political Science* 28:165-79.

McGuire, Martin C. 1974. "Group Size, Group Homogeneity, and the Aggregate Provision of a Pure Public Good Under Cournot Behavior." *Public Choice* 18:107-126.

McKelvey, Richard D. 1976. "Intransitivities in Multidimensional Voting Models and Some Implications for Agenda Control." *Journal of Economic Theory* 12:472-82.

McPherson, Charles P. 1971. "Tariff Structures and Political Exchange." University of Chicago: PhD. Dissertation.

Meadows, Dennis, D. Meadows, J. Randers, and W. W. Behrens. 1972. *The Limits to Growth.* New York: Universe Books.

Mearsheimer, John J. 1990. "Back to the Future: Instability in Europe After the Cold War." *International Security* 15:5-56.

Merrit, Richard L., and Bruce C. Russett, eds. 1981. *From National Development to Global Community* London: George Allen and Unwin.

Michalski, Anna, and Helen Wallace. 1992. *The European Community: The Challenge of Enlargement.* London: Royal Institute of International Affairs.

Milner, Helen. 1991. "The Assumption of Anarchy in International Relations Theory: A Critique." *Review of International Studies* 17:67-85.

——. 1992. "International Theories of Cooperation Among Nations." *World Politics* 44:466-96.

Milward, Alan S. 1984. *The Reconstruction of Western Europe, 1945-51.* Berkeley: University of California Press.

——. 1992. *The European Rescue of the Nation-State.* Berkeley: University of California Press.

Mitrany, David. 1966. *A Working Peace System.* Chicago: Quadrangle Books.

——. 1975. *The Functional Theory of Politics.* London: St. Martin's Press.

Money, Jeannette, and George Tsebelis. 1992. "Cicero's Puzzle: Upper House Power in Comparative Perspective." *International Political Science Review* 13:25-43

Moravcsik, Andrew. 1991. "Negotiating the Single European Act: National Interests and Conventional Statecraft in the European Community." *International Organization* 45:19-56.

——. 1993. "Preferences and Power in the European Community: A Liberal Intergovernmentalist Approach." *Journal of Common Market Studies* 31:473-524.

Morrow, James D. 1987. "On the Theoretical Basis of a Measure of National Risk Attitudes." *International Studies Quarterly* 31: 423-38.

——. 1991. "Alliances and Asymmetry: An Alternative to the Capability Aggregation Model of Alliances." *American Journal of Political Science* 35:904-33.

——. 1994. "Modeling the Forms of International Cooperation: Distribution versus Information." *International Organization* 48:387-424.

Mueller, Dennis C. 1989. *Public Choice II.* New York: Columbia University Press.

Mueller, John. 1989. *Retreat from Doomsday: The Obsolesence of Major War.* New York: Basic Books.

Mundell, Robert. 1961. "A Theory of Optimum Currency Areas." *American Economic Review* 51:657-65.

Mutimer, David. 1989. "1992 and the Political Integration of Europe: Neo-functionalism Reconsidered." *Revue d'intégration européenne* 13:75-101.

NATO (North Atlantic Treaty Organization). 1989. *Facts and Figures.* Brussels: NATO.

Neidhart, Leonhard. 1970. *Plebiszit und pluralitäre Demokratie.* Bern: Francke.

Nell, Philippe. 1990. "EFTA in the 1990s: The Search for a New Identity." *Journal of Common Market Studies* 28:327-358.

Nelson, Richard R., and Sidney G. Winter. 1982. *An Evolutionary Theory of Economic Change.* Cambridge, MA: Belknap.

Nisbet, Robert A. 1993. *The Sociological Tradition.* New Brunswick: Transaction Publishers.

Norpoth, Helmut, Michael Lewis-Beck, and Jean-Dominique Lafay. 1991. *Economics and Politics: The Calculus of Support.* Ann Arbor, MI: University of Michigan Press.

North, Douglass C. 1981. *Structure and Change in Economic History.* New York: W.

W. Norton.

———. 1990. *Institutions, Institutional Change and Economic Performance.* Cambridge, MA: Cambridge University Press.

Nugent, Neill. 1989. *The Government and Politics of the European Community.* London: Macmillan.

———. 1992. "The Deepening and Widening of the European Community: Recent Evolution, Maastricht, and Beyond." *Journal of Common Market Studies* 30:311-328.

Nye, Joseph S. 1971. *Peace in Parts. Integration and Conflict in Regional Organization.* Boston: Little, Brown and Company.

Oakland, William H. 1972. "Congestion, Public Goods and Welfare." *Journal of Public Economics* 1:339-357.

OECD (Organization for Economic Cooperation and Development). 1984. *National Accounts.* Paris: OECD.

———. 1992. *National Accounts.* Paris: OECD.

———. 1992. *OECD Economic Outlook.* Paris: OECD.

———. 1993. *National Accounts.* Paris: OECD.

Olson, Mancur, and Richard Zeckhauser. 1966. "An Economic Theory of Alliances." *Review of Economics and Statistics* 48:266-279.

Olson, Mancur. 1965/1971. *The Logic of Collective Action.* Cambridge, MA: Harvard University Press.

Oneal, John R., and Hugh Carter Whatley. 1994. "The Effect of Alliance Membership on National Defense Burdens, 1953-88: A Test of the Theory of Collective Action." Paper prepared for the 1994 Annual Meeting of the International Studies Association: Washington, DC.

Ordeshook, Peter C., and Thomas Schwartz. 1987. "Agenda and the Control of Political Outcomes." *American Political Science Review* 81:179-200.

Padoa-Schioppa, Thomaso. 1990. "Fiscal Prerequisites of a European Monetary Union." Paper presented at the Conference on Aspects of Central Bank Policymaking: Tel-Aviv.

Pahre, Robert. 1994. "Multilateral Cooperation in an Iterated Prisoners' Dilemma." *Journal of Conflict Resolution* 38:326-352.

Papadopoulos, Yannis. 1991. *La Suisse: Un Sonderfall pour la théorie politique.* Université de Lausanne: Travaux de science politique.

———. 1994. "Les votations fédérales comme indicateur de soutien aux autorités." In *Elites politiques et peuple. Analyse des votations fédérales 1970-1987,* ed. Yannis Papadopoulos. Lausanne: Réalités sociales: 113-160

Peltzman, Sam. 1976. "Towards a More General Theory of Regulation?" *Journal of Law and Economics* 19:211-40.

Persson, Torsten, and Guido Tabellini. 1993. "Designing Monetary Institutions for Stability." CEPR working paper.

Peters, B. Guy. 1992. "Bureaucratic Politics and the Institutions of the European Community." In *Euro-Politics,* ed. A. Sbragia. Washington, D.C.: Brookings.

Pinder, John. 1992. *European Community: The Building of a Union.* Oxford: Oxford

University Press.

Poggi, Gianfranco. 1978. *The Development of the Modern State: A Sociological Introduction*. Stanford: Stanford University Press.

Prigogine, Ilya, and Isabelle Stengers. 1984. *Order out of Chaos: Man's New Dialogue with Nature*. New York: Bantam.

Puchala, Donald J. 1988. "Integration Theorists and the Study of International Relations." In *The Global Agenda*, eds. Charles W. Kegley and Eugene R. Wittkopf. New York: Random House:198-215.

Putnam, Robert D. 1988. "Diplomacy and Domestic Politics: The Logic of Two-Level Games." *International Organization* 42: 427-60.

Reed, Laurence. 1967. *Europe in a Shrinking World*. London: Oldbourne Book.

Richardson, George P. 1991. *Feedback Thought in Social Science and Systems Theory*. Philadelphia: University of Pennsylvania Press.

Riker, William H. 1962. *The Theory of Political Coalitions*. New Haven: Yale University Press.

———. 1964. *Federalism: Origin, Operation, Significance*. Boston: Little Brown.

Rogoff, Kenneth. 1985. "The Optimal Degree of Commitment to an Intermediate Monetary Target." *The Quarterly Journal of Economics* 100:1169-90.

Romer, David. 1993. "Openess and Inflation: Theory and Evidence." *Quarterly Journal of Economics* 4:869-904.

Rubinstein, Ariel. 1991. "Comments on the Interpretation of Game Theory." *Econometrica* 59:909-924.

Rucker, Rudy. 1987. *Mindtools: The Five Levels of Mathematical Reality*. Boston: Houghton Mifflin.

Ruggie, John Gerard. 1993. "Territoriality and Beyond: Problematizing Modernity in International Relations." *International Organization* 47:139-174.

Rühl, Lothar. 1994. "Europäische Sicherheit und Osterweiterung der NATO." *Aussenpolitik* 2:115-12.

Russett, Bruce M. 1970. *What Price Vigilance? The Burdens of National Defense*. New Haven: Yale University Press.

Sandholtz, Wayne. 1993. "Choosing Union: Monetary Politics and Maastricht." *International Organization* 47:1-39.

Sandholtz, Wayne, and John Zysman. 1989. "1992: Recasting the European Bargain." *World Politics* 42:95-128.

Sandler, Todd. 1992a. *Collective Action: Theory and Applications*. Ann Arbor, MI: University of Michigan Press.

———. 1992b. *The Theory of Collective Action*. Ann Arbor, MI: University of Michigan Press.

———. 1993. "The Economic Theory of Alliances: A Survey." *Journal of Conflict Resolution* 37:446-483.

Sandler, Todd, Jon Cauley, and John F. Forbes. 1980. "In Defense of a Collective Goods Theory of Alliances." *Journal of Conflict Resolution* 24:537-47.

Sandler, Todd, and John T. Tschirhart. 1980. "The Economic Theory of Clubs: An Evaluative Survey." *Journal of Economic Literature* 18:1481-1521.

Sardi, Massimo, and Eric Widmer. 1993. "L'orientation du vote." In *Citoyenneté et démocratie. Compétence, participation et décision des citoyens et citoyennes suisses*, ed. Hanspeter Kriesi. Zürich: Seismo.

Satz, Debra, and John Ferejohn. 1994. "Rational Choice and Social Theory." *Journal of Philosophy* 91:71-87.

Sbragia, Alberta M. 1992. "Thinking About the Future: The Uses of Comparison." In *Euro-Politics: Institutions and Policymaking in the "New" European Community*, ed. Alberta M. Sbragia. Washington, D.C.: Brookings Institution.

Scharpf, Fritz W. 1988. "The Joint-Decision Trap: Lessons From German Federalism and European Integration." *Public Administration* 66:239-78.

Scheingold, Stuart A. 1970. "Domestic and International Consequences of Regional Integration." *International Organization (special issue)* 4.

Schlesinger, Philip R. 1994. "Europe's Contradictory Communicative Space." *Daedalus* 123:25-52.

Schneider, Gerald. 1994a (forthcoming). "Agenda Setting in European Integration: The Conflict Between Voters, Governments, and Supranational Institutions." In *The Political Economy of European Integration*, ed. Finn Laursen. Maastricht: European Institute of Public Administration.

———. 1994b (forthcoming). "Ein Opfer des eigenen Erfolges: Mehrheitsentscheide als Sprengsatz für die Selbsterneuerung der Europäischen Union." *Homo Oeconomicus.*

———. 1995. "The Limits of Self-Reform: Institution-Building in the European Community." *European Journal of International Relations* 1:59-86.

Schneider, Gerald, and Lars-Erik Cederman. 1994. "The Change of Tide in Political Cooperation: An Limited Information Model of European Integration." *International Organization* 48:633-662.

Schneider, Gerald, and Patricia A. Weitsman. 1994. "European Cooperation and the Revival of Regional Integration Theory." University of Bern/Ohio University, mimeo.

———. 1996 (forthcoming). "The Punishment Trap: Integration Referendums as Popularity Contests." *Comparative Political Studies.*

Schneider, Gerald, and Claudia Seybold. 1995. "Twelve Tongues, One Voice, An Evaluation of the European Political Cooperation." Paper prepared for the ISA Convention 1995 in Chicago.

Schofield, Norman. 1978. "Instability of Simple Dynamic Games." *Review of Economic Studies* 45:575-94.

Sciarini, Pascal. 1992. "La Suisse dans la négociation sur l'Espace économique européen: de la rupture à l'apprentissage." *Annuaire suisse de science politique* 32:297-322.

Sciarini, Pascal. 1994 (forthcoming). *La Suisse face à la Communauté européenne et au GATT: le cas-test de la politique agricole.* Genève: Georg.

Seeley, John Robert. 1885. *The Expansion of England.* London: Macmillan.

Sen, Amartya K. 1970. *Collective Choice and Social Welfare.* San Francisco: Holden-Day.

Shambaugh, George, and Patricia Weitsman. 1992. "First, Second, and Third Wave Approaches to the Study of Institutions in International Politics: Is Progress Ever Possible Without Reinventing the Wheel?" Paper prepared for the 1992 Annual Meeting of the American Political Science Association.

Shapiro, Martin. 1992. "The European Court of Justice." In *Euro-Politics,* ed. A. Sbragia. Washington D.C.: Brookings.

Shepsle, Kenneth A. 1979. "Institutional Arrangements and Equilibrium In Multidimensional Voting Models." *American Journal of Political Science* 23:27-57.

Shepsle, Kenneth A., and Barry R. Weingast. 1984. "Uncovered Sets and Sophisticated Outcomes with Implications for Agenda Institutions." *American Journal of Political Science* 1:49-74.

——. 1987a. "The Institutional Foundations of Committee Power." *American Political Science Review* 81:85-104.

——. 1987b. "Why Are Congressional Committees Powerful?" *American Political Science Review* 81:935-45.

Sidjanski, Dusan. 1992. *L'avenir fédéraliste de l'Europe. La Communauté européenne, des origines au Traité de Maastricht.* Paris: Presses universitaires de France.

Spokkereef, Annemarie. 1993. "Developments in European Community Education Policy." In *The European Community and the Challenge of the Future,* ed. Juliet Lodge. New York: St. Martin's Press.

Steiner, Jürg. 1974. *Amicable Agreement versus Majority Rule: Conflict Resolution in Switzerland.* Chapel Hill: University of North Carolina Press.

——. 1982. Switzerland: "Magic Formula Coalition." In *Government Coalitions in Western Democracies,* ed. E. Brown and J. Dreijmanis. New York: Longman:315-334

——. 1983. "Conclusion : Reflections on the Consociational Theme." In *Switzerland at the Polls,* ed. H. Penniman. Washington-London: American Enterprise Institute for Public Policy Research.

——. 1994. "Preface." In *Swiss Democracy: Possible Solutions to Conflict in Multicultural Societies,* ed. Wolf Linder. New York: St. Martin's Press.

Stephen, Roland. 1992. "Domestic Interests, Interstate Bargains and European Integration: The Case of the Automobile Sector." Paper presented in APSA meetings.

Sterbenz, Frederic P., and Todd Sandler. 1992. "Sharing Among Clubs: A Club of Clubs Theory." *Oxford Economic Papers* 44:1-19.

Stigler, George J. 1971. "The Theory of Economic Regulation." *Bell Journal of Economics and Managment Science* 1:137-46.

——. 1974. "Free Riders and Collective Action." *Bell Journal of Economic and Management Science* 5:359-365.

Stigler, George J., and Gary S. Becker. 1977. "De Gustibus Non Est Disputandum." *Amercian Economic Review* 67:76-90.

SIPRI (Stockholm International Peace Research Institute). 1993. *SIPRI Yearbook 1993: World Armaments and Disarmament.* Oxford: Oxford University Press.

Strayer, Joseph R. 1970. *On the Medieval Origins of the Modern State*. Princeton: Princeton University Press.

Sugden, Robert. 1985. "Consistent Conjectures and Voluntary Contributions to Public Goods: Why the Conventional Theory Does Not Work." *Journal of Public Economics* 27:117-124.

Summers, Robert, and Alan Heston. 1991. "The Penn World Table (Mark 5): An Explained Set of International Comparisons: 1950-1988." *Quarterly Journal of Economics* 106:291-303.

Swann, Dennis. 1990. *The Economics of the Common Market*. London: Penguin Books.

Taylor, Paul. 1983. *The Limits of European Integration*. New York: Columbia University Press.

Thomas, H. G. 1988. "Democracy and 1992—Integration Without Accountability?" *The Liverpool Law Review* 10:185-201.

Thomas, R. 1978. "Logical Analysis of Systems Comprising Feedback Loops." *Journal of Theoretical Biology* 73:631-656.

————. 1979. "Kinetic Logic: a Boolean Analysis of the Dynamic Behavior of Control Circuits." In *Kinetic Logic: A Boolean Approach to the Analysis of Complex Regulatory Systems*, ed. R. Thomas. Berlin: Springer-Verlag:107-119.

Tilly, Charles. 1975. "Reflections on the History of European State-Making." In *The Formation of National States in Western Europe*, ed. Charles Tilly. Princeton: Princeton University Press.

————. 1985. "War Making and State Making as Organized Crime." In *Bringing the State Back In*, eds. Peter B. Evans, Dietrich Rueschemeyer and Theda Skocpol. Cambridge, MA: Cambridge University Press.

————. 1990. *Coercion, Capital, and European States, AD 990-1990*. Oxford: Basil Blackwell.

Tocqueville, Alexis de. 1986 [1835]. *De la démocratie en Amérique*. Paris: Gallimard.

Tollison, Robert. 1982. "Rent Seeking: A Survey." *Kyklos* 35:575-602.

Tönnies, Ferdinand. 1957. *Community and Society*. Transl. East Lansing: Michigan State University Press.

Tsebelis, George. 1990. *Nested Games. Rational Choice in Comparative Politics*. Berkeley: University of California Press.

————. 1994. "The Power of the European Parliament as a Conditional Agenda Setter." *American Political Science Review* 88:128-142.

Tsebelis, George, and Jeannette Money. (forthcoming). "Bicameral Negotiations: The Navette System in France."

Tullock, Gordon. 1967. "The Welfare Costs of Tariffs, Monopolies and Theft." *Western Economic Journal* 5:224-32.

————. 1969. "Federalism: Problems of Scale." *Public Choice* 6:19-29.

Van Evera, Stephen. 1986. "Why Cooperation Failed in 1914." In *Cooperation Under Anarchy*, ed. Kenneth Oye. Princeton: Princeton University Press:80-117.

Van Hamme, A. 1989. "The European Parliament and the New Cooperation Procedure." *Studia Diplomatica* 291-314.

Vickers, John S. 1984. "Delegation and the Theory of the Firm." *Economic Journal*

(Conference Proceedings) 95:138-147.

Von Bertalanffy, Ludwig. 1960. *Problems of Life; An Evaluation of Modern Biological and Scientific Thought*. New York: Harper.

———. 1968. *General System Theory: Foundations, Development, Applications*. New York: G. Braziller.

Von Hagen, Jürgen, and Michele Fratianni. 1993. "The Transition to European Monetary Union and the European Monetary Institute." *Economics and Politics* 5:167-185.

Wallace, Helen. 1985. *Europe: The Challenge of Diversity*. London: Routledge & Kegan Paul.

Wallace, Helen, William Wallace, and Carol Webb, eds. 1983. *Policy Making in the European Community*. New York: Wiley.

Wallace, William. 1982. "Europe as a Confederation: the Community and the Nation State." *Journal of Common Market Studies* 21:57-68.

———. 1983. "Less than a Federation, More than a Regime: The Community as a Political System." In *Policy Making in the European Community* (2d ed.), eds. Helen Wallace, William Wallace, and Carole Webb. New York: J. Wiley and Sons.

Walsh, Carl. 1992. *"Optimal Contracts for Central Bankers."* Mimeo, Santa Cruz: University of California.

Walt, Stephen M. 1987. *The Origins of Alliances*. Ithaca, N.Y.: Cornell University Press.

Waltz, Kenneth W. 1979. *Theory of International Politics*. New York: McGraw-Hill.

———. 1993. "The Emerging Structure of International Politics." *International Security* 18:44-80.

Ward, Michael Don. 1982. "Research Gaps in Alliance Dynamics." Monograph Series. In *World Affairs*. Graduate School of International Studies: University of Denver.

———. 1988. "Things Fall Apart: a Logical Analysis of Crisis Resolution Dynamics." *International Interactions* 15:656-79.

——— ed. 1991. *The New Geopolitics*. New York: Gordon and Breach.

Warr, Peter G. 1983. "The Private Provision of a Public Good is Independent of the Distribution of Income." *Economics Letters* 23:207-211.

Webb, Carole. 1983. "Theoretical Perspectives and Problems." In *Policy Making in the European Community* (2d ed), eds. Helen Wallace, William Wallace, and Carole Webb. New York: J. Wiley and Sons.

Weber, Shlomo, and Hans Wiesmeth. 1991. "Issue Linkage in the European Community." *Journal of Common Market Studies* 29:255-67.

Wendt, Alexander. 1994. "Collective Identity Formation and the International State." *American Political Science Review* 88:384-396.

Wessels, Wolfgang. 1991. "The EC Council: The Community's Decisionmaking Center." In *The New European Community,* eds. Robert Keohane and Stanley Hoffman. Boulder, CO.: Westview Press.

Wiener, Norbert. 1950. *The Human Use of Human Beings: Cybernetics and Society*.

Boston: Houghton Mifflin.

——. 1961. *Cybernetics: or, Control and Communication in the Animal and the Machine* (2d ed.). New York: MIT Press.

Williams, Shirley. 1991. "Sovereignty and Accountability in the European Community." In *The New European Community,* eds. Robert Keohane and Stanley Hoffman. Boulder, CO.: Westview Press.

Wilson, Thomas M. 1993. "An Anthropology of the European Community." In *Cultural Changes and the New Europe: Perspectives on t-he European Community*, eds. Thomas M. Wilson and M. Estellie Smith. Boulder, CO: Westview.

Wittman, Donald. 1991. "Nations and States: Mergers and Acquisitions; Dissolutions and Divorce." *AEA Papers and Proceedings* 81:126-129.

Yannopoulos, George. 1990. "Foreign Direct Investment and European Integration: The Evidence from the Formative Years of the European Community." *Journal of Common Market Studies* 28:325-259.

Zinnes, Dina A. 1970. "Coalition Theories and the Balance of Power." In *The Study of Coalition Behavior: Theoretical Perspectives and Cases from Four Continents,* eds. Sven Groennings, M. Leiserson, and E.W. Kelley. New York: Holt, Rinehart, and Winston:351-68.

INDEX

ABOUT THE EDITORS AND CONTRIBUTORS

Thomas Bernauer is a Senior Lecturer and Research Associate at the Department of International Relations, University of Zurich, Switzerland. From 1988 to 1992, he was a Research Associate at the United Nations Institute for Disarmament Research in Geneva, and from 1992 to 1994 a Research Fellow at Harvard University. His recent publications have appeared in *Security Dialogue*, *Environmental Politics*, and *International Organization*.

Lars-Erik Cederman is Lecturer in International Relations at Oxford University and Fellow at Somerville College. His recent publications have appeared in the *International Studies Quarterly* and *International Organization*.

Simon Hug is chargé d'enseignement at the Department of Political Science, University of Geneva. He has written a dissertation and several articles on new political parties in Western democracies. Other publications include contributions to a volume on direct democracy in Switzerland and a forthcoming book (co-authored with Stefano Bartolini and Daniele Caramani) on the development of the literature on political parties in Western Europe.

Corey L. Lofdahl is a Ph.D. candidate in International Relations and Political Theory at the University of Colorado, Boulder. His primary research interests address environmental issues from a complex systems perspective.

Philippe Martin is Assistant Professor in international economics at the Graduate Institute of International Studies in Geneva, and a Research Affiliate at the Center for Economic Policy Research in London. His research focuses on the political economy aspects of trade and monetary integration, the impact of public infrastructure on economic geography, and the relation between growth and stabilization policy.

Walter Mattli is Assistant Professor in the Department of Political Science at Columbia University in New York. He has published in *International Organization, Conflict Management and Peace Science* and is currently working on a book on regional integration.

Robert Pahre is Assistant Professor of Political Science and Public Policy at the University of Michigan. His primary research interests are foreign economic policy, the political economy of Scandinavia, and the philosophy of social science. He is co-author, with Mattei Dogan, of *Creative Marginality: Innovation at the Intersections of Social Science*.

Gerald Schneider is Program Director and Assistant Professor of Political Science at the University of Bern, Switzerland. He is the author of *Strategic Integration: Domestic Politics and Regional Cooperation in Europe* (forthcoming). His recent work is published in *Comparative Political Studies, International Interactions, European Journal of International Relations* and *International Organization*.

Pascal Sciarini is maître-assistant at the Faculty of Social and Economic Sciences (European studies programme), University of Geneva. He has written a dissertation on the reform of the Swiss farm policy in the context of the Uruguay Round and European integration, several articles dealing with relations between Switzerland and the European Union, as well as other various topics of Swiss politics (direct democracy, political parties).

George Tsebelis is Professor of Political Science at UCLA. He is the author of *Nested Games: Rational Choice in Comparative Politics*. He has published numerous articles on the impact of different political institutions like bicameralism, presidentialism, multipartism, etc. Currently he is the recipient of a Guggenheim fellowship to study the institutions of the European Union.

Michael D. Ward is Professor of Political Science and Director of the Center for International Relations at the University of Colorado, Boulder. He has published widely in political science, economics, and geography.

Patricia A. Weitsman is Assistant Professor of Political Science, Ohio University. In addition to the study of European integration, her areas of research and publications include international security, and U.S. foreign policy making.

ISBN 0-275-94865-X

9 780275 948658

HARDCOVER BAR CODE